Face to Face with Body Dysmorphic Disorder

In *Face to Face with Body Dysmorphic Disorder*, BDD expert Arie M. Winograd shares his unique insights as a psychotherapist who has spent thousands of hours treating patients with this uniquely complex disorder. By specifically focusing on the patient-clinician relationship and exploring treatment options beyond the cognitive-behavioral model, this groundbreaking new text offers a new perspective designed to help practitioners truly understand the emotional inner-workings of the BDD client, and in turn, how to genuinely connect with them in order to facilitate recovery. Also included are two chapters written by former BDD sufferers chronicling their personal struggles with the disorder.

Arie M. Winograd, MA, LMFT is the founder and director of the Los Angeles Body Dysmorphic Disorder & Body Image Clinic. Having dedicated the majority of his professional career as a psychotherapist to treating individuals with the complex psychiatric condition termed body dysmorphic disorder (BDD), Mr. Winograd has worked extensively to diversify and expand treatment strategies while emphasizing interpersonal relationships as the epicenter of BDD treatment and recovery. Mr. Winograd's formal education includes a Bachelor of Arts from Carnegie Mellon University and a Master's Degree in Clinical Psychology from Pepperdine University, along with clinical training via the University of California, Los Angeles.

Face to Face with Body Dysmorphic Disorder

Psychotherapy and Clinical Insights

Arie M. Winograd

Routledge
Taylor & Francis Group

NEW YORK AND LONDON

First published 2017
by Routledge
711 Third Avenue, New York, NY 10017

and by Routledge
2 Park Square, Milton Park, Abingdon, Oxon, OX14 4RN

Routledge is an imprint of the Taylor & Francis Group, an informa business

Library of Congress Cataloging in Publication Data
Names: Winograd, Arie M., author.
Title: Face to face with body dysmorphic disorder : psychotherapy &
    clinical insights / Arie M. Winograd.
Description: New York, NY : Routledge, 2016. | Includes
    bibliographical references and index.
Identifiers: LCCN 2016019708| ISBN 9781138890732 (hardback) |
    ISBN 9781138890749 (pbk. : alk. paper) |
    ISBN 9781315710082 (ebk)
Subjects: | MESH: Body Dysmorphic Disorders—therapy |
    Psychotherapy
Classification: LCC RC480 | NLM WM 170 | DDC 616.89/14—dc23
LC record available at https://lccn.loc.gov/2016019708

ISBN: 978-1-138-89073-2 (hbk)
ISBN: 978-1-138-89074-9 (pbk)
ISBN: 978-1-315-71008-2 (ebk)

Typeset in Sabon
by Swales & Willis Ltd, Exeter, Devon, UK

The body is the servant of the mind
Kunkhen Mipham—Entry to the Wise

The mind is the servant of the body
Body Dysmorphic Disorder

Contents

Preface

The inspiration for writing this book has come from the people whom this manuscript is about, the individuals who are plagued by a condition that has been named body dysmorphic disorder; a condition in which those inflicted experience relentless tormenting thoughts and emotions. In my many years of working with this group of individuals, what has never ceased to amaze me is how they remain some of the most kind, compassionate, and courageous people that I have ever met even while they themselves are experiencing profound emotional agony. Having witnessed their capacity to still have empathy for others even in the midst of their own anguish has significantly motivated me to remain in the treatment trenches with them, and now to tell their story. I hope that by relaying their narrative and passing on this knowledge, the next person inflicted with body dysmorphic disorder will not have to traverse as many obstacles on their way to recovery.

This book would never have come into fruition without the internal strength of the individuals who made the choice to battle back against their body dysmorphic disorder. The information dispersed in this text is a result of your bravery, so I first and foremost would like to thank you. This is your story. I would also like to thank the many people who have been instrumental in the creation of this book and in my development as a psychotherapist. In alphabetical order, I would like to thank: Thomas Brauner, PhD for mentoring me in the art of psychotherapy; Michael Cameron, PhD; Scott Fears, MD; Jamie Feusner, MD; Scott Granet, LCSW who understands body dysmorphic disorder better than most; Ali Ghassemi, PsyD; Karron Maidment, LMFT for giving me that first opportunity; the entire staff of the Los Angeles Body Dysmorphic Disorder & Body Image Clinic; Charles Mansueto, PhD; Malin McKinley, LCSW; Sanjaya Saxena, MD for answering the telephone that summer day in 1996; Jason Schiffman, MD; my editor Chris Teja of Routledge Press for his direction, flexibility, and openness to my ideas; both Isaac and Linda Winograd and also the people of the Kingdom of Bhutan for teaching me empathy and compassion. Without the wisdom, insight, caring, and knowledge of the previously named individuals, you would not be reading this text today.

I could not have created this manuscript alone, without the love and support of other people. Recovery from body dysmorphic disorder also cannot be achieved alone. My hope is that the information within the pages of this book will assist someone in becoming free from the shackles of body dysmorphic disorder so that they, in turn, can someday be of service to someone else. Although this book contains psychological jargon and concepts that someone without a psychotherapy background may not be familiar with, this book is ultimately about relationships. Recovery from body dysmorphic disorder transpires within the realm of genuine, unconditional relationships, and it is within this realm that I believe every individual with body dysmorphic disorder has the capacity to recover and live a much higher quality of life. There is hope. There is absolutely hope.

1 The Experience of Body Dysmorphic Disorder

Imagine experiencing pervasive and perpetual sensations of dread and shame, the sort of visceral response that you might have when your body reacts to a physical threat. Envision how distressing it would be if you experienced these exact same feelings after viewing yourself in a reflective surface or a photograph. Imagine what it might be like if your body was the source of extreme feelings of anger, disgust, anxiety, fear, and hopelessness. Try to visualize how it might be if viewing your outward appearance triggered a reaction usually associated with a perilous situation, and how disconcerting it would be if every time you looked at yourself you experienced primal feelings of terror. If you have not had such an experience, it is probably quite difficult to comprehend how it is possible to have such a reaction to one's own body. This, though, is the very tormenting reality for individuals who suffer from body dysmorphic disorder (BDD). This book is about that reality, the experience of millions of people who silently suffer from a profound anguish about their most outward identity, their bodies.

Human beings have been equipped with physical characteristics that enhance our chances of survival. Whether these are internal or external physical attributes, they are all necessary to allow us to function and survive. Internally, the human brain serves as our control center while the heart pumps oxygenated blood to our muscles that in turn allows us to be mobile. Other vital organs are necessary for survival, such as the liver that filters blood coming from the digestive tract and the kidneys that extract waste from our blood. External physical characteristics such as skin, the largest organ in the human body, assists in protecting the body against pathogens. The nose filters and conditions inhaled air and also contains specialized cells for smelling. Hair on the human head is a primary source of heat insulation and also serves as a cooling mechanism when sweat soaked hair evaporates. Each physical characteristic interfaces with the others and contributes to our well being to insure that we will persevere. An increased chance of survival in turn improves the possibility that our genetics will be passed onto the next generation.

It is the appearance of the external physical features that is at the epicenter of the psychiatric condition called body dysmorphic disorder, a malady in which aesthetic characteristics take on an exaggerated sense of value far beyond any biological function of survival. For the individual with body dysmorphic disorder, an inverse phenomenon exists in which the visual attributes of the body are associated with survival and the biological role of body parts hold far less importance. The human body evolved in order to provide the optimal possibility of survival for the individual. Body parts are not built to become the repository of emotional torment, that is, until body dysmorphic disorder hijacks the process.

Picture your worst fear or most shameful experience becoming associated with an area of your body, and then magnify this image many times over. Within the construct of body dysmorphic disorder, a body part takes on an identity of its own. The body area of concern becomes profoundly associated with the individual's sense of self: The individual with BDD misses the forest through the trees, and rather than seeing many different body parts that together shape outward appearance, the despised physical feature becomes the focal point of their existence. It can easily become the singular element within the person's life and a gauge that determines the entirety of their self-worth.

In contemporary Western culture there is no denying that appearance does matter. In countries such as the United States of America there is a constant barrage of visual messages driven by the commercial marketing apparatus that reminds us what we do not have, what others have, and what we need in order to keep up with our neighbors. Visual images of people that appear content, successful, and aesthetically attractive are often associated with a product in order to convey that you, the consumer, will obtain these characteristics if you purchase the item advertised. This message becomes even more pronounced if the item being promoted pertains directly to one's physical being, delivering a not-so-subtle message that the product will remedy aesthetic imperfections and simultaneously improve quality of life. The bar of what is aesthetically normal is raised so high that inevitably many people will feel substandard and turn to the advertised product in an attempt to minimize feelings of inferiority. This, however, is only a very epidermal layer of the tumultuous relationship that body dysmorphic disorder sufferers have with their bodies.

Body dysmorphic disorder is a very, very lonely experience. Those with BDD often languish in silence. To openly speak about what is perceived as an aesthetic defect would mean drawing attention directly to the source of profound shame. Shame, the internal experience that something might be inherently defective about one's self, is frequently the primary emotion percolating just beneath the body related preoccupation. Shame leads to silence, silence leads to secrecy, and secrecy leaves the BDD sufferer feeling very alone and hopeless. It is also the shame that hinders many individuals with body dysmorphic disorder from seeking appropriate treatment.

There is also the embarrassment that no one else will believe or can truly understand why they care as much as they do about their appearance. Those with body dysmorphic disorder do not want to think about their bodies, in fact, they are very ashamed that they are unable to stop focusing on their physical appearance. Because people on the outside do not perceive the supposed physical defects as problematic, it leaves the sufferer feeling even more alone. The discrepancy between how other people view the appearance of the BDD patient and how they view themselves is often very confusing and only emphasizes how different they already feel in relation to others.

We live in a society that emphasizes individual performance and consumerism. Success is generally measured and defined by the accumulation of external, tangible commodities such as wealth, fame, academic degrees, popularity, and material objects that prove to the outside world that we have succeeded and thus hold individual value. The need for individual success is intricately woven into the fabric of Western culture and is often the barometer for how we fundamentally feel about ourselves. Our happiness is often contingent upon if we successfully reach the next goal in our lives; once we achieve the goal we quickly realize that happiness is ephemeral. We then rush to the next performance driven objective in order to quench the inner experience that something is missing in our lives. For many, outward appearances of success are a necessity in order to achieve an internal feeling of tranquility.

Our physical appearance is one of multiple components that contribute to the formation of our identity. We live within a society that rewards and validates us based on our individual external accomplishments, thus it should come as no surprise that our aesthetic appearance has also become a canvas in which external values are painted. This creates a fertile environment for profit: If we are told that our appearance is such an important element of our identity and then through advertisements we are exposed to images of how we should strive to appear, we will never feel as if we are good enough. This cycle perpetuates itself because if the preponderance of our identity has evolved around outward presentation, then naturally the only way we could conceive to maintain our identity would be to further chase external validation.

Advertisements evoke envy. We are constantly bombarded by advertising: Sports arenas are named after corporations, billboards litter urban landscapes, infomercials are continuously broadcast on television, and the Internet distributes product information the world over. Advertisers are masters at playing into our insecurities, anxieties, fears, and primal instincts. If we are made to feel inferior or different from others then we may be more easily exploited into purchasing the promoted product. The utilization of beauty as a marketing device is just another method of manipulating us into feeling fundamentally inadequate about ourselves. We are so inundated by advertising that we are probably not even aware of the influence it can have on our internal sense of identity.

Is commercialism responsible for body image disturbances because of its unrelenting message that physical appearance is of the utmost importance? When we are constantly being made to feel that our skin is not smooth enough, our hair is not as lush as it should be, our teeth need to be whiter, and our bodies must be more toned, it should come as no surprise that many of us might become somewhat self-conscious about how we appear to others. We are made to feel that we will not be accepted by our peers or cannot fit in with the masses if our bodies do not look a certain way. Perhaps on a subclinical level we all have body image distortions because we begin to lose the capacity to decide for ourselves how our bodies should appear. According to the self-ideal discrepancy and social comparison theories, people frequently compare their appearance to cultural ideals and find that they are inadequate, and this may result in increased body dissatisfaction (Thompson and Heinberg 1999). Although we live in a society that places exorbitant value on our external presentation, I do not believe that this is the primary etiology of the condition we call body dysmorphic disorder.

I am frequently contacted by media sources that are looking to produce stories about body image and body image disturbances. Flattered by an image of themselves, they often presume that there is an epidemic of body image disorders as a result of our media induced cultural influences emphasizing the importance of appearance. They are often perplexed when I explain to them that the media's influence may not be as significant as they had concluded. They often assume that Los Angeles must be the body dysmorphic disorder capital of the world because of Hollywood's notable influence on our culture. There is no doubt that the movie industry and other media outlets utilize beauty to market their products, but this may not necessarily have anything to do with an individual developing body dysmorphic disorder.

Multiple research studies established that upward of 2% of the general population suffer from symptoms of body dysmorphic disorder. If societal and commercial emphasis on beauty was a significant factor in determining the development of BDD, we would probably have a much higher incidence of the disorder because everyone is exposed to the same deluge of beauty driven messages. Because the majority of the population does not develop symptoms of body dysmorphic disorder, there must be other more significant maladies that evoke BDD symptomology. But, individuals who are genetically and environmentally predisposed to developing BDD are also probably more susceptible to the societal communications connecting beauty with self-worth.

Both men and women suffer from body dysmorphic disorder. There have been research studies that show a preponderance of male BDD sufferers, while other studies have demonstrated that the incidence of women with body dysmorphic disorder is slightly higher than the percentage of men experiencing similar symptoms (Phillips and Dufresne 2002). People are usually astonished when I explain to them that many men suffer from BDD, their surprise probably deriving from the belief that women are mostly proselytized by the beauty industry. Men are also recipients of beauty marketing campaigns, but perhaps not to the same extent as women. If body dysmorphic disorder were a culturally based phenomenon then we would probably see a much higher incidence of female sufferers. Since this is not the case, again there must be many other factors determining who is inflicted.

The body dysmorphic disorder sufferer often lacks an integrated identity, and with this comes a very amorphous sense of self. With a fragile identity and a preoccupation with appearance they are very vulnerable to external messages, including those emphasizing beauty as a source of self-worth. A person with an integrated sense of self is exposed to the same media-biased information, but because they have the capacity to define themselves internally they will not be nearly as influenced by the constant barrage of marketing chatter.

It is not unusual that body dysmorphic disorder patients will interpret these messages at face value. They often see themselves and the world in a very all-or-nothing and inflexible way that includes an emphasis on perfectionism. Individuals with BDD tend to ignore or distort information that is not consistent with their rigidly held beliefs about appearance (Cororve and Gleaves 2001). This in turn only reinforces the dysfunctional convictions involving extreme value attributed to aesthetic presentation. Whereas a person without a diathesis for BDD may become insecure from a beauty based advertisement, the individual with body dysmorphic disorder will often internalize this information as evidence that they must be defective. The very profound underlying experience of inadequacy is not purely the result of cultural influences: Perhaps these external cultural factors activate pre-existing inherent negative beliefs about themselves.

Body dysmorphic disorder lies on the extreme end of the body image continuum. The amalgamation of psychiatric, psychological, emotional, environmental, familial, and cultural components align to create a tormenting experience that can readily disable the sufferer. Because we are so accustomed to beauty driven images, the average person probably cannot fathom the devastating experience that the individual with BDD endures. I always attempt to explain to the media and the layperson that this is not just another body image disturbance but rather a very severe condition with as many as 80% of sufferers contemplating suicide. Upward of 28% of those with body dysmorphic disorder have attempted suicide (Phillips 2007). It is unknown how many of these suicide attempts are completed.

The quantity to which the mainstream media has contributed to body image disturbances is debatable, but regardless of influence, the

Hollywood media has begun to toss around their own version of body dysmorphic disorder, which they have titled *body dysmorphia*. This term is often used in the context of a commentary about a celebrity who either appears to have an eating disorder or has received a plethora of cosmetic procedures. Neither an eating disorder or cosmetic procedures are evidence that an individual has body dysmorphic disorder. In fact, individuals who actually have BDD would very likely not be in the spotlight to begin with. The media's version of body dysmorphic disorder often portrays it as an excessive preoccupation with appearance stemming from vanity or narcissism, an angle that is much more sexy and conducive to business ratings. This inevitably does a major disservice to those who languish from true body dysmorphic disorder and who are the antithesis of vain or narcissistic; in fact, many BDD sufferers avoid treatment because they do not want to be perceived as self-absorbed.

The greater purpose of this book is to help mental health practitioners better understand the experiential workings of the body dysmorphic disorder condition so that they can better relate to these individuals. It is also written to the BDD sufferer who feels very misunderstood and so alone because they rarely encounter someone who can genuinely understand or relate to their emotional torment. This is not meant to be a technical, scientific, or academic manuscript of the psychiatric diagnosis. The intention is to provide insight to clinicians who are working with someone with a BDD diagnosis so that the sufferer will finally feel heard and validated. Knowing that someone else truly believes them and at least somewhat understands their struggles can determine whether or not they feel comfortable to proceed in treatment. Hopefully this book will provide you, the clinician, friend, or family member, with an insider's understanding of the body dysmorphic disorder experience.

2 The Genesis

Where Does Body Dysmorphic Disorder Begin?

Psychotherapists are in a profession that strives to reduce the emotional distress of their patients. Because of this, they can easily become programmed to dive into rescuing, solving, or fixing mode when working with an individual who is experiencing emotional agony. The body dysmorphic disorder patient initially presents extremely stuck, and usually it does not take a long time for the clinician to discern how emotionally tormented these individuals can be, even if to the outside observer there seems to be nothing wrong with their appearance. It can be very tempting for the clinician to plunge into the epicenter of the overt body image symptoms in an attempt to reduce the patient's internal angst; after all, the patient has entered treatment seeking symptom relief.

There is absolutely nothing wrong with slowing down the therapy process, especially early in treatment. If the patient is ready to do so, I most definitely allow them to elaborate on their body related symptoms. What patient, or human being for that matter, does not want to be heard or understood? Early in the treatment process I also begin learning about the patient's formative years as well as their family of origin. Some patients readily discuss this material while others can be perplexed about what their past has to do with their current symptoms. These individuals will usually report that before the advent of their body image symptoms, their life was normal. This may very well be true, but in my experience this is even more reason to explore what life looked like prior to the onset of symptoms. It is usually only a matter of time until the patient and therapist stumble upon past material that is related to what brings them into the therapy.

I believe it is very important for the patient to eventually understand the genesis of the shame and dread that has become associated with their body. It can be very liberating to correctly label the true source of these negative emotions rather than mislabeling the body as the problem. Within the paradigm of the body dysmorphic disorder experience, the body becomes the conduit by which the individual fights a battle. Every patient with untreated BDD is convinced that the body area that they loathe is the problem, and that it needs to be fixed in order to reduce how poorly they feel about themselves.

I explain to my patients that they are in a tug-of-war with their body dysmorphic disorder and that they cannot win if they continue fighting it head-on. Using the tug-of-war analogy, I explain that the BDD symptoms represent big, burley, hyper-muscular challengers, while the BDD sufferer is all alone on the other side of the rope attempting to pull down the massive competition. It is obvious who is going to win this battle every time it is fought, so I point out that doing more of the same will only result in a comparable outcome. I explain that we need to understand how and why these competitors became so powerful in order to have a chance of defeating them. "Fighting the battle of the BDD" head-on has proven not to work, thus it is time to shift paradigms and change how this struggle is waged. This paradigm transition includes understanding the origins of the patient's psychosocial development.

Infants need food, water, and shelter to survive. If these three basic needs are not met, the child will perish. Infants also need nurture. When I use the term nurture, I am referring to everything the child receives from a primary caregiver besides food, water, and shelter. Nurture is the warm, connective, loving bond between the infant and the parent. The parent becomes the first mirror for the child; the parent is also the child's first interpersonal relationship. When an infant looks upward from its crib it sees the face of a parent looking down: The facial reactions and facial characteristics of the caregiver become the original template from which the infant receives information about the world, thus the parent's face becomes the mirror by which the baby learns about himself and about how to relate to people. The emotionally well-adjusted parent will be attuned to the infant's needs, thus providing appropriate mirroring. If good enough, stable, and consistent mirroring is provided by a caregiver, the baby's first experiences relating to another human being are those of security, safety, trust, and love (Bowlby 1969).

I often refer to nurture as a nutrient. We probably can survive without the nutrient of nurture, but we likely will not thrive if we lack it. A secure, stable attachment with a primary caretaker sets the stage for the child's future interpersonal relationships as they leave the crib and begin to explore the world. The initial secure attachment provided by the primary caregiver sends the message to the child that relationships with people are a positive experience. This secure attachment reinforces the relational blueprint that interpersonal relationships are normal, healthy, and are associated with good feelings (Strathearn 2011).

The origin of a child's sense of self, or identity, may also derive from initial healthy mirroring experiences. When a child arrives in the world, they physically exist, but since they have not been exposed to life, do they have a sense of self? This question will not be answered in the pages of this book, but it can be speculated that if an infant is receiving consistent mirroring from a parent then this can only contribute to the foundation of a healthy sense of self. If the primary caregiver is not physically or emotionally present when a child peers upward from its crib, there can be no mirroring. If the child stares upward from its crib and there is limited or no reflection back from a parent, there likely will be deficits in identity formation. If the most fundamental building blocks of identity are not instilled, this may manifest later in a person's life as the experience that something is inherently wrong or different about them or that somehow they are not loveable.

Assuming that a parent intentionally made the decision to have a child, what might be going on with them that they would not be present to provide at least sufficient nurture and mirroring for their infant? There are of course innumerable possibilities why this might occur; this being stated, perhaps it is not always what did occur but rather what did not occur during the process of attachment. A parent will likely parent their own children based upon what had been modeled for them.

A child's family of origin is the initial paradigm by which they understand interpersonal relationships, attachments, and how to care for others. Even when a person leaves home and is exposed to others, their family system model is still their reference point for how they should interact with people. Although being exposed to the outside world can provide the opportunity to learn from others and grow, it is the original information instilled from the family of origin that permeates how an individual navigates interpersonal interactions.

If a parent was not provided with adequate nurture when he or she was a child, how would this individual know to provide this to their own child? If a person was never exposed to something, how would they even know that it exists in the first place? The answer is that they do not know. We cannot conceptualize something that we never knew existed, thus perhaps what did not occur in a person's formative years might explain why it is that they are not even aware that nurture and mirroring need to be passed on to the next generation. For individuals who have received adequate nurture, attunement, and mirroring from their parents, the concept that someone does not know how to attach to their child might seem unfathomable.

A primary caregiver may have been provided with sufficient nurture as a child and have the intellectual understanding of its importance, but this does not necessarily guarantee that they will bond with their own children. Just because a parent is physically present with their infant does not automatically equate emotional attachment. If a primary caregiver is having personal struggles, this will inevitably interfere with their capacity to be attuned to their child. Examples of this might be a caregiver who is grappling with substance abuse, a highly narcissistic parent, one who is suffering from mental illness, or a parent who is experiencing prolonged external stressors such as financial or relational stress. Any scenario where a parent is either distracted from or is incapable of providing consistent attachment and nurture will inevitably disrupt the process of healthy emotional mirroring.

If a child does not receive ample nurture from a parent, this does not automatically condemn him to a life of inner emptiness and loneliness. There are many factors that contribute to the development of an individual's sense of self including their temperament, genetics, the disposition of the other parent, as well as environmental determinants. Insufficient attachment by the primary caregiver may not completely impact a child's future, but it most certainly will deprive the child of the nutrient of nurture that can determine if he thrives or just survives. Quality mirroring by a parent also lays the framework for a child to begin learning how to self-soothe (Bowlby 1988). The consistent, emotionally well-regulated caretaker will naturally model that emotions are normal and healthy. The infant internalizes these emotionally stable interactions and this contributes to the initial development of an integrated sense of self.

Many body dysmorphic disorder patients that I have worked with have reported that they knew something was amiss when they were very small children, they just did not know what it was. Someone who did not receive adequate parental connectivity as a child is often not able to identify the feeling that something is wrong or missing even when they are an adult. The "something is wrong or missing" feeling is often experienced as a profound sense of emptiness, loneliness, defectiveness, or a very vague sense of not being loveable. These feelings are often quite ambiguous because if appropriate nurture and love were not present when someone was a child, they would not be able to emotionally identify it as an adult. They might be able to intellectually understand love, attachment, and nurture, but this is very different from a true emotional understanding.

If a child does not receive nurture and consistent mirroring from a primary caregiver, then where does it come from? In the best case scenario, other members of a family system will be able to provide an infant with emotional sustenance. If this is completely lacking in the family system, then a child will seek love and connectivity elsewhere. The source of the very abstruse experience of emptiness and loneliness is nearly impossible for someone to identify if they have never experienced sufficient nurture to begin with; it is also difficult to fix something that never existed. It is much easier to work with and repair something that is tangible than to identify and solve an ambiguous, abstract experience.

The human body is not abstract or ambiguous. It can be seen, touched, smelled, and even heard. It physically exists: We can be concretely identified by many a somatic cue including our facial features, height, finger prints, and skin-hair-eye color. These tangible characteristics provide factual evidence of our existence because they can be measured, weighed, and photographed. This drastically differs from the concept of sense of self, that even when it is very solid cannot be quantitatively documented. If an individual does not have an integrated sense of self because they did not receive sufficient bonding, nurture, and mirroring, it would make sense that they turn toward something that they can distinctly distinguish as their own: This would be their body.

Individuals with body dysmorphic disorder utilize the body, or specific body parts, as the filter from which they understand, experience, and interpret their existence. Not every individual with body dysmorphic disorder lacked emotional connectivity with their primary caregiver, and not every person who experienced an insecure attachment with a parent develops a body image disturbance. This being stated, the majority of BDD patients that enter treatment will report that they feel as they do because of the perceived physical defect, rather than the other way around. I usually inquire if it is possible that they are having an uncomfortable internal experience and are focusing on their body in an attempt to find a solution to their emotional distress.

Patients who are new to treatment or those with very overvalued ideation are usually convinced that they would feel better if the body part looked different. I do not challenge their belief because this is body dysmorphic disorder and to challenge it would also be invalidating their experience. Later in treatment I might point out to them that there is no scientific evidence that feelings actually come from a body part: A nose, eyebrow, hair follicle, skin, ear, forehead, or jawline do not cause feelings. The experiences they are having are coming from somewhere else and are being filtered through the area of the body deemed defective.

So how can emotions become attached to physical appearance if body parts do not cause feelings? Sometimes body dysmorphic disorder patients are very aware of how a feeling became associated with an area of their body; on other occasions these associations are not so overt and sometimes are even very subtle. I have worked with patients who are acutely aware of the origins of their body related feelings; there are also many individuals who are so hyper-focused on the visceral feelings that there is absolutely no insight into anything beyond the body area that they are preoccupied with.

Case Study: Hazel

Hazel, a 27-year-old woman, entered treatment with multiple concerns regarding her facial features as well as an overall feeling that her face was "just wrong." She described her nose as too big for her face, her forehead as too high, her teeth as crooked, her eyes as not symmetrical, and felt that her skin was blotchy. She stated that she felt she looked "hideous and like a monster." Sitting in front of me in my office was an attractive young woman who truly could not objectively see how she appeared. Like so many of the BDD patients that I work with, Hazel stated that she was so ashamed to talk to me about this because she assumed that I would think she was vain or narcissistic and that I would not truly understand that she felt her face appeared monstrous.

I expressed to Hazel that I 100% completely believed that she was having these feelings about her appearance. I also made sure to explain that I believed that *she* was having this experience so that my comments were not misinterpreted. Individuals new to BDD treatment will either assume the clinician sees how unattractive they are, or, will conclude that the clinician has to be nice thus is not telling the truth about the body area of concern. It is important to validate the BDD patient's experience rather than focus on their appearance: This is a battle the clinician will not win.

During the process of getting to know Hazel, it soon became very apparent that she did not randomly wake up one morning not liking her appearance. Although initially tentative to do so, she began to share about the extensive bullying that she had experienced in elementary school. She admitted that she was even very ashamed to disclose that she had been teased constantly as a child and that much of the taunting was about her appearance. She stated that she had never spoken about this before not only because it was very shame inducing, but also because she assumed that everyone was teased as children and that this was normal. Hazel had not told her parents about the daily ridicule because she was too embarrassed, and she had not told her teachers because she thought that if her peers found out about this then she would be teased even more. Until sharing this information with me years later, Hazel had been enduring these traumatic experiences alone.

I thanked Hazel for trusting me enough to disclose this very shameful information. I explained that her experience was most definitely not normal, and although most children may get teased on occasion, the daily bullying that she endured was considerable and a prolonged trauma. Hazel seemed perplexed when I stated this because for years she had blamed herself, especially the appearance of her face, for why she was treated so poorly. She intellectually believed what I was saying, but emotionally it was difficult for her to fathom that perhaps she and her appearance were not to blame. To Hazel, it just felt so real that something must be really, really wrong with her face.

Even prior to sharing with me her traumatic childhood experiences, Hazel had been able to identify that the source of her BDD concerns were directly linked to the constant taunting about her appearance. Although Hazel had this insight prior to treatment, it was still not enough to disconnect the profoundly tormenting feelings associated with her facial features. However, this insight was a valuable therapeutic building block: Just the realization that perhaps she was not to blame for the abuse gave her a sense of hope and served as a major incentive to move forward in the therapeutic process.

Case Study: Andrew

Andrew, a man in his late thirties, arrived in therapy after a recent breakup with his long-time girlfriend. Andrew had been diagnosed with body dysmorphic disorder in his twenties and had been treated with cognitive-behavioral therapy. He reported that although his BDD symptoms had been temporarily reduced, the symptoms would resurface when he was tired or under stress. The break-up with his girlfriend had seemingly activated the worst episode of his BDD since prior to entering treatment the first time.

Andrew was preoccupied with hair loss. He admitted that he had been concerned about losing his hair ever since his early twenties when someone had made a comment to him that his hair was thinning. What had begun as a comment from an acquaintance soon turned into a tormenting preoccupation surrounding losing his hair. Andrew explained that not only was he fearful of losing his hair, but that he was very concerned how the shape of his face would appear if he was bald, thus hair loss represented an agonizing double bind for Andrew.

After getting to know Andrew better, he eventually revealed that he had been ashamed of the shape of his face ever since childhood because he had felt his face was too long and this in turn made his facial features appear "stretched out and not normal like others." He acknowledged that it seemed likely that he had body dysmorphic disorder symptoms much of his life, but that it was not until he received the hair loss comment that he began to experience full-blown symptoms. Andrew explained that he already felt as if his face looked different from that of other people, but that he was able to tolerate this. If he lost his hair, he believed he would "look like a Martian with a bald head and long face."

Andrew was terrified about losing his hair. He had insight that he suffered from body dysmorphic disorder, but he was still tormented by continuous thoughts about how he might look if he was bald. Besides not wanting to "look like a Martian," Andrew had no idea why something as seemingly innocuous as hair follicles held such power over him. He was able to articulate that he knew that hair does not cause feelings and that there is no physical danger associated with his hair, but his physiological response to observing what he perceived as hair loss was real. He would describe an "internal sinking-in-his-stomach" feeling that he would experience every time he saw one of his hairs on a pillow, in his brush, or in the shower drain. Or, if he was viewing his hair under bright light or in photos and believed that he saw hair loss, he would also experience this intense emotional reaction.

Although Andrew's hair and hairline did not resemble that of a male teenager, it did not appear out of the norm for a man in his late thirties. Andrew perceived his hair as much more thin than I observed it to be, believing that he was soon to be completely bald. He explained that his experience of hair loss felt equivalent to Chinese Water Torture: Drop by drop, hair by hair, he was heading toward becoming bald. This slow, tortuous process made him feel a sense of impending doom, that it was only a matter of time until the last remaining hair would fall out and his scalp would be completely exposed.

Because Andrew had previously experienced some success with cognitive-behavioral therapy, I decided to return to this modality at the very beginning of his treatment. I usually do not jump into behavioral therapy, specifically exposure and response prevention, so early in the treatment process; because of Andrew's former treatment record and fairly good insight, I decided that this could be conducive to giving him some relief from the tormenting, obsessive thoughts about hair loss. Simultaneously, we began to take a look at his personal history as well as his family of origin. Growing up he had not been bullied or teased about his appearance and denied any significant traumas during childhood or adolescence. He stated that as far as he knew, there was no mental illness in his immediate family besides his BDD; his extended family history consisted of several relatives with histories of major depression and alcoholism. Andrew did not feel that there was anything significantly out of the norm during his childhood, thus assumed that he must have "gotten a bad genetic draw" when it came to his BDD symptoms.

After several months of twice-per-week therapy, Andrew's body image symptoms began to decrease. He had refrained from participating in BDD compulsions and reported that there was an overall decrease in the intrusive thoughts about his hair. The terror connected with possible future hair loss still remained even though his day-to-day existence returned to how it had been prior to the break-up with his girlfriend. Both Andrew and I agreed that he was back to status quo, but unlike his first round in therapy, he realized that his hair was not the primary problem and that it could not be his actual hair causing the feelings of terror. Even while acknowledging that his hair was not truly the issue, he still had no idea why his hair held such dominance over how he felt.

Fast forward one year: A lot had come out in therapy. Issues regarding relationships, trust, intimacy, and his break-up had been discussed and processed. His BDD symptoms had become negligible. During one therapy session, with only a few minutes remaining, Andrew told me that he just remembered something that he did not think was too important but he figured he would tell me anyhow.

Andrew told me about a childhood experience regarding friends of his family. He explained how his family would usually spend Thanksgiving at another family's home and would also get together with them on other occasions. The father of this family was very much into fitness and was in superb physical health, that is until he was diagnosed with cancer. Andrew recalled how he witnessed this very strong, vibrant adult become crippled with the disease and how every time his family would go to visit, he would see the man become weaker and more disabled. He also observed a very obvious change in the dying man, that being significant hair loss. He did not know or understand that hair loss was the result of chemotherapy, and clearly remembers how a healthy man with a full head of hair so quickly became incapacitated and bald. Andrew recalled how the rapid hair loss really, really "freaked him out."

Andrew reiterated that he was not sure why he was even bringing this up in therapy, but that he had recently thought about the death of this family friend and how terrifying it had been for him. This had been the first person he knew who had died, and it happened so quickly. Andrew and I continued to explore this event during subsequent therapy sessions and it soon became evident to both of us that there was an association between this frightening childhood experience and his current fear regarding hair loss. Andrew began to remember other things that he would think about as a child and how this might be associated with his body related concerns. He remembered watching many science fiction movies growing up and recollected how Martians were usually portrayed as bald, along with having elongated faces that made them look different from humans. He admitted that he had never spoken about this before and had not even thought about it in many years.

We theorized that along with probably having a predisposition for body dysmorphic disorder, a conditioned response had likely transpired between hair loss and the frightening emotions associated with seeing someone rapidly become incapacitated and then die from cancer. For Andrew, hair loss was the most obvious, tangible change in the dying man, thus it is possible that balding was paired with these disturbing feelings. The experience of observing a person die may have been too overwhelming for Andrew, who as a child was not able to process these intense emotions. Hair is much more perceptible than feelings, thus the emotions associated with the death had possibly become paired with the obvious physical change of hair loss.

Whereas Hazel was aware of the likely origins of her body dysmorphic disorder symptoms, Andrew's hair loss preoccupation had diverged far from any conscious awareness between balding and the associated feelings of dread. Whether or not the individual with BDD is mindful of the symptom etiology, how does a body part become so closely linked with a feeling? Even BDD patients with poor insight will admit that feelings do not come directly from a body part. How then can we explain that so many individuals with body dysmorphic disorder report having literal feelings attached to the body area of concern?

The Body: An Emotional Conduit

When an emotionally mature adult endures an uncomfortable emotion, they understand that this is an ephemeral experience that will eventually dissipate. Either they have the capacity to self-soothe or they have healthy mechanisms to cope with these feelings such as expressing themselves to another person. If an individual is never taught that emotions are a normal human occurrence that should be embraced rather than avoided, then they will likely develop seemingly adaptive mechanisms to defend against these uncomfortable feelings. It is human nature to avoid distressing emotions, thus ridding oneself of these feelings is not in itself unusual. But what might initially appear as an adaptive mechanism to cope with bad feelings may eventually become maladaptive.

When explaining emotions to my patients, especially to those who are very analytical or intellectual and emotionally disconnected, I give the example of blowing up a balloon: If air was analogous to emotions, and you blew a breath into a balloon every time you felt bad, the balloon would soon become inflated. There will become a point where the balloon begins to get over-inflated and if air is not released it will eventually burst. I explain that we all experience emotions, but if we do not have healthy means of releasing the emotions, we will eventually rupture like the over-inflated balloon. Although temporary relief may be experienced when avoiding emotions or when participating in compulsive behaviors to reduce uncomfortable feelings, this is highly problematic because the feelings are never properly processed and released, thus remain within us. The problem is not the emotions, but rather the maladaptive means by which they are dealt with.

If a child is not raised in a nurturing and emotionally safe environment, chances are that there will be deficits in understanding emotions and knowing how to manage these internal experiences. If a parent or parents are emotionally off the mark when mirroring their child, it is highly likely that the child will not acquire the most fundamental foundation of being emotionally attuned. If a child is raised in an environment conducive to healthy emotional development, it increases the chance that they will be able to manage distressing experiences. Even if they are not able to self-regulate their emotions in a particular situation, having a safe environment at home to return to allows them to at least have an outlet to process the experience rather than turn it inward.

Both Hazel and Andrew came from relatively emotionally stable family systems, but the intensity of the emotions that they were experiencing were such that they were unable to adequately process the information. Hazel experienced extreme humiliation and did not disclose her situation for fear of reprisal from her peers along with having profound shame associated with the traumatic events. Andrew was frightened by the drastic bodily changes he witnessed in a healthy man who rapidly deteriorated toward death. The intensity of both their emotional experiences were way too overwhelming for them to comprehend as children, thus the feelings were internalized.

Infants and very young children do not have the cognitive capacity to grasp and process abstract concepts, but they do understand the relationship between actions and objects (Hoffman et al. 1988). Emotions are not concrete, but the physical body is a tangible object. If a child is stimulated by a distressing emotion over and over again in conjunction with a particular physical feature, the emotion may eventually become associated with the body part. Classical conditioning is the process of learning in which a strong stimulus is elicited in response to a stimulus that was previously neutral. This occurs when there is a consistent pairing of the neutral and potent stimulus (Pavlov 1927). If a virulent event occurs in relation to the body—which initially may have been a neutral stimuli—it may become paired with distressing emotions elicited by the negative experience.

Shame is the emotion that a person has when there is a deep-rooted, inherent belief that there is something so very wrong with them, and because of this, they must conceal this from others to avoid being negatively judged and feeling humiliated. Hazel would feel shame and humiliation every time she was teased about her appearance. She did not disclose her traumatic experiences to her parents or teachers because she was so humiliated, thus was left to her own accord in trying to make sense of why her peers would be so mean to her. As a child, Hazel did not have the life experience or cognitive acumen to understand why she was being bullied. At the time she only understood that there must be something very unattractive about her appearance and because of this she deserved to be treated so badly.

Hazel's body dysmorphic disorder symptoms were so intense that looking at her face, feeling her face, and even thinking about her face would stimulate intense feelings of shame and embarrassment. Several years of daily taunting about her appearance accompanied by acute feelings of shame likely became coupled such that anything associated with her appearance had become associated with negative emotions. She expressed how she had felt extremely lonely during the time she was being regularly taunted, and that she had turned to the mirror and photographs to attempt to figure out what was so wrong with her. After school she would go home and gaze in the mirror and make different facial expressions in an attempt to appear less ugly. The mirror became a safe haven for her because even though she strongly disliked her reflection, at least she was not being bullied, or at least she was not being bullied by her peers.

Hazel interpreted how people treated her as evidence that something must be fundamentally wrong with her. Her reflection represented something tangible that could help her comprehend the stinging feelings of shame; the emotions that Hazel had internalized were now being filtered through her facial features. Whereas at school Hazel was being bullied by her peers, at home she became the bully as she spent hours in front of her bedroom mirror critically scrutinizing all aspects of her face and head. Mirror checking and related compulsive behaviors developed as mechanisms to emotionally soothe herself and as an attempt to make sense of a dreadful situation. These compulsive behaviors persisted long after Hazel had switched schools and was no longer being verbally and emotionally abused.

Body dysmorphic disorder compulsions and avoidance behaviors reinforce the association between the distressing emotion and the body part. A pattern of engaging in compulsions begins when it is realized that emotional distress decreases following one of these behaviors. Whether the compulsion is as blatant as viewing or touching the body or as subtle as avoiding situations that activate body related sentiment, it assists in temporarily mollifying emotional duress. The next time the individual experiences the negative emotion attributed to their body, they will repeat the compulsion that previously provided relief. This cycle reinforces itself because more and more compulsions become necessary in order to maintain the initial experience of symptom alleviation.

The relief experienced after performing a body related compulsion strengthens the association between the disliked body part and the negative emotion. If an individual experiences relief after participating in a body related compulsive behavior, the message interpreted by the brain must be something to the degree of, "I was feeling danger and defectiveness connected with my body, but now I am not, thus it must be this area of my body that is the problem." The continuous repetition of compulsions will inevitably intensify the belief system that the body part is the source of the emotional pain and this in turn exacerbates the hyper-focus on the body. The relationship between the supposed defect and the related negative emotion can become so entrenched that the BDD sufferer may be incapable of identifying that their emotional affliction may have a genesis beyond that of their appearance.

Years of body related compulsions fortify the connection between a physical feature and the negative emotions. This is very problematic because not only do BDD symptoms worsen, but the body part becomes an external object employed to regulate emotions. If emotions are being regulated by way of an external object, then the individual cannot be self-soothing from within. If the identified body area becomes a filter for how the individual experiences emotions and interprets interpersonal relationships, then it will inevitably take on excessive value because it becomes the mechanism by which they interface with the world. If the body takes on such profound value that it replaces an individual's internal locus and becomes the barometer for regulating emotions, then any feeling—body related or otherwise—will be interpreted through the vortex of the supposed defect.

Many of my patients have reported that the perception of their bodily defect can fluctuate week-to-week, day-by-day, and even from hour-to-hour. The majority of these individuals report that they intellectually know that these physical changes are not possible, but even with this awareness they may still see themselves differently at any given time. Patients have often referred to this experience as "shape-shifting." Needless to say, this can be quite disconcerting for someone whose mood is so dependent upon how they feel they look. If feelings are determined by how one perceives their appearance but at any given time the perception of their appearance drastically differs, there will inevitably be a fluctuation in emotional states.

Many body dysmorphic disorder sufferers attribute their negative emotions to their perceived defect, but perhaps this is a two-way street: If years of repetitive compulsive behaviors have conditioned certain negative emotions to a particular area of the body, might it be possible that unrelated activating feelings and other internal experiences could also manifest through the body part? Could uncomfortable and activating emotions that are percolating from within, and that have not been adequately processed, surface through the body area that is deemed defective? If this does occur, then this may explain why individuals with BDD have such a diffuse and easily altered perception of how they appear. This may also explain why so many individuals with BDD describe having very distinct physical experiences within the body area that they interpret as defective: They are feeling and experiencing a multitude of emotions that are accumulating and being regulated through certain physical points in their body. As the repository for unprocessed emotions, the amount of distortion that the individual experiences surrounding a body part may be correlated to the intensity of the emotions being activated.

External events may also stimulate what material is internally triggered. My patients consistently report an exacerbation in their symptoms when they are under stress. I often observe this when archaic pathological themes from the individual's past become activated. For individuals new to psychotherapy or for those who have limited insight into their symptoms, the body area of concern is usually identified as the source of duress. For those individuals who are much further along in their recovery, they soon become aware of particular emotional states and external situations that regularly coincide with increased bodily preoccupation.

3 Psychotherapy and Body Dysmorphic Disorder

All human beings organize their world in a manner that makes sense to them and feels comfortable and safe. Not fully understanding our surroundings and why we exist leads us to gravitate toward ideologies that comfort and enlighten us. Within the field of psychology, clinicians often drift toward the therapeutic modalities that best fit within their life paradigm. It is not uncommon that the modality that a therapist feels comfortable working with is the same as the one they used in their own personal therapies that contributed to a sense of improved self-awareness, an integrated identity, and feelings of security. If a particular philosophy makes us feel better about ourselves, it only makes sense that we share these beliefs with other people. If a particular therapeutic ideology resonates with us and answers many questions regarding our own life experience, this likely will be the therapeutic stance that we feel most comfortable with when assisting patients. This may also be the bane of treatment when working with complex psychotherapy cases, such as with individuals suffering from body dysmorphic disorder.

When using the term psychotherapy, I am referring to any and all techniques, modalities, and processes that a clinician utilizes in order to provide relief from emotional and psychological distress. Clinicians who have practiced psychotherapy for many years are well aware that there is not a quick fix for psychological or psychiatric disorders. Recovery from many of these disorders, especially body dysmorphic disorder, exists on a continuum of gradual progress rather than on a cured or not-cured Western medicine model. This is not what most people want to hear, especially those who suffer from this tormenting body image disturbance. Although there is no magical panacea, many BDD sufferers do significantly improve such that life is no longer about trying to just survive.

I do not believe that there is one correct method of treating body image disturbances: Body dysmorphic disorder evolves by way of multiple psychological, psychiatric, familial, environmental, and behavioral origins. This in itself is not unusual for psychiatric syndromes, but I have observed that patients with body image disturbances often present with a much more complex amalgamation of symptoms that complicate treatment and frustrate even seasoned psychotherapists. Working with BDD cases can be very confusing because there are often so many variables to contend with. If we are the practitioner treating a difficult, multifaceted case that confuses us, it is not unnatural to resort to therapeutic methods and techniques that we have used successfully in the past and that make us feel more secure and competent. There in lies the dilemma in treating body dysmorphic disorder patients: If we consistently organize our treatment approach based upon what is most familiar to us, it is very likely that sooner rather than later we will encounter a BDD patient that does not fit into our therapeutic model.

There is no place for therapeutic dogma when treating body dysmorphic disorder. We all would like to think that our treatment paradigm is the most effective for conceptualizing therapy cases, thus we frequently utilize the modalities with our patients that are most comfortable for how we organize our own lives. Although I do not feel there is one correct approach to BDD treatment, I do believe that an incorrect system of treatment entails rigid and inflexible doctrinaires regarding how treatment should proceed. Body dysmorphic disorder patients exist with the unyielding and dogmatic belief that their appearance holds the key to a higher level of functioning and better quality of life. It is exactly these stringent beliefs that keep them stuck and in a perpetual cycle of reverting to these principles in the desperate attempt to feel attractive.

If you are treating BDD patients, you should be very mindful of not taking a fixed stance on how a case should proceed; to do otherwise is in essence mimicking the firmly entrenched schemas of the patient. If both the patient and the psychotherapist have very rigid stances then it is more than likely that the treatment process will soon stall. Therapists working with this patient population need to model flexibility in thinking and feeling (Feusner, Winograd, and Saxena 2005). Clinicians who do not feel comfortable working outside of a singular therapeutic modality should probably refer body dysmorphic disorder patients to practitioners who feel more comfortable employing multiple psychotherapy methodologies.

I realize that when I say there is not one correct way of treating body dysmorphic disorder that this may seem quite ambiguous, especially to a practitioner who is reading this material intentionally to gain insight, direction, and treatment recommendations. This does not mean that all therapeutic modalities are equally conducive to achieving long-term symptom reduction, but one approach does not fit all BDD patients. It is important to not completely rule out a particular technique because this might be the one that the patient best responds to.

Having done psychotherapy with this patient population for many years, I have adapted, adjusted to, and become comfortable with a variety of therapeutic techniques that these individuals respond well to, and of course I will share these. This being stated, with every new BDD patient

I make sure not to assume that they will respond to treatment like the hundreds of patients that I have worked with before them. Of course there are usually analogous themes between body image patients, but I reiterate that one or even two styles of therapy do not fit all patients and to assume so will increase the likelihood that the clinician will become stuck in the same inflexible quagmire in which the patient has been sinking.

No therapist wants to fail their client, and no therapist enjoys the experience of feeling stuck and not knowing what to do with a patient who is not responding to treatment. In life we often panic when we feel out of control, lost, or trapped, and this is also applicable to the therapy practitioner who is witnessing their patient descend further into emotional oblivion. If this occurs when working with the body dysmorphic disorder patient—and I guarantee you it will—it is imperative not to revert to the safety of the therapeutic realm that makes you feel competent, especially if this is the modality that you have been actively using while treating the patient who is lapsing.

To rapidly return to the safety of our accustomed therapeutic cubicle only imitates the reaction of the patient who always returns to the familiarity of their body every time they are feeling out of control or emotionally overwhelmed. It is during the times where the patient is not responding to our direction and is experiencing emotional torment that the clinician needs to tolerate the patient's frustrations and not over-react by frantically trying to fix them. This panicked need to fix the patient or rescue them from their anguish may at times be the psychotherapist's need to diminish their own feelings of incompetence as they see that the patient is not responding to their recommendations.

The need to urgently fix the patient because the clinician is feeling inept is a major pitfall when working with complicated patients such as those with body dysmorphic disorder. The clinician needs to have the capacity to tolerate the emotional intensity and ambiguity of the BDD population. To not have the ability to tolerate this unpredictability increases the chances that the clinician will respond by utilizing therapeutic techniques that may feel most organized to them, but that might not be best for the patient.

In Chapter 5 I talk about body dysmorphic disorder compulsions and how these contribute to the BDD patient remaining so stuck. BDD sufferers participate in ritualistic body related behaviors that they believe will free them from emotional duress; it is also these behaviors that keep them perpetually trapped because they are inhibited from experiencing and adapting to the perturbing emotions that eventually manifest as a body image disturbance. Regardless of the variety of therapeutic modalities that can be employed with the body dysmorphic disorder patient population, it is very necessary to allow the patient to experience these uncomfortable emotions without the distraction of the clinician constantly attempting to solve the overt body image disturbance. The clinician needs to be aware that fixing the obvious problem may at times be contraindicated because it diverts attention away from the patient experiencing uncomfortable feelings. Thus sometimes less can be more: This is the first therapeutic technique that I recommend when treating this patient population.

Body dysmorphic disorder patients who are beginning treatment often ask me if I am going to help them like how they look. The patients who ask this are generally skeptical about entering therapy and are convinced that their appearance must be fixed first and foremost before their lives can change. My response to them is one that they are mostly not interested in hearing: "Your life will get better when your appearance does not determine how you fundamentally feel about yourself. You will know when you are recovering from body dysmorphic disorder when you become neutral regarding how you look and your identity is not dependent upon a body part." I do not expect the individual entering treatment to completely absorb this, but it sets the stage for the therapy process emphasizing that recovery will not result from altering one's external characteristics.

Like all psychiatric disorders, body dysmorphic disorder exists on a continuum of severity. There are those patients who appear to function and carry out normalized daily activities even though they are tormented by negative intrusive thoughts about their appearance. There are also individuals who have not left their homes in years because they truly believe that they are too physically horrifying to be seen. Most body dysmorphic disorder sufferers experience symptoms somewhere in between these extremes. I have observed that an individual's emotional development is often correlated to symptom severity as well as to the duration of time that the BDD has actively disrupted their life. A patient who has been struggling with BDD symptoms for many years will probably have a less integrated sense of self and usually their emotional development does not match their chronological age. For those with fewer symptoms, emotional growth is less impeded.

Adolescents are excessively concerned about their appearance and what other people think of them. They are transitioning between childhood and young adulthood and are struggling to establish an identity that they can call their own (Hoffman et al. 1988). They frequently turn to the most obvious and concrete method of distinguishing themselves, that being their appearance. This is not unlike the individual with body dysmorphic disorder who chronologically may have passed adolescence, but is still emotionally stranded in an adolescent psychosocial stage of development. As they struggle in an attempt to correct, change, or perfect their appearance, other areas of psychosocial development are hindered which in turn leaves the BDD patient emotionally stranded. They automatically assume that they are not functioning as a result of the perceived body defect, when actually it is the thoughts about the importance of appearance that blatantly interferes with the establishment of a definitive sense of self. Emotional evolution is delayed as the individual continuously fixates on perceived body imperfections; the external distraction of appearance is in direct conflict with the individual developing an identity from within, thus an endless cycle is perpetuated.

Recovery from body dysmorphic disorder does not only entail decreasing the overt body image symptoms but necessitates stimulating emotional development from the point where it became delayed. It is not unusual that the onset of emotional delay is correlated with the initial exacerbation of the patient's BDD symptoms. When working with BDD clients I am always asking myself the question, "Did the BDD cause the emotional stranding, or, is the BDD serving a greater purpose?" Any psychiatric condition can significantly interfere with emotional maturation processes especially if it occurs during formative developmental years, and body dysmorphic disorder is no exception. I believe that it is important to examine the possibility that perhaps the disorder is more than what meets the eye and at times may be the symptom of a more deeply rooted condition.

To recover from body dysmorphic disorder involves becoming an autonomous adult who has the ability to cope with life's adversities as well as the capacity to internally regulate one's own emotions. Many individuals with BDD have not had the opportunity to do so because of the constant external distraction of their appearance. Many body dysmorphic disorder patients are not aware that their emotional development has been delayed and they continue to attribute many personal deficits to their perceived aesthetic defects. These emotional developmental reprieves can significantly impact the person's ability to function as an adult and it is the clinician's responsibility to bring this to the attention of their patient. In my experience it is not uncommon that BDD symptoms will worsen when the therapist begins having this conversation with their client. To acknowledge that perhaps a body part is not the sole determinant of why one's life is in shambles means that the individual may have to delve into uncomfortable thoughts and feelings. As miserable as body dysmorphic disorder can be, it may provide a diversion from emotionally activating material.

Concurrent with the emotional delay are deficits in social skills and interpersonal appropriateness. Not only does the body image disturbance hamper the individual's ability to integrate a solid sense of identity, but it also may interfere with the acquisition of normalized interpersonal acumen. Social feedback from others may be misinterpreted or altogether avoided, resulting in a paucity of evidence from the outside world that could otherwise serve to challenge the rigidity and inaccuracy of BDD thoughts and beliefs. Deficits in interpersonal skills also increase the possibility that social cues will be misinterpreted or missed altogether.

The individual with BDD often delineates external feedback in a way that matches their biased body image paradigm and this only reinforces their belief system that their appearance is at the origin of their limited quality relationships. The deficiency of accurate external feedback and the deprivation of internal self-efficacy leaves the individual stuck: Without alternative feedback from either direction, the intrusive body dysmorphic disorder thoughts remain as the focal point of the individual's existence.

The enduring challenge for the treating clinician is to get the patient "unstuck." The patient may intellectually begin to understand that their emotional development was delayed, but this does not mean that emotionally they are prepared to progress. They usually understand that recovery might mean a higher quality of life but this does not necessarily translate into their emotional experience. Patients frequently remark, "If I could only get back to how I used to feel." They often remember a period of time prior to the onset of symptoms during which the feelings of shame and disgust were less pronounced or even seemingly nonexistent. This particular point of time is their reference point of what quality of life should look and feel like. This though is problematic and "getting back to this point in time" should not be the goal of the therapist or patient.

The attempt to "get back to before" is not possible because we are all constantly changing for better or worse and this in itself is an accumulation of our life experience. Also, struggling to retrieve a past life experience will interfere with emotional maturation in the present. This does not mean that the patient should not discuss what life was like previous to the onset of symptoms, but the purpose should not be to replicate a previous era in their life.

It is acceptable for the therapist to process these dynamics with their body dysmorphic disorder patient. It is important for the patient to understand that the excessive focus on their appearance mimics themes of adolescent development: Most individuals who are not predisposed to body image disturbance are able to traverse the insecurities of adolescence and progress toward young adulthood. This may not occur with those who have a diathesis for the psychiatric condition body dysmorphic disorder. Even though physically they may have matured into adults, the emotional delay can leave them stranded in a developmental stage comparable to adolescence. This discrepancy can be quite disruptive to identity development and is not conducive to the navigation of autonomy, relationships, and other themes of young adulthood. The body dysmorphic disorder sufferer will often attribute their inability to fully function as an autonomous adult as a result of their supposed aesthetic defects rather than as a consequence of developmental deficits.

The patient may feel overwhelmed when it is brought to their attention that there have been emotional developmental delays that may be partially responsible for their limited functioning. I explain to the individual that it is feasible to restart emotional growth and that the process of assimilating emotional and chronological maturation can occur fairly rapidly with consistent psychotherapy. I do emphasize that their attempts to improve their lives by way of their appearance have not been working and that something different needs to occur in order to catalyze emotional growth. It is not unusual that this is met with resistance because this would also involve admitting that years and years of maladaptive behaviors were for naught. It would also entail having to trust another person and accept feedback regarding a paradigm that is likely the antithesis of their own.

As psychotherapy proceeds, the process of emotional maturation will inevitably gain momentum. The therapist can expect to witness an individual emotionally evolving through incomplete psychosocial stages of development within a very condensed span of time. Assuming that the individual's emotional arrested development began prior to adolescence, it is predictable that this person will have to traverse the emotional terrain that did not occur during their chronological adolescence. Thus the clinician needs to expect the possibility of turbulent therapy sessions as the rebellion of adolescence unfolds as the individual attempts to establish their own identity. The acting out process needs to occur so that the patient can begin to individuate into the psychosocial stage of young adulthood. Fortunately for the therapist, the period of defiance that occurs while overcoming years of emotional stagnation does not last nearly as long as it would during actual adolescence.

I have observed that the body dysmorphic disorder patients who are the most emotionally stranded often have much more difficulty reconciling physical changes that result from the natural process of ageing. Individuals with BDD have enough difficulty accepting their appearance as is, thus natural bodily reformations are often experienced as highly disturbing. To observe the natural changes in the body provides concrete evidence that one is chronologically growing older; this can also be experienced as moving further away from the point in time in which emotional development decelerated.

The BDD patient is usually actively focused on the changing body part and may not be aware that seeing this physical change is activating fears of growing up, as well as moving further away from the incomplete developmental phases of their life. Gradual physical changes in appearance become tangible evidence that ageing is occurring, thus the body may become the object of distress. I hypothesize that the body part is only the transitional object that serves as an insecure but concrete alternative to the more profound aversion of becoming an individuated adult. Becoming an autonomous adult would entail having to acknowledge and experience emotions that perhaps have never been examined or processed.

For those individuals who are ambivalent toward intimacy, physical evidence of ageing may also render an increased preoccupation with appearance. Body dysmorphic disorder patients often erroneously deduce that being loved is directly connected to attractiveness: Aesthetic changes that come with age are experienced as a direct threat to ever achieving physical normalcy and is often interpreted as conclusive evidence that they can never be loved. Inevitably it is this concern that will interfere with the individual formulating an intimate connection with another person.

Some body dysmorphic disorder patients may not be directly disturbed by the ageing body part itself, but are still preoccupied with the change because of its implications for other areas of the body. Julian, a man in his mid-twenties, entered treatment stating he could not stop obsessing about his skin, nose, dark circles under his eyes, and the shape of his jawline. These areas of concern were soon to shift to that of his hair, which he began to believe was thinning, and his hairline, which he perceived was receding. He explained to me that of course he did not want to lose his hair, but that his greatest fear was that if he became bald there would be nothing to distract from his face, which he thought was ugly.

Rita, a woman in her late twenties, entered therapy expressing anger about a recent rhinoplasty that she felt had gone awry and that made her nose appear even less attractive than prior to the surgery. Although her primary concern was that her nose was misshapen, it was not long before she admitted that she was also concerned about "fine facial lines around her mouth and crows feet by her eyes." She stated that she had never really had a major concern about wrinkles, and that her skin had always been the only body part that she did not dislike; she believed that her skin over-compensated for her unattractive nose. Her skin had never been a primary preoccupation, but it was soon to become a major area of concern because she felt it could no longer be used as a diversion from what she perceived as her unattractive nose.

Another theme surrounding the ageing process is the concern that other people will notice and comment on these physical changes. Having to see people from the past often activates the fear that the aesthetic changes due to ageing will be readily observed, especially the body areas that are overvalued. The possibility that these changes in appearance might draw attention to the perceived defect is the source of major shame. It is not unusual that individuals with body dysmorphic disorder will avoid situations where there is the possibility of meeting people from the past. I have worked with individuals who have skipped going to high school reunions, weddings, and even funerals rather than risk the possibility that they will see someone from past times and receive a comment about how their appearance has changed.

Attunement

Most individuals with body dysmorphic disorder feel as if no one truly understands their inner torment and many do not dare disclose their experience because of the pervasive shame that fuels their symptoms. For those who do manage to reveal their shameful preoccupation, they often feel as if the other person either does not believe them or cannot fully comprehend their experience. Individuals with this condition really,

really want to be heard and understood but are often hesitant to reveal their innermost secrets. To unveil this information exposes them to the very familiar experience of feeling very alone because no one seems able to fully identify with them. This only perpetuates archaic feelings that somehow they are inherently different from anyone and everyone else.

In my opinion, one of the most important, necessary, and valuable skills that a clinician can utilize when working with this patient population is the capacity for attunement. Attunement is the process by which one human being authentically connects to another: Listening while not judging, mirroring the patient's emotional state, and letting them know that you believe that they are having the thoughts and feelings that they are describing. Attunement cannot be measured, nor should it be measured. Attunement is not a therapeutic modality: It is not about fixing, finding a solution, or making interpretations. Attunement is not evidenced based. Although no two people will ever have identical thoughts and feelings, a person feels attuned with another when there is an exchange of genuine compassion and acknowledgement that the other person's experiences do exist.

Attunement is the essential cornerstone of treatment that needs to be laid from the very first contact with the body dysmorphic disorder patient and needs to be maintained throughout the course of the therapeutic relationship. The treating clinician has to become highly attuned with the inner experiences of the BDD patient: This is a very sensitive patient population that is acutely aware when anyone, including the practitioner, is emotionally off the mark. As in all quality psychotherapy, becoming emotionally attuned with a patient lays the foundation of trust; this in turn allows the patient to feel safe disclosing very intimate information.

Because with the body dysmorphic disorder patient population these intimate details are usually doused in significant shame, discussing the shame-evoking material is a crucial component of emotional and psychological healing. The clinician has to remain attuned not only to foster a secure environment in which shameful material can be divulged, but also to serve as a model to the patient of what healthy attunement and mirroring involves. BDD patients often have major deficits in interpersonal relationships stemming from a paucity in mirroring earlier in their lives: Many have experienced insufficient attunement with people as a result of having been so attached to a body part. Good enough attunement strengthens the attachment between the clinician and patient, a relationship that needs to be very secure during the process of recovery.

The Therapeutic Trajectory

The path toward recovery from body dysmorphic disorder rarely follows a linear trail. In fact, the clinician should expect a seemingly well-organized and sensible therapeutic route to go off course sooner rather than later.

The pervasive themes of deep-rooted shame, fear of intimacy, and the ambivalence surrounding interpersonal relationships will inevitably enter the therapeutic arena. The psychotherapist should not be surprised that when these themes arise, it coincides with interruptions in the treatment process. This may present as an increase in external chaos, "fires" that need to be extinguished that divert attention and therapy time away from addressing underlying themes. It is also not uncommon that at this juncture the patient takes a hiatus from therapy.

When working with a new BDD patient, I explain that during the process of treatment there will always be uncomfortable emotions that will surface. I explain that it is during these times that I would hope they could express to me how they are feeling and if they are getting the urge to bolt from therapy. Even having pre-emptively communicated this does not guarantee that the patient will remain in treatment. Individuals with body dysmorphic disorder tend to have avoidant personality traits; just being their clinician provides no assurance that they will attempt to avoid addressing certain issues. Just when you believe that a breakthrough is occurring in the therapy milieu is when you may receive the voicemail message that they need to take a break from therapy, or can no longer attend.

The most common rationalizations that I encounter are that "I no longer can afford to come to therapy" or "my insurance is no longer reimbursing me for sessions." If the patient is employed, they may report that they are unable to participate in therapy because of their work schedule. These justifications might very well be the truth, but they also serve as a rationalization defense against having to explore and acknowledge emotionally painful material (Diehl et al. 2014). Hopefully the patient will provide notice to the clinician regarding their predicament so other accommodations can be made and so the emotions behind the rationalization can be processed. Unfortunately, too often, this is not the case as the patient will notify the therapist in the closing minutes of their final session or by way of a voicemail message stating that they will be discontinuing treatment. If this occurs, I recommend contacting the patient and letting them know that when their circumstances change they are more than welcome to continue the therapy process.

I have observed over the years that psychotherapy for body dysmorphic disorder infrequently occurs on a straight trajectory. A patient may begin and withdraw from treatment multiple times, sometimes even spanning multiple years from the commencement of therapy to when they are ready to address the more shameful material that festers beneath the overt body image symptoms. It is usually an exacerbation of their BDD symptoms that brings them back into therapy. I do not view this inconsistent psychotherapy process as either good or bad, but rather the gradual process that may have to occur with this very sensitive and avoidant patient population.

Although it is acceptable to discuss with the patient your concerns that he may be avoiding addressing uncomfortable material, I recommend respecting this elongated process rather than attempting to persuade the client to remain in treatment. It is likely that your attempts at convincing them to remain under your care will not alter their decision and may also be interpreted as you disapproving of them; this will only strengthen the patient's shame and deep-seated beliefs that somehow they are bad or defective.

In the following chapters I discuss therapeutic genres and techniques that I often utilize when treating body dysmorphic disorder patients. By no means do I feel that these are the only methods that can be used when working with this patient population, but these are the ones that I have found to be conducive to getting BDD sufferers unstuck. If you are not familiar with any of these, this does not necessarily mean that you cannot treat body image patients, although it could only contribute to your therapeutic arsenal if you were to learn. I have worked with body image patients with whom I have used all of these therapeutic modalities, and there have been those patients with whom I used none or maybe only one of these techniques. Regardless, the essential ingredient of these treatments is less about which modality is utilized: The success of each therapeutic variation reflects the quality of attunement as well as the flexibility exhibited in adapting to the patient rather than imposing rigid and systematic therapeutic boundaries upon them.

4 Furry Caterpillars on My Forehead

Sadie's Story

My name is Sadie. My earliest memories of body dysmorphic disorder began in grammar school when I was only 11-years-old. I remember sitting in class and having this very strange sensation that my eyebrows, my eyes, my cheekbones, and the corners of my mouth were drooping. I would be very distracted by this feeling and because it was so uncomfortable I would regularly leave class and go to the bathroom to check my face in the mirror. While gazing in the mirror I would experiment with different ways that I could stop my face from feeling as if it was drooping. I was very ashamed about how I felt my face appeared, thus I needed to come up with clever ways to do this without other people noticing. I figured out that if I squeezed the muscles in my forehead then I would not experience the falling sensation in my eyebrows. Although I thought that this was very subtle, I must have been walking around with a surprised look on my face because I was constantly scrunching up my forehead in order to make my eyebrows feel taught.

The best way I can describe the sinking experience that I was having in my face is to compare it to a Salvador Dali painting where everything is melting. Besides continually scrunching up my forehead, I needed another tool that I could use to mask my appearance: This is when I discovered make-up. When my mother was not home, I would go into the room where she kept all her make-up and women's magazines. I would scrutinize every female image in these magazines, studying their facial features, especially their eyes and eyebrows. I wanted to figure out how I could literally recreate their eye shape and change the shape of my eyes to minimize the feeling that they were dipping downward. In retrospect, I began to use make-up in a pretty extreme way and ironically it must have made my eyes look quite strange.

I believed that my face looked monstrous and that I could not be seen in the world without offending or disgusting people. I learned that when I used make-up I could create an illusion that made my eyes and eyebrows appear as if they were not sinking. What began as an experiment in an attempt to make my face feel normal soon turned into spending six, seven, and even eight hours a day putting on cosmetics. It felt as if every moment of the day my face was morphing and I found that by using make-up I could temporarily have the experience of "freezing" my face. I also believed that if I kept my mouth in a certain position then this would keep my cheekbones propped up; this in turn would make my eyes feel as if they were not hanging lower on my face. It was as if I wanted my features to stay as still as a statue so that I could recall every facial movement that I made. This was the only way I could experience my face as feeling somewhat normal.

I always wore make-up even when I was at home. I was afraid that if there was an instance where a family friend stopped over unannounced that they would see my bare face and be repulsed. The only time that I would ever look at my face without wearing cosmetics was when I would wake up early in the morning to begin the arduous process of putting it on before I left for school. It was very difficult for me to look at myself without wearing it, and when I did so I would wonder why my face looked so distorted and why nobody else had facial features like mine. I had thought about getting plastic surgery to change my face but I was a teenager and did not have the financial resources, so I did the next best thing, which was to attempt to make the structure of my face look and feel different with make-up.

Even though I spent hours putting my make-up on, I never felt like I could get it exact enough to leave my home and to be seen in public. I would try to draw a straight line with my eyeliner, but then I would look in the mirror and it did not seem like a straight line and did not appear level with my other eye. I would get the make-up remover and take off the eyeliner and then do it all over, again and again, to the point where my eyes would get red and swollen. Since I could rarely get my eyes and eyeliner to look right, I would move on to what I perceived was my lack of obvious cheekbones. I would try to use foundation and blush to create the illusion that I had cheekbones. This would also be a process of taking the make-up on and off, over and over again. I would also attempt to balance out the shape of my lips because I felt they were offset and that my upper and lower lip were different sizes. If I did not have to leave for school, this process would have continued all day. It was very tormenting for me to leave the mirror: Even though I hated looking at myself, I would feel like a failure if I could not correctly put on my cosmetics. To not perfectly apply my make-up would leave me feeling hopeless and very depressed.

During school hours there was no way that I could be in front of the mirror all of the time, so I needed to figure out a way to know if my face was severely offending people versus moderately offending them. I began to mentally catalog the eye contact that I had with every person I interacted with, whether they were classmates, teachers, the lunch lady, or strangers on the street. In my mind I would assign a value to every interaction, for instance, if the person looked at me and then looked away, I would catalog this as a negative reaction to my appearance. If a person maintained eye contact with me for a longer period of time,

I would interpret this as a neutral or maybe even a positive reaction to my face. I believed that if I cataloged more positive than negative reactions then this must mean that I was offending fewer people.

The majority of the interactions that I mentally cataloged I would label as negative, and this would be evidence to me that I should not go anywhere in public besides school. I dreaded the negative looks because to me these felt incredibly judgmental, as if I did not deserve to exist. I felt that if my appearance offended someone and this received a negative label, I could not return to this location because I was much too ashamed. I also did not want to offend them for a second time and felt as if I was being a burden by causing them anguish when they saw my face. Growing up in a small town, I quickly ran out of places that I could go because I never wanted to return to a location where I had previously cataloged a negative interaction. This became an exercise of avoiding on a massive level.

My make-up ritual was very private, and I always did this alone because it was so embarrassing for me and I was so afraid that people would assume I was vain. It may have seemed to other people that I was wearing so much make-up because I wanted attention, but actually I just wanted to blend in because I thought I looked like a monster without it. When I lived at home during high school I was able to hide out in my bedroom and work on my make-up in secret. I was terrified to go to college because I knew it would be very difficult to conceal my extensive make-up rituals if I had to share a dormitory room with another person.

My body dysmorphic disorder became much worse once I went to college. Just like in high school, I would spend hours in the mirror fixing my make-up before I could even leave my dorm room. It was very difficult for me to even make it to class; many times I would be so preoccupied with desperately trying to make my face look acceptable that hours would go by and I would miss class altogether. Going to a lecture not only entailed the hours of make-up preparation, but it also meant having to be seen by people on campus and then being surrounded by people when sitting in the lecture hall. I would create very circuitous routes to make sure that I could avoid the most crowded areas of campus; often going far out of my way to insure fewer people would see me. I also became very familiar with all the reflective surfaces on my path across campus so that I could check to see how my make-up and face looked. These included bathroom mirrors, plexi-glass windows, car windows, and any other reflective surface where I could view my appearance before I entered the classroom.

Sitting in a classroom encircled by people felt extremely intolerable. I would go to the bathroom as many times as possible in an attempt to fix my make-up. But if someone else was already in the bathroom this posed a problem because I was too ashamed to have them see me do my make-up. When I was sitting in class I was focusing on if the other students were noticing how bad I looked, and if they looked in my direction I would assign a value to their glance. Constantly going to the bathroom mirror and cataloging how other students in the class viewed me made it almost impossible to concentrate on anything the professor was teaching. It is hard to believe that I was able to graduate from college; the irony of all my avoidance of people meant that I spent a lot of time studying.

During college I had an appendectomy and because of this I lost a lot of weight. I observed that my face looked a little thinner after the operation and because of this my cheekbones and eyes seemed to appear more proportional. It also felt as if they were not drooping as much as before the weight loss; after this observation I began to restrict my diet. I was not at all preoccupied by how my body appeared from the neck down, but what I cared about was how my cheekbones appeared in relation to my eyes. My parents became concerned that I was losing too much weight and they sent me to an eating disorder program. I felt like a fish out of water at this program because the other patients were mostly concerned about the weight of their bodies; I did not care if I was thin or fat as long as my cheekbones looked proportional on my face in relation to my eyes and eyebrows. It was difficult to be in eating disorder treatment because I felt that I was very different from the other patients, but I was too ashamed to disclose that my preoccupation was not about my weight or body size and that I believed my face looked atrocious. I felt like no one understood me and I felt very alone.

Believe it or not, I had a boyfriend during college. He never saw my face without make-up and I truly believed that he would leave me if he saw me without it. He was a very devoted and kind person, but I could not accept that he really loved or cared for me. My entire sense of self-value was based upon how I thought my face appeared, so needless to say I believed I was valueless. I found it intolerable to have my boyfriend too close to my face, and this made it difficult to be intimate with him. I am not one to push someone away, after all, I am very sensitive to rejection myself. But to have my boyfriend so close to my face was very shameful and I would pull away from him so that he could not see my face up close for an extended period of time.

When he did see my face close up, I would feel the necessity to ask him for reassurance about my appearance. For instance, I would ask him if my eyes and eyebrows looked acceptable. He would always respond that I looked fine, but then I would question what fine meant: Did fine mean they looked good? Did it mean that they looked just average? Was he just saying this to appease me? If he said that I looked good, I would believe that he was just saying this to be nice. If he said something such as I looked a little tired, I would interpret this as he was saying that I looked horrendous. I thought that he must be embarrassed to walk next to me or take me anywhere and I could not fathom how he could be seen with me in public because I was sure I was so repulsive to him. Nothing he would say was ever good enough. I knew this intellectually, but emotionally I felt very guilty about asking him for reassurance and this was more confirmation to me that I was not good enough for him and must be a burden. I was too ashamed to communicate to him about how I thought my face looked monstrous, but I still needed to ask him for reassurance or else I would go into a downward spiral.

I sought out other relationships, not because I wanted to be involved with another man, but because I needed reassurance so badly. I now realize that there is nothing that my boyfriend could have said that would have made me believe him. I loved him and wanted to be in a relationship with him, but I needed further reassurance that my face did not offend people. I was of course uncomfortable around people in general, but I felt that women were more judgmental than men. Also, when I would compare my facial features to those of other women I felt vastly inferior, so it was hard for me to have any sort of relationship with them. I turned to men to seek the reassurance that I was so desperate for.

I would get involved in different relationships with men solely for seeking value based on my appearance, and some were strange relationships, including one with my professor who was 30 years older than me. When I got involved with him I do not think I was fully aware that I was seeking reassurance about my appearance. I think that subconsciously I could not accept that I was intelligent unless I knew my appearance was okay. In retrospect, I believe I became involved with him because as a professor he represented education and intellect and that I needed him to approve of my face as confirmation that I was intelligent. Everything in my life had to filter through my appearance, and I could not accept that I was intelligent without reassurance that my face was not offensive. Of course this did not solve anything because even after this relationship, I still did not believe I looked normal and did not believe that I was intelligent. These relationships would never quench my need for reassurance, and I would always end up going back to my boyfriend.

By the time I graduated from college, nothing had been resolved with my body dysmorphic disorder symptoms. My excessive mirror checking and make-up compulsions had only become worse throughout the last four years. Another body dysmorphic disorder ritual that I was spending a lot of time on was the accumulation of a massive collection of peoples' faces. I would compile these facial images on my computer, and these could be of anyone ranging from celebrities, to friends on Facebook, to random people on the Internet. I know it sounds kind of creepy, but having these images on my computer allowed me more time to analyze their facial features. I could take my time doing this without being in their presence and having to worry if they were scrutinizing my face. I would especially study the distance between their eyes and their eyebrows in an attempt to figure out if I could get mine to look normal.

It was also around this time that I came up with an elaborate idea regarding my eyes and nose. I could never get my eyes to look right, so I thought that if I got the bridge of my nose lowered then there would be less of a shadow cast on my eyes and that this somehow would make them look better. Cosmetic surgery had always been on my mind because I believed that if my facial features were changed then I might look somewhat normal. All I wanted was relief from the drooping sensations around my eyebrows, eyes, and cheeks and to be free of the make-up ball and chain that I had been fastened to since adolescence. Somehow I convinced my parents to pay for my rhinoplasty.

After I had the rhinoplasty operation my eyes turned black and blue and my nose remained swollen for a very long time. I experienced these changes as entirely distorting the previous image I had of my face. This was psychological torture. After my nose and face finally healed I realized that nothing had been resolved. I think the surgeon did an acceptable job, but I did not feel that the procedure changed my appearance that much. People would not even notice that I had a nose job and this was difficult: I was very embarrassed that I had had my nose done and I did not want people to notice it, but if they did not notice it I interpreted this as evidence that I must look exactly the same. I was so ashamed about getting the rhinoplasty that I made sure no one would know and I sequestered myself in my house for weeks. For others to know that I had undergone cosmetic surgery was equally as shameful as having people see me doing my make-up: I thought that this would be confirmation that I was vain and self-centered and this would mean I must be a horrible person for caring so much about my appearance.

I eventually moved away from the state that I had lived in the majority of my life and I found employment in California at a real estate company. One of my duties was to make daily coffee runs for the office. It was terrifying for me to go to the same coffee establishment each day because to become a regular meant that the baristas would frequently see me and I believed that my appearance might offend them. When working I was on the clock, thus I had no choice but to visit the closest coffee location because my boss expected me back in the office as soon as possible. My strategy was to try to hide behind someone else in line when I was placing my order, and then while my order was being processed I would rush to the bathroom. The café bathroom provided a secure place where I could hide and also try to fix my make-up in the mirror. I would listen at the bathroom door to hear if they called my name, and when they did, I would dash out and grab the coffee before anyone could see me. This was my solution to having to go to the same establishment over and over again.

I was more or less able to perform at my job, but I would still be in the bathroom examining myself in the mirror during work hours. I was of course still preoccupied with my eyes and eyebrows, but I was increasingly becoming more fixated on my cheekbones. I decided to get buccal-fat-removal, a procedure that would remove the residual pockets of fat in my cheeks. I was not concerned about the fat itself, but wanted my cheeks to look and feel more pronounced in order to create the illusion that my face was not drooping downward. Also, if my cheekbones looked bigger I believed that my eyes would look more deep-set. It would have been very embarrassing to tell people that I just wanted to have fat taken out of my cheeks. As with my rhinoplasty, I was very ashamed that I had undergone another cosmetic procedure, so I told people that my face was swollen because I had my wisdom teeth removed. Getting my teeth extracted would be considered a necessary procedure and would not be construed as vanity.

It was around the time of my second cosmetic procedure that I decided to seek treatment. I had read about body dysmorphic disorder on the Internet, but had always assumed that it could not be applicable to me because I had been convinced that my appearance was the problem. I was still unsure if I really had body dysmorphic disorder or if I was just unattractive, but I did know that I could no longer go on living like this so I decided to give treatment a chance. One of my fears going into therapy was that the therapist would confirm that I did not have body dysmorphic disorder. I was so scared of this because if I did not have it, then this would be confirmation that my face just looked abnormal.

On the day of my first therapy appointment I spent hours trying to get my make-up perfect. I was already very anxious about going and I wanted to make sure that I did not look too hideous. I was worried that the therapist might not want to work with me if she saw how truly ugly I was and I even considered skipping the appointment. Although I arrived very late for my first therapy session, I am so glad that I decided to show up. It was on this day that I began my journey of recovery from body dysmorphic disorder.

Having decided to address the body image issues that had been plaguing me since grammar school once and for all, I also made the choice to disclose personal details. This had not been the case when I had previously received treatment because I had been much too ashamed to openly talk about my facial features. At the time I did not want to draw further attention to my face and I also assumed that it was obvious that I looked very unsightly. I mustered up the courage and over my first few therapy sessions I shared that I felt my appearance was scary and how this had been tormenting me for years. This was not easy for me to do but I am very happy that I went through with this. My therapist had heard this many times before, something that really surprised me because I felt that I must be crazy and I also believed that I was the only person in the entire world who felt this way about their appearance.

During the early stages of my therapy it was explained to me that I engaged in many body dysmorphic disorder compulsions. One of my most prominent BDD compulsions was that of collecting and cataloging peoples' reactions to me, information I would interpret as positive or negative affirmations regarding my appearance. My therapist explained that these rituals would give me a temporary sense of relief, but in the bigger picture they would also strengthen the very negative beliefs about my appearance. Slowly but surely I began decreasing my cataloging compulsions. This was very scary at first because for so much of my life my identity had been based around collecting this data in a desperate attempt to discern if I was or was not repulsive to other people.

I practiced not giving into the cataloging compulsions during therapy as well as after the sessions. I eventually got to the point where I could walk past people on the sidewalk and would refrain from scanning their faces and facial expressions. This was a pretty huge hurdle for me because I never would have imagined that I could live without the safety and familiarity of this body related ritual. Decreasing the body dysmorphic disorder compulsions did give me a sense of freedom, but during this process I realized that I was going to have to experience scary emotions that I had been avoiding for a long time.

As I began to experience success with reducing my cataloging of BDD compulsions, my therapist asked me if I thought I was ready to address my behaviors revolving around make-up. My first reaction was ABSOLUTELY NOT! My make-up had been such a part of me for over half of my life, and I was not even convinced that it was a compulsion. No one had seen me without make-up for years, including past boyfriends and my family. As frightening as this sounded, I had already trusted my therapist by refraining from the cataloging rituals, and by doing so I was already experiencing some relief. As much as I wanted to avoid anything to do with changing my make-up routine, I took the plunge and chose to address it.

My therapist recommended that I, very, very slowly, begin reducing the amount of make-up that I wore. We agreed that prior to attending the next therapy session I would slightly reduce the amount of eyeliner that I put on. As terrifying as this was for me, I followed through and attended my next appointment wearing less eyeliner than I had in years. Driving to this session I tried my best to make it through all the green traffic lights because I did not want to be sitting at a red light and have the person in the car next to me see how bad I looked. Even though I arrived at my therapist's office on time, I did not enter the waiting room until five minutes after the hour because I was afraid that other patients might see me without my full mask of make-up.

I trusted and felt very comfortable with my therapist, but I will admit that I was very ashamed for her to look at me without my usual eyeliner. She assured me that she was not judging me and brought to my attention that perhaps it was me who was having this shameful experience, not her. I really, really wanted to ask her for reassurance about how my eyebrows and eyes appeared, but I refrained, mostly because I knew that she would not give me reassurance even if I asked. This was one of the most difficult therapy sessions, but it also was a significant breakthrough session as well. My therapist did not treat me any differently, something that I assumed would happen when she saw how bad I looked with less make-up. Now it seems so backward, but at the time I really believed that if she saw my face like that she would not want to work with me anymore.

Each therapy session thereafter I would slightly lighten my eyeliner. After several sessions it was becoming much less difficult and I was soon able to attend a session without wearing any eyeliner at all. I then began to reduce other aspects of make-up, such as not putting on excessive eye-shadow and sometimes not even wearing mascara. Reducing make-up around my eyes was a challenge because the drooping feeling that I experienced in my face had originated with my eyes and eyebrows. I soon attended therapy wearing only foundation and nothing else. This was becoming fairly normalized, so my therapist suggested that we up-the-ante and take a walk outside of the office. This was at first very scary and made me very anxious, but once again I started to acclimatize and after a while this too became easier.

Consistently practicing these behavioral changes had notably made a difference and they were rapidly becoming much less challenging. I eventually began to attend morning therapy sessions which also meant that I would need to go directly to work afterward; I began going to work only wearing minimal cosmetics. In the past I never would have attended work without wearing loads of make-up and would have also been constantly checking it in bathroom mirrors; anything less than this would have been unimaginable. Now I was doing the opposite at my job: I was barely wearing any make-up and I was not using bathroom mirrors or other reflective surfaces to check my appearance. Taking the behavioral changes from the controlled environment of my therapist's office and bringing them into the real world was really hard but it definitely helped my recovery enormously because it made a therapeutic theory very applicable to my own life. It became very apparent to me that the more I practiced this, the better I would become.

My therapist explained to me that the long-term goal was not that I could never wear make-up again, but that I could wear it if I wanted to rather than absolutely having to wear it. As I adapted to going to work and other activities without having it on, the next step was to be able to wear it like a woman who does not have body dysmorphic disorder. In my therapy sessions I started to practice putting on my make-up in a very limited period of time and intentionally doing so imperfectly. In retrospect, it probably looked perfect to anyone else but to me at the time it felt very incomplete. I would then go to work and continue with the rest of my day without checking reflective surfaces and just having the feeling that my face and make-up did not feel right. By doing a lot of repetition of these behavioral activities I began to experience a differentiation between my BDD and myself. This experience of feeling as if body dysmorphic disorder was not actually me but a separate entity was a huge step in my recovery. I was able to begin identifying if I was having a BDD moment: Previously in a similar situation I would have interpreted it as absolutely being about what I perceived as my horrendous appearance.

There were definitely times that I felt like I was going backward in therapy. This was of course discouraging, but what I soon learned was that this was part of the recovery process and that I would make my biggest gains after temporary setbacks. I experienced what felt like an insurmountable setback about a year into therapy. I had long since disclosed to my therapist all of my very shameful secrets and feelings about my face and appearance, including my distain for how my eyebrows appeared in relation to my eyes. I had not left anything out, but I also did not elaborate on the extent to which my eyebrows horrified me. I am not sure what prompted me to finally admit this to my therapist, but at some level I knew that this needed to be discussed if I was to continue progressing in recovery.

I had been plucking my eyebrows for years. I viewed my eyebrows as growing straight across rather than arching above my eyes like those of normal people. I also thought they were way too bushy and between this and the lack of arch I felt that they made me look like Groucho Marx. This was all interconnected with the rest of my face because when I experienced my eyebrows as too thick, then this would exaggerate the feeling that my eyebrows were drooping and in turn would make my other facial features feel as if they were also drooping. I would excessively pluck my eyebrows in an attempt to make them look less bushy and to try and give them a normal looking arch. But similar to my make-up routine, I could never get my eyebrows to look like what I perceived as normal, and on numerous occasions I would pluck them until barely any hairs remained. I would then have to draw my eyebrows on with make-up and this in itself would become another tormenting ordeal.

It was really, really shameful to tell my therapist that I had somewhat omitted the details of my eyebrows, but now in hindsight I am very glad that I did bring this up. To not address this would have meant that a significant aspect of my body dysmorphic disorder was still a secret and this likely would have stalled my recovery process. Acknowledging that this was extremely shameful as well as processing this shame with my therapist was a very important part of dislodging my BDD. Along with openly talking about this shame, I needed to reduce the compulsion of plucking my eyebrows. I began by bringing all my tweezers into my therapist's office and I left them with her. This was going to be different from the reduction of my other BDD compulsions because this would entail the extremely slow and agonizing process of seeing my eyebrows grow into what I feared would look like furry caterpillars on my forehead.

My concern that this was going to be a very gradual and emotionally strenuous experience was only partially accurate. My therapist suggested that I speed up the process, something that confused me when she mentioned this because I did not know how my eyebrows could grow any faster. I should not have been surprised when she proposed that I do my eyebrow make-up to intentionally create the look that I loathed. If this had been recommended earlier in treatment I probably would have already been out the door, but because I had already experienced substantial success with many other behavioral exercises I decided to again trust my therapist.

At the following session I began the process of turning my eyebrows into exposure therapy exercises. Using a compact mirror, I quickly put make-up on my eyebrows so that they appeared slightly darker and wider. My therapist instructed me to only use the mirror briefly to put on the eyebrow make-up and not to scrutinize the rest of my face. After doing an imperfect job of making my eyebrows more obvious, I put the compact away. My eyebrows felt as if they were incredibly heavy and this also made my eyes and cheekbones feel as if they were drooping downward. This was the exact feeling that I had been trying to avoid for so much of my life and here I was sitting in my therapy session intentionally creating the frightful feeling. My therapist encouraged me to experience the feeling rather than fighting it: She pointed out that for years I had been battling against having the drooping facial feeling and that the more I fought it, the worse it had become. As intolerable as it felt, I again trusted her and by the end of the therapy session the drooping sensation seemed less intense.

I practiced this in therapy over the next few weeks. I would use the make-up to create an eyebrow look that was thicker and more distinct, and each session I would exaggerate it a little bit more than the previous time. My therapist and I would also leave her office and walk around the neighborhood, something that would have been unthinkable for me to do in the past. It was very anxiety provoking at first because I feared that somebody might notice how ridiculous my eyebrows looked, but this never happened. We would pass people walking their dogs, parking their cars, and jogging and no one ever made a comment. In fact, most people were either too busy looking down at their smartphones or they seemed too preoccupied with other things. Occasionally someone would say good morning, but nobody ever seemed to take special notice of my eyebrows. They still felt very heavy and strange to me, but I was beginning to accumulate evidence that my experience of my eyebrows and face was very different from how other people perceived me.

I became much more accustomed to the behavioral therapy exercises that we were doing outside of the office, and soon my therapist encouraged me to add more interpersonal interactions. Around the corner from the therapy office was a café, and we began intentionally going there so that I could have interpersonal interactions with the employees. Like every previous behavioral exercise, this was at first very nerveracking. Walking around the neighborhood without make-up and with thick, made-up eyebrows had become fairly easy, but the difference was that now I had to directly speak to someone opposed to only walking past them.

The first time I walked into the café I became very self-conscious about my face and I began to feel the drooping feeling from my eyebrows. As I went up to the counter to order a coffee, I did so with the assumption that the woman taking my order would instantly notice how outrageous my eyebrows looked. She smiled at me and was very friendly. She took my order and asked me how I was doing. I cannot remember how I replied because I felt somewhat discombobulated, but I survived the experience. I began to ruminate whether or not the woman had taken notice of and was thinking about how unattractive I looked. I discussed this with my therapist who asked me to provide factual evidence that she was having this thought. I was not able to do so. This was the first of many behavioral excursions to this café, and in fact I would say much of my recovery from body dysmorphic disorder occurred there. After every therapy appointment I would utilize what I had learned in session while interacting with people at the café.

What was so cool was that I actually became a regular there. I would walk in and they would know my name and already know how I liked my coffee. Prior to starting treatment I would scamper into a coffee establishment, hide in the bathroom while waiting for my order, and then grab my coffee while dashing out, all in an attempt to not let my face be seen. It was now drastically different: I actually had interpersonal relations with the staff at the café. I would take my time ordering the coffee, I would drink it there, and I would often have conversations with the employees. What is so interesting is that the more I interacted with people at the café, the less I was concerned with what they thought about me. In fact, there were times that I even forgot that I was doing behavioral therapy exercises. It was as if the intrusive BDD thoughts and feelings were gradually beginning to dissipate.

There were definitely times where I had the desire to avoid or altogether bolt from therapy because the process can be scary. A lot of emotional material from my past that had been buried was beginning to surface. Prior to treatment I would not have been able to address this material and instead would have instantly resorted to trying to fix my drooping face with make-up compulsions. Now that I had significantly reduced many of my BDD rituals, I was exposed to emotions that had never been processed or expressed in healthy ways. During sessions my therapist would always make time to process these feelings with me. I learned that there is a spectrum of emotions and that experiencing the uncomfortable feelings is not necessarily bad. My compulsions had always blocked me from feeling so I was unaware that to feel also means that I am actually normal. I learned to tolerate and sit with uncomfortable emotions like anger, jealousy, shame, and fear.

For so much of my life BDD had inhibited me from freely experiencing emotions, but now I was learning that rather then doing compulsions

I could express these feelings in healthy ways. When I would experience confusing and scary feelings during therapy and nothing bad actually occurred, I realized that it was safe to begin to trust myself. I would never have been able to do this on my own because these emotions were the sort of thing that I was not able to process by myself because I would either start doing compulsions or just shut down and feel numb. I began to understand that experiencing emotions associated with my appearance is actually about past material and unprocessed feelings and not necessarily about how I look.

These changes helped me in many areas of my life. For instance, going to work was no longer an exercise in attempting to merely make it through the day in between bathroom mirror checks. I had already become much more comfortable at work from doing so many behavioral therapy exercises, and I decided to apply these same techniques in the workplace. I made a point of frequently stopping and having mini conversations with a lot of different people at my job. This is something that I previously would never have considered doing; in fact, I used to do my best to avoid as many people as possible. I also began to participate in activities outside of work, something that I was unable to do before I received treatment. With this have come friendships, something that had been very difficult for me to maintain over the years because of the severity of my body dysmorphic disorder. I missed out on so many opportunities to cultivate quality relationships, but now that my symptoms have decreased I am experiencing many more meaningful connections with people.

My life is very different today. I will not say that my life is perfect and it is not as if my body dysmorphic disorder is completely gone, but my overall quality of life is much improved and my symptoms are greatly reduced. It feels so strange because for so many years of my life I felt like I was shackled in a cage. Now, less than two years after entering therapy, I am not only unshackled but I am outside looking back at the cage where I was imprisoned. In retrospect it seems so surreal to imagine how I had been so trapped for so long. I had always thought that it would be impossible for me to live my life the way I wanted to because of my appearance. My quality of life has improved to a point that I did not realize was possible: As someone with body dysmorphic disorder I had always assumed that I was the exception and that there was something wrong with me. I now realize that there was not something wrong with me, rather the problem was with my body dysmorphic disorder. For the majority of my life I had just been trying to survive, but now I have finally begun to thrive.

5 "If Only I Could Fix It"
Body Dysmorphic Disorder Compulsions

The vast majority of body dysmorphic disorder patients engage in compulsive behaviors in an attempt to reduce the distress associated with their perceived physical defect. Compulsions may occasionally provide the individual with relief from the emotional torment they experience, but relief is only ephemeral: The intrusive thoughts about their appearance and the resulting uncomfortable feelings always return and activate further obsessions about appearance. The individual becomes trapped in a cycle of attempting to ward off unwanted emotions related to their appearance by acting on compulsive behaviors that subsequently only fuel the unwanted negative thoughts. Veale differentiates compulsions from safety-seeking behaviors. He explains that individuals participate in safety-seeking behaviors to avoid aversive incidents, whereas the purpose behind compulsions are to undo an aversive experience (Veale and Neziroglu 2010:73). Body dysmorphic disorder sufferers perform both compulsions and safety-seeking behaviors.

As the individual desperately attempts to fix what they perceive are imperfections, they are distracted from all other areas of life: Work or school productivity decreases, natural personal strengths are ignored, social skills atrophy, and relationships fizzle. Patients entering treatment frequently exclaim, "If I could only fix my appearance, then everything in my life would be better." Ironically, the opposite occurs: The more they fixate on correcting perceived defects, the more they become embroiled in a never-ending quest that only perpetuates shame, disappointment, and self-hatred. These feelings are interpreted as a result of the supposed defect rather than being recognized as underlying factors that cause the individual to be so self-critical in the first place. Compulsions not only serve to neutralize profound feelings of shame but in turn they can divert attention away from other issues that may be too difficult for the individual to acknowledge.

Almost all body dysmorphic disorder compulsions are done in an attempt to seek reassurance that a body part is not defective. Because so much of a BDD sufferer's identity is derived from their appearance, a perceived physical flaw is internalized as *I must be defective*. Rather than experiencing the extremely negative feelings, they will employ multiple compulsive behaviors in order to avoid supposed evidence that they are fundamentally inadequate as human beings. The most drastic BDD compulsion is undergoing cosmetic procedures. Although it is common that individuals with body image disturbances resort to cosmetic solutions, many do not: This is often out of concern that the body part that they already view as defective might be further misshapen or damaged.

Cosmetic procedures may be one of the more invasive body dysmorphic disorder compulsions, but there are many other ritualistic behaviors that BDD patients engage in on a regular basis. Many of these are very subtle and secretive and will continue unless identified by the clinician. The individual performing the compulsions may have been doing so for so many years that they are not even aware of how pervasive these behaviors have become. The following are descriptions of very common body dysmorphic disorder compulsions.

Cosmetic Procedures

Individuals with body dysmorphic disorder that do resort to cosmetic solutions are very rarely ever satisfied with the outcome (Sarwer, Crerand, and Didie 2003). In my experience, this patient population usually endures an exacerbation of symptoms after receiving cosmetic procedures. The fantasy of what the reconstructed body part should look like never matches reality, leaving the individual more distraught, angry, and ashamed, and feeling more hopeless than prior to the operation. On the rare occasion that the individual is satisfied with the procedure, they usually soon begin obsessing about another aspect of their appearance.

Because so many body dysmorphic disorder patients have very poor insight into their symptoms, they often seek dermatological and cosmetic solutions prior to receiving mental health treatment. They usually do not believe that they have a psychiatric, psychological, and emotional problem, rather they are convinced that the issue is with their appearance so they seek out physicians who can fix their perceived defect. Even BDD patients who do not have overvalued ideation or delusional thinking are not always convinced that they suffer from a psychiatric and psychological condition. Patients with more insight into their symptoms may at least consider receiving care from a mental health practitioner, foregoing cosmetic procedures.

The patient who is either considering plastic surgery or who is convinced that a cosmetic procedure is necessary usually has a fantasy of what the surgical outcome will look like and how this will transform their life. There has been such profound value placed on the perceived imperfection that it becomes the metaphoric lightning rod for anything in their life that they are dissatisfied with or disappointed about. Because the body part that is considered so flawed becomes the repository for fundamental feelings of inadequacy, it also becomes the central character in a fantasy based on the belief that an alteration in appearance would catalyze a drastic improvement in quality of life. This imaginary scenario sets the stage for a massive let down after a cosmetic procedure is performed and the individual's life does not radically change. What is not included in the fantasy—usually because the excessive emphasis on the supposed defect nullifies any capacity to view the bigger picture—is that perhaps there are many, many other issues going on that may be at the root of why the person feels inherently defective and unloveable.

Although it is not unusual that an individual with body dysmorphic disorder sometimes experiences an initial burst of exhilaration immediately after the completion of a cosmetic operation, it is only a matter of time until reality surpasses fantasy. It is during this time that preliminary euphoria gives way to feelings of hopelessness and subsequent depression as the BDD sufferer recognizes that their life has not dramatically changed. The disillusioned individual will usually begin to excessively scrutinize their post-operative body part and frequently consider pursuing another operation to repair what they believe was not fixed during the initial procedure.

Throughout the years I have learned that attempting to convince a patient not to get a procedure is for naught. I make the recommendation that they give psychotherapy a try for at least a year and then revisit their cosmetic plans at a later date. Educating the patient regarding how and why cosmetic procedures may not be the solution to their life disappointments is acceptable, but I do not recommend trying to talk them out of it. Overt attempts to dissuade the person will often lead them toward a clandestine operation, and then they will likely mislead their psychotherapist about this and the events surrounding the procedure. It is much more therapeutic to create an atmosphere of honesty where the patient can openly discuss their decision to undergo the cosmetic procedure. Because BDD symptoms usually increase after these cosmetic compulsions, the patient will need a safe and trusting relationship with their psychotherapist post-surgery. I have found that the majority of BDD patients will give psychotherapy a chance. Knowing that cosmetic procedures are an option in the future is often comforting enough for them to begin the psychotherapy process.

There will always be patients who go against clinical recommendations and proceed with dermatologic or other cosmetic procedures. Phillips and Diaz (1997) reported that 70% of their sample of 188 body dysmorphic disorder patients had at least sought medical or cosmetic surgery for their perceived defects while 58% had followed though with at least one operation. A study conducted by David Veale (Veale et al. 1996) of fifty BDD patients seen in psychiatric settings unveiled that 81% of these individuals were dissatisfied or very dissatisfied with the outcome of the nonpsychiatric, medical operations. I rarely encounter a BDD patient who is content with the results of a cosmetic procedure; in the very infrequent case that an individual is satisfied, their appearance preoccupation usually soon morphs to another body part.

Case Study: Layla

Layla, a woman in her early thirties, entered psychotherapy several weeks after receiving her third nose job. She tearfully explained that she had endured her most recent rhinoplasty with the hope that finally her nose would "look and feel right" on her face. This latest procedure entailed the surgeon removing cartilage from the back of her left ear so that it could be used to improve the contours of her nose. Layla was convinced that three would be the lucky charm; she believed that this one final operation would once and for all cure her preoccupation with her nose and free her to move forward with her life.

Layla had been brought into treatment by her husband. She acknowledged that there were probably some psychological issues connected to her nose obsession, but believed that these issues were a result of her nose looking imperfect and that they would dissipate after her nose was fixed. Her husband was very supportive of her attending treatment for what he viewed was body dysmorphic disorder. Layla was unsure that she even had BDD, believing that it was her nose that was causing emotional distress. She was hesitant to begin the therapy process because she was concerned that the money going toward therapy could be used for a possible fourth nose procedure, and she was also skeptical that therapy would "make her like her nose."

She stated that she received the third rhinoplasty for several reasons: Not only did she detest how the previous procedure turned out aesthetically, but explained that ever since the first nose job she experienced the inside of her nostrils as feeling radically differently, as if "a piece of her nose was now missing." She would vividly experience the feeling anytime she made facial movements, whether this would be smiling, squinting, or even talking. Having the disconcerting feeling that she was missing a piece of her nose would activate feelings of hopelessness that would leave her feeling very depressed. For Layla, having this feeling was a constant reminder that she probably would not be able to get back to how her nose felt pre-surgery, and because of this she believed her life was ruined. Her desperation and despair kept her fixated on the idea that a fourth procedure was imperative.

* * *

When I explain to a patient who is considering a procedure that it is very unusual for a satisfactory outcome, they often believe that they are the exception to the rule. For those patients with very poor insight or who are delusional, they will be convinced that this is not applicable to them. An individual who is bent on getting a procedure will find a doctor who will operate. Although many more medical doctors, especially dermatologists, dentists, and cosmetic surgeons are becoming aware of body dysmorphic disorder, this does not mean that a BDD patient will be identified as a poor candidate for a procedure. The BDD patient is proficient in hiding, denying, or disguising their symptoms and to the untrained eye it can be very easy for these individuals to fly under the radar. They often have the where-with-all to be on their best behavior when seeking a cosmetic consultation.

Even if the prospective surgery patient has insight regarding their body dysmorphic disorder symptoms, they will not reveal this to the doctor performing the cosmetic procedure out of concern that they will be refused treatment. If treatment is denied, the individual will shop for a doctor that will perform the operation. I have worked with patients who have received multiple surgeries on the same body part from the same surgeon and they report that the doctor never questioned their motives. Fortunately there are responsible and alert surgeons who do notice discrepancies with patients with body image disturbances. Patients who have received multiple procedures, who frequently cancel and reschedule appointments, and refuse to allow the surgeon to speak with anyone, may be clues to a case of body dysmorphic disorder (Sarwer et al. 2003).

Mirror Checking and Mirror Avoidance

Mirrors and other reflective surfaces are inevitably the primary venue by which individuals with body dysmorphic disorder examine their external physical characteristics. Most people use the mirror to perform daily grooming activities prior to moving on with much more important aspects of their day. The individual with body dysmorphic disorder regularly utilizes reflective surfaces to inspect the body area of concern. Reflective surfaces are not limited to generic mirrors, but can include anything in which the individual can examine their body such as tinted car windows, the glass of storefronts, computer screens, cellular telephone surfaces, smartphone mirror applications, the front of microwave ovens, shiny metal spoons, and even the reflection from other peoples' sunglasses. Many BDD patients report having "good mirrors and bad mirrors," in other words, mirrors that make their body area of concern look less defective or more defective. Lighting may also determine what is considered to be a "good or bad" mirror: Body dysmorphic disorder clients frequently report that florescent mirror lighting is the bane of their symptoms because every aesthetic flaw appears exaggerated.

Some individuals with body dysmorphic disorder alternate between excessive mirror usage and avoidance, while others completely avoid reflective surfaces altogether. Mirror checkers do so in the attempt to have just one good glimpse of themselves so that they can go on with their day with this image stored in their memory. Rarely is this accomplished, thus they continue returning to the source of their reflection with the expectation that this time they will see the body part as less defective. Mirror avoiders become so distraught when viewing themselves that they choose to avoid reflective surfaces entirely. Their internal image of their body is already so negative that it is very difficult for them to tolerate any further evidence supporting the belief that they are physically defective.

The BDD sufferer who constantly checks reflective surfaces can be compared to a casino gambler: The gambler is intellectually aware that their chances are slim that they will win the jackpot, but their motivation to return to the card table or slot machine is reinforced knowing they eventually may prevail. They easily overlook the amount of time and money squandered during their attempts to experience the bonanza. Individuals with BDD who regularly engage in mirror checking rituals are hoping that eventually they will be satisfied with their reflection. Just like the occasional win in gambling, the individual with body dysmorphic disorder will like how they look on rare occasions, but these instances are few and far between. Even when they are satisfied with their appearance, the experience is ephemeral; they will eventually need to return to the mirror in an attempt to regain the moment in time where they viewed themselves as less defective.

Touching the Perceived Defect

Engaging in mirror checking rituals is not the only method by which the body dysmorphic disorder patient monitors their appearance. Touching the supposed defect is a very common BDD compulsion. Examples of this include, but are definitely not limited to, rubbing the nose to make sure it is not too big or that its contours are acceptable; stroking head hair to monitor its thickness or texture; touching skin to check for imperfections such as blemishes; pinching the arms, stomach, or thighs to determine body fat levels; feeling the cheekbone or jawbone to discern if it is adequately defined; or using the tongue to touch teeth in order to make sure that they are straight enough or at least not crooked. Multiple body areas may simultaneously be the focus of tactile compulsions. Some individuals with BDD intentionally avoid touching the body area deemed defective because they believe that they may somehow further damage it or cause it to become contaminated. This is frequently the case with individuals who are preoccupied with their facial complexion and who believe that touching their skin will cause blemishes.

From my experience, individuals who have overvalued ideation are much more likely to believe that they will damage their body by merely touching it. While some of these individuals will avoid touching a body part altogether, others will only do so after they have washed their hands excessively. This can be misconstrued as obsessive-compulsive disorder: It is not uncommon that an individual will be given an OCD diagnosis unless they eventually disclose that they are washing their hands because they fear that they may contaminate their skin or another aspect of their appearance.

Photographs and Video

Reflective surfaces are not the only means by which body dysmorphic disorder sufferers visually inspect their appearance. Many analyze their supposed defects in photographs or by watching video of themselves. With the advent of cellular phones that incorporate digital camera and video technology, using one's photograph to examine the body has become almost as common a BDD compulsion as mirror checking. Even prior to digital photography becoming commonplace, individuals with body dysmorphic disorder would study themselves in pictures not only to scrutinize the perceived defect but to compare themselves to how they used to look and how the body area of concern has changed.

I once worked with a man who was preoccupied with what he considered to be his receding hairline and thinning hair, and who created a chronological timeline of pictures of himself starting from when he was an infant. He brought this chronology of photographs into one of our therapy sessions to emphasize to me that he had evidence that his hairline was receding. Even though his hairline looked like that of an average male his age, the patient was convinced that he must be going bald since his hair looked different as an adult compared to when he was a child.

Many individuals with BDD avoid having their photograph taken altogether. They are so ashamed or disgusted by their own appearance that they do not want their image permanently "frozen" in time. They may also avoid photographs because they become too distraught when seeing an image of themselves that they conclude must be objective evidence that they are so unattractive. BDD patients are often more confused by photographs than reflective surfaces because in the mirror they at least have some control over the reflection, for instance with different lighting and the distance they stand from the mirror. They frequently comment that the photograph must be evidence that they do not have body dysmorphic disorder because "can't you see how bad I look in the picture?" They explain that "because in the photograph everyone else looks like they do in reality, I must be seeing things normally; thus I must be seeing myself realistically as well, and I look so unattractive."

As I previously explained, individuals with BDD look in the mirror hoping to see themselves as normal or at least as not unattractive. They are hoping to get that "good mental snapshot" that they can remember for the remainder of the day. Photographs are analogous to these "mental snapshots" because they represent a moment in time that their appearance is suspended. A person without body dysmorphic disorder would view a photograph of themselves and not rigidly interpret the picture as permanent, concrete evidence of how they will always look.

Even if they did not find the photograph flattering, they would not automatically utilize the particular snapshot as definitive evidence that they are unattractive. They would probably admit to not liking the picture and would conclude that they have been and will be satisfied with other photographs. This is not the case with many BDD sufferers who hyperfocus on the details of an unflattering photograph and use this as steadfast proof that they are physically unattractive.

Comparing Aesthetic Features

One of the most common body dysmorphic disorder compulsions is comparing and scrutinizing the physical features of other people. In fact, I have yet to work with a BDD patient who at some point has not studied the aesthetic characteristics of others, especially the areas of the body that they are most preoccupied with. This compulsion is not limited to interpersonal interactions but includes analyzing the physical characteristics of people by way of the television, movies, magazines, and images found on the Internet. Regardless of the source of the image, the individual with BDD uses the aesthetic features of other people as a barometer to measure their own appearance and overall self-worth.

Because this patient population perceives themselves as much less attractive than they actually are and because many of them have such an ambiguous sense of self, they look beyond their own reflection in an attempt to establish some concrete image of their physical being. This BDD compulsion is highly prone to selective bias because the individual inspecting another person's bodily features often observes and pays closer attention to the people who have what they consider to be aesthetically attractive characteristics. They are usually unaware that the majority of people do not meet their hyper-criteria for aesthetics. The continual focus on those select individuals who have body parts that they would like only reinforces their feelings of being aesthetically inferior.

I have observed that this is one of the more difficult body dysmorphic disorder compulsions for patients to reduce even if they are quite motivated to do so. When we interact with another person we usually look at their face, specifically into their eyes and sometimes at their mouth. We are aware that they have a nose, skin, hair, ears, forehead, eyebrows, and other facial features, but we do not concentrate on these. Many individuals with BDD are preoccupied with areas of their face or head, thus when they speak with someone they are inevitably looking at the other person's face and often their gaze gravitates to studying their facial features. This not only distracts from the connectivity of the conversation itself but can also make the other individual feel uncomfortable if they notice that their face is being scrutinized. I recommend to my patients that they attempt to focus on making eye contact with the other person. I explain that when they interact with other people they need to remain mindful that studying the other person's physical features are not only a BDD compulsion but it also interferes with truly hearing and connecting to the other person.

Sometimes body dysmorphic disorder patients will watch other peoples' eyes in order to discern if that person is looking at the supposed defect. They erroneously assume that other people are as equally consumed with physical aesthetics as they are, and so naturally conclude that other people are examining them. They often do not realize that if they stare at someone else, the other person will eventually look to see why they are being stared at. As is the case with many other cognitive errors that exist with BDD patients, this information is misinterpreted as evidence that there is something wrong with how they look because they see another person looking at them. This in turn only further perpetuates all body dysmorphic disorder compulsions, including that of scrutinizing the physical characteristics of other people.

Case Study: Christopher

Christopher was terrified of losing his hair. During his late teens and into his mid-twenties he had experienced mild body dysmorphic disorder symptoms involving the concern that his ears protruded too far from his head. He had also felt that his head was too small for his body. Although both of these aesthetic concerns bothered him, he kept them in check by growing out his curly hair: His ears did not look like they stuck out as far when his hair was grown out, and he also felt that all the hair made his head look bigger and more proportional to the rest his body.

The day after his 26th birthday, Christopher was getting a haircut from the same hairstylist that had been cutting his hair for years. She made the comment that it looked like his hair was beginning to recede in the corners of his forehead. Christopher was not sure that he had heard her correctly and asked her to repeat what she had said: She told him that he may be in the early stages of male pattern balding. He remembers experiencing a wave of dread flowing through his body as if he had just been told that a family member or good friend had passed away. This was only the beginning of many years of obsessing about hair loss.

Christopher had always found comfort in his hair. As a child he received much attention because of it, and as a young adult it served as camouflage for aspects of his appearance that he disliked. This was soon to change as comfort and safety surrounding his hair abruptly morphed into a shameful, anxiety provoking preoccupation with hair loss. With this preoccupation came many classic body dysmorphic disorder compulsions, but the one that Christopher found the most necessary to do was to study the hairlines of other men.

What began as an occasional glance quickly turned into an endless routine of inspecting the foreheads and hairlines of every man he saw, whether it was in person, on television, in magazines, or on the Internet.

When speaking to other men he would find himself examining their hair rather than making normal eye contact. Christopher was also aware that he would sometimes make the other person uncomfortable because they would notice that he was constantly looking upward. To avoid the discomfort of having the other person notice his upward glances, he became quite adept at discreetly peeking at their hairline when they broke eye contact with him.

He would especially study the hairlines of men who were close to his age. For Christopher, this became a barometer to try and discern if he was balding at a rate slower than his peers, the same as, or more rapidly than them. If he came into contact with a male peer who had a hairline showing no signs of recession, he would experience a sense of hopelessness and also feel inferior to this individual. This sense of inferiority also applied to men who were older than him and who did not have a receding hairline. If he interacted with a man his age whose hairline was overtly drifting upward, he would feel a strange sense of relief that somehow he was not that far along in the balding process. With individuals who were losing their hair, Christopher would also analyze the size and shape of their head as well as how their ears appeared in relation to their head in order to discern how he might look if his hairline continued to recede.

Reassurance Seeking

Although some body dysmorphic disorder suffers will never ask for reassurance about their appearance out of concern that this will draw attention to the supposed defect, many do compulsively ask other people if they look acceptable. This behavior usually entails questioning people that they are very familiar with, such as a family member or a significant other. In a desperate attempt to get reassurance, the BDD sufferer places the other person in a problematic position: Assuming that the person being asked does not have body dysmorphic disorder, they most likely do not perceive there to be a defect and thus respond accordingly. The person with BDD will often interpret this as either "they are just being nice because they are my friend/parent/significant other" or "they are lying to me because they know that my defect looks awful and they just don't want to say it because they feel sorry for me." The individual seeking reassurance is never satisfied with the response, and the person being asked to give reassurance experiences a help-reject interaction that leaves them feeling invalidated.

This particular compulsion not only reinforces the body dysmorphic disorder symptoms, but also effectively impacts relationships with other people leaving everyone feeling stuck and unheard. I explain to my patients that seeking validation from other people is analogous to gazing into the mirror because both involve seeking an external source of validation to compensate for deficits in a sense of self. This perpetuates itself because the more a person pursues authentication from outside sources, the more this interferes with developing an integrated sense of self from within. Also, this compulsion is unintentionally utilizing another person as an object to gain reassurance and this is not conducive for healthy connectivity: The other person begins to feel as if their role in the relationship is that of a mirror rather than a mutual friend. If the clinician has the opportunity to speak with the person who is the source of the reassurance, it should be explained that by participating in this compulsion they are colluding with the BDD symptoms and are reinforcing this behavior every time they do so.

Another method of reassurance seeking involves individuals posting pictures of themselves on different Internet forums. These can include forums that specifically rank peoples' appearances by way of votes from forum members, dating websites where pictures are posted as part of a personal profile, or even on BDD websites where individuals post their images and ask other sufferers to "honestly tell them if they look hideous or okay and if they truly have BDD or if they are just ugly." Even though the venue is cyberspace, this is still a body dysmorphic disorder reassurance seeking compulsion because the individual is fishing for external feedback as a means to dispel their belief that they are somehow misshapen or unattractive.

Indirect reassurance seeking is a term I use for those individuals who are too ashamed to directly ask for reassurance but still desire feedback about their appearance. This often takes the form of the individual making an openly derogatory statement about their own appearance when in the presence of someone who has not yet been educated regarding the complexities of body dysmorphic disorder. As an example, if an individual believes that they have dark circles under their eyes, they may "randomly" make the following statement in front of an enabler: "The dark circles under my eyes make me look so tired and unattractive." They have learned that the enabler (or the person who is not familiar with BDD) will most likely respond with reassurance that they look fine and that there is nothing to worry about. Like all body dysmorphic disorder compulsions, the BDD sufferer only experiences impermanent relief from acting on a reassurance seeking behavior and the need to pursue further indirect reassurance will soon occur. And as is the case with all BDD rituals, indirect reassurance seeking can take place with any aspect of the body.

The body dysmorphic disorder patient may also seek discrete reassurance from their therapist without overtly mentioning anything at all about a specific appearance concern. It is usual for a patient starting therapy for their body related symptoms to inquire if they really do have BDD and perhaps are not seeing themselves like others see them. This becomes an indirect reassurance seeking compulsion if they regularly ask this question. They want to hear from the professional that they have a psychiatric disorder which would explain that maybe they really are not unattractive and that their "brain is making them see themselves as ugly" when in reality they are not.

It is acceptable for the clinician to answer this question the first time it is asked and to explain to the BDD patient that yes, the nature of the disorder is such that they see themselves differently from how other people view them. But if the patient continues to inquire about this, it should be brought to the patient's attention and explained that they are participating in a BDD compulsion in an attempt to feel convinced that they look acceptable.

Avoiding Eye Contact

Another prevalent body dysmorphic disorder behavior, and one that is frequently overlooked by clinicians, is the avoidance of making eye contact with other people. BDD patients often assume that other people experience the world as they do, so naturally they also believe that everyone else is preoccupied with their appearance. It is as if they are seeing themselves through another person's pupils and erroneously assuming that this person is observing their physical imperfections. Ironically, it is not the supposed aesthetic defects that are observed by the other person as much as the obvious lack of culturally appropriate eye contact. It is inaccurately ascertained that other people are looking at them and scrutinizing their supposed defect. This of course is probably not the case, but the individual with BDD often does not realize that other people do not experience a world in which aesthetic appearance is of utmost value.

It is common that patients beginning treatment for their BDD symptoms will not look up or make eye contact during the initial therapy sessions. This is not something that needs to be corrected or even worked on at first; at least the individual has arrived for therapy and this is most likely a difficult first step. I may mention to the patient that I notice they are not making eye contact: I will explain to them that I can accommodate this for the time being if it makes them more comfortable as they become accustomed to the psychotherapy process. Practicing eye contact during the therapy session can be addressed once the patient and therapist have built rapport.

Many of my body dysmorphic disorder patients have explained to me that they avoid making eye contact with others because they presume that the other person is examining their physical flaws and this makes them very uncomfortable. Also, the individual with BDD may simultaneously be studying the other person's appearance, thus two compulsions are occurring simultaneously. Regardless of the compulsion that is responsible for a lack of eye contact, it is difficult to genuinely connect to another person if these behaviors are occurring during interpersonal interactions. The supposed defect is again held culpable for inadequate relationships and a mediocre quality of life. As is the case with any avoidant behavior, it is important to address this with patients because it significantly interferes with appropriate social interactions.

Food Regimen

It is not uncommon for individuals with body dysmorphic disorder to avoid consuming certain foods or liquids that they believe may somehow alter the appearance of or cause damage to the body area of concern. Alternately, some individuals will intentionally consume particular foods that they trust will catalyze change in the body area that they consider defective; others take any precaution to avoid or to deliberately eat certain foods as a preventative measure against ageing. Although the basis of some of these culinary compulsions may be evidence based (for instance, most people would agree that soda and other sugary drinks cannot be conducive for healthy teeth), there is frequently selective reasoning and overvalued ideation that contribute to the misinterpretation of factual information. Sometimes these beliefs can take on delusional levels of intensity where the patient is convinced that a body part is "getting worse" because of an ingredient in a food despite any evidence to the contrary.

Sometimes an individual with a BDD based food aversion may avoid eating particular things that they think will immediately damage a body part. An example that I have come across multiple times is the fear that certain foods will discolor, fracture, or create larger spaces in between teeth. This particular concern may also be associated with how the teeth appear in relation to the gum-line and if the consumption of a particular food is affecting this.

Body dysmorphic disorder patients who have concerns about their skin may avoid eating certain messy or greasy foods such as salads and pastas that may touch areas around their mouth. They worry that the grease from the food may clog the pores of their skin and cause them to break-out. While some individuals may shun these foods completely, others will eat them but in a very regimented manner taking all precautions to prevent any food from touching the outside of their lips. It is not uncommon that extensive facial cleansing rituals will follow the consumption of messier foodstuffs in an attempt to ward off the anxiety that grease may have touched the skin and entered into pores.

Medication Compliance Behaviors

Similar to body dysmorphic disorder compulsions related to food is the hesitation to follow medication recommendations because of the concern that it might damage the appearance or functionality of the body area deemed defective. Many patients with BDD have a predisposition for obsessions and can have limited insight into their symptoms, overvalued ideation, and even somatic delusions, thus medication management is usually highly recommended. If a patient is very tentative about following through with medication recommendations it is useful to inquire if their worry is that the medication may affect the body area of concern. Common side effect concerns include the fear of hair loss, acne or other skin blemishes, and weight gain (including weight gain in the face that in turn may make other facial features "look different").

Body dysmorphic disorder patients are extremely proficient at scouring the Internet for information, including material regarding side effects of medications. I point out to my patients that if they look hard enough they will inevitably find something on the Internet that confirms their fears, while missing all the examples of people who may not have had adverse reactions. I explain that their hesitation to take medication because of the apprehension it may harm their appearance creates a paradox: Perhaps they have the firmly held belief that medication will alter their appearance because they have overvalued ideation or they are delusional.

Without proper medication management, the rigidity of these thoughts are unlikely to become more flexible and the patient will remain stuck focusing on their body. Because therapists usually meet with patients much more frequently than prescribing psychiatrists, the therapist may become the arbitrator, clarifying the necessity of following through with the medication recommendations. The BDD patient may feel more comfortable disclosing medication side effect concerns to their therapist and may not report this same information to their psychiatrist, thus it is very helpful for both treating clinicians to communicate with one another.

Hair Counting

For individuals with body dysmorphic disorder who are preoccupied with hair loss, hair counting is a frequently performed compulsion. Although these rituals are more common with men because male pattern balding is a natural feature of the male ageing process, women with BDD may also engage in hair loss focused compulsions. These rituals can include: Checking pillows to see how many hairs were lost while the individual was sleeping; examining the bathtub and drain after a shower; counting hairs in a hairbrush or comb; looking for hair in a towel used to dry off after a shower; and, running one's hand through their hair in order to observe how many hairs fall out.

Many of these individuals have read, whether it is accurate or not, that the average person sheds 100 hairs per day. Thus this number is frequently used as the reference point by which hair loss preoccupation is measured: If they count fewer than 100 lost hairs each day they feel relief, but if they count more than 100 they become distressed because they believe hair loss is happening to them more rapidly than the average person. There are also individuals who become very distraught at the sight of seeing their hair that is anywhere besides on their head, regardless of the number.

Concerns about hair loss and the related hair counting compulsions may be associated with other body area preoccupations, especially facial features, ears, or the shape and size of the forehead or the head. The fear of hair loss and becoming bald is a very common body dysmorphic disorder theme, but sometimes the concern regarding hair loss is less about the actual hair itself. It is not uncommon that the excessive worry about hair loss is associated with the preoccupation that certain facial features that are already deemed undesirable will become more apparent without hair serving as a distraction. Hair is frequently used as a camouflaging apparatus, and to lose this as a distraction from other body parts leaves the BDD sufferer feeling extremely exposed and ashamed. Sometimes hair loss preoccupation involves a concern about both the hair itself and how a paucity of hair will alter the appearance of facial features.

Compulsive Tanning

Some individuals with body dysmorphic disorder excessively tan. This is done for multiple reasons including trying to camouflage skin that they perceive is too blotchy or discolored, darkening skin that they feel is too pale, or because of the belief that darker skin will help distract from facial features that are considered unattractive. Other individuals with BDD believe their skin is too dark, and attempt to make it lighter, either by avoiding direct sunlight as much as possible or by using lotions that supposedly will lighten the skin. Patients who do utilize tanning as a BDD compulsion often become trapped in a cycle of desperately needing to maintain a certain skin complexion while also fearing the skin damage that might occur from frequent and continuous exposure to the sun. These individuals may alternate between spray tanning and sun tanning in an attempt to maintain their color while minimizing possible epidermis damage.

While tanning might be a preferable compulsion for some body dysmorphic disorder patients, others will do whatever they can to avoid being exposed to the sun. The excessive application of sunscreen is not an unusual BDD compulsion: Many times individuals who partake in this particular compulsion are excessively preoccupied that their skin will become damaged by the sun and will look even more flawed than they already believe it to be. I have worked with body dysmorphic disorder patients who are not of Caucasian decent who do not want their skin to become darker, thus they meticulously cover their face and other exposed areas of their body with sunscreen.

I once worked with a college student who was so fearful of his skin becoming darker that not only would he go through multiple bottles of sunscreen each week but he also would choose his class schedule based around what direction the sun would be shining at that time of year. He would make these calculations in order to determine where shadows would be on campus in relation to the buildings that his classes were in; this way he could minimize sun exposure by walking in shaded areas. Although this may sound extreme, this is not necessarily that excessive by body dysmorphic disorder standards: The feelings of shame, disgust, anxiety, and terror associated with an aspect of the body can motivate the BDD sufferer to go to any length in order to reduce these dreadful emotions.

Dieting, Exercise, and Body Building

Restricting food intake, excessive or compulsive exercising, or an obsession with building muscle mass are frequently associated with symptoms of anorexia nervosa, bulimia nervosa, pathorexia, or even borderline and narcissistic personality disorders. Body dysmorphic disorder patients may also participate in these behaviors, but this may not be because they have a comorbid diagnosis (although this may also be the case) but because they are attempting to alter another aspect of their appearance that they consider unattractive. This may entail exaggerating one part of the body in order to distract from or camouflage an area considered unattractive, or to change the size or shape of the body that in turn can make the perceived defect look more proportional.

In my earlier years working with body dysmorphic disorder, I treated a young man who was concerned about the size of his forehead that he described as "too small and made him look like a Neanderthal." He was also concerned about other areas of his body including his legs that he felt were "too skinny" and his upper body that he believed "needed to be bigger and more defined" to divert attention away from his forehead. He would also regularly tan his skin in order to look as "ripped" as possible. He admitted that he had considered using steroids in order to get as big as possible as quickly as possible, but had decided against this because of the long-term repercussions that might include future health problems that would prevent him from keeping very fit. He was fully aware that there could be consequences from long-term excessive tanning, but would rationalize this by proclaiming "that at least it is not as dangerous as taking steroids." The patient admitted to me that he really did not enjoy compulsively exercising and tanning and in fact was tired of spending so much time doing so. But by doing this, he believed that other people would notice his body and this would decrease some of the shame about how abnormal he felt his forehead appeared. He also eventually confessed that if it was not for how "bad" his forehead looked, he would never workout or tan.

The previous example is not an isolated case. In fact, many times the body area that a body dysmorphic disorder patient seems hyper-focused on may not necessarily even be the physical feature that causes them the most distress. It is important that clinicians treating body image disturbances inquire with the patient whether there may be another area of their body that they are actually even more concerned about than the one that they openly discuss. Sometimes this is not the case, but it is still important to at least examine the possibility so not to miss another body theme that is shrouded with shame. Sometimes a patient is so profoundly ashamed about the area of their body that they consider defective that they will not share this information until after an extended process of developing a trusting therapeutic relationship with the clinician.

Altering Posture and Manipulating the Body

Body dysmorphic disorder patients will often alter their posture or "manipulate" the body part that they dislike. This entails attempting to change or camouflage a disliked physical feature without a surgical procedure in a desperate attempt to either change its appearance or to prevent other people from seeing its supposed defectiveness. This is different from when compulsive exercise, fitness, and building muscle mass is utilized to distract from facial features.

I recall working with a male patient who when interacting with women would inhale through his nose and hold his breath to make his nose look more narrow. Inevitably this caused difficulties in his interpersonal interactions because he would have difficult speaking while holding his breath. He would say that women would "look at him funny" and believed that this was because his nose was too broad. He was probably correct and not necessarily having referential thinking when interpreting women as "looking at him funny" because he was attempting to have a conversation with them while holding his breath through his nose. But like many individuals with BDD, his interpretation of why the women were looking at him oddly was tainted by his erroneous thoughts that everyone was as concerned with his nose as he was.

Other examples of manipulating the body include, but are not limited to: Attempting to speak with lips as closed as possible in order to not expose areas of the mouth that are interpreted as defective, for instance, concerns that teeth are too yellow, that gaps between teeth are too wide, and that gums appear too exposed; "scrunching" the forehead in an attempt to make it look smaller; looking downward to minimize others from seeing a full frontal view of the face; "puffing up" or "sucking in" cheeks to make the face look larger or smaller; and "stretching-open" eyes so that they look bigger or distract from areas that are considered to be unattractive such as dark circles under the eyes.

Case Study: Samantha

Samantha hated her eyebrows. She described them as "growing very different from other peoples' eyebrows, that they were straight across rather than arched, and that they were too close to her eyes." She experienced her eyebrows as being so far from the norm that she felt they must be instantly noticeable and offensive to anyone she would interact with. To counter this feeling, she would raise her eyebrows any time she interacted with someone. She would do this compulsion because she believed that by scrunching her eyebrows upward, they would appear more normal and make her feel less like a "freak."

Interactions with other people are usually uncomfortable for the individual with BDD because of the concern that their perceived defect will be noticed and judged by the person they are interacting with. When having a conversation, they may stand at a distance greater than what is culturally considered the norm or shift their posture in order to hide the body area they consider flawed. Although this may mollify some of the shame that they experience during the interaction, they may actually be drawing attention to themselves because of the socially awkward behaviors. It is not uncommon that a BDD patient entering therapy will sit as far away from the clinician as possible, or be seated in a position that leaves a side of their face shielded from view. Although it is not necessary to discuss this with the patient early in therapy, it is important to do so eventually because the unwieldy behaviors detract from connectivity with others.

Patients with untreated body dysmorphic disorder sometimes speak with their hand covering their mouth or in front of the supposed facial defect. Many of these individuals have done this for so long that it has become habit and until it is brought to their attention they are not even aware that they are doing it. Not only is this a BDD compulsion but it interferes with the other person being able to read facial expressions and cues that are integral in interpersonal interactions.

Another reason that a body area may be manipulated is in an attempt to experience symmetry. The ambiguous feeling that a body feature is "wrong" or "defective" is a quite common BDD occurrence, and this can include the feeling that the body area of concern is asymmetrical. Sometimes the BDD sufferer may report that they visually observe a lack of symmetry; it is also not uncommon that patients report that the body part appears symmetrical but simultaneously "it just feels" disproportionate. This disconcerting experience of a body feature feeling asymmetrical may induce body related compulsions.

Case Study: Anthony

Anthony experienced his left cheek as being more bulky and bigger than his right cheek, leaving him with the feeling that his face was asymmetrical. He would engage in numerous rituals in an attempt to "even out the feeling of being disproportional." When chewing food, Anthony would only chew on the right side of his mouth because he worried that to chew on the left side would "build up the jaw muscles" and this would make his left cheek protrude even more. Also, he believed that if he only chewed on the right side, he would build the muscularity of the right jaw and this would assist in balancing out the symmetry of his cheeks. Anthony would frequently use his tongue to push against the inside of his right cheek in the hope that this constant pressure would neutralize the disconcerting feeling that his face was not symmetrical. He also would intentionally sleep on his left cheek believing that perhaps the pressure of sleeping on it would push it inward.

Make-Up and Camouflaging

The behavior of camouflaging areas of the body is very similar to the BDD compulsion of altering posture and "manipulating" the body in that it is an attempt to draw attention away from or disguise an area that is considered unappealing. Camouflaging frequently entails using objects such as hats, bandanas, scarfs, sunglasses, reading glasses, make-up, baggy clothes, and related items to hide the body area of concern. This can also be achieved with facial and head hair: Sometimes men with body dysmorphic disorder may use facial hair to cover skin that they consider imperfect or to hide a jawbone that they feel is not well defined. Women with BDD commonly utilize their hair to hide their profile, their forehead, or any other aspect of their face that they consider defective.

Hats and other headgear may be used not only to hide hair concerns, but also to shadow the face. I once worked with a body dysmorphic disorder patient who would always wear a baseball cap: He was not thrilled with his hair, but this was not his main BDD preoccupation. He disliked his complexion and wore a baseball cap because he believed that it shadowed his face and made his perceived skin flaws look less obvious. Reading glasses are sometimes avoided or over-utilized, both cases being a BDD compulsion. An individual who may actually need to wear glasses or contact lenses may choose to go without and have mediocre vision rather than have 20/20 eyesight: To have very clear vision and to view other peoples' appearances in detail reminds them that other people must be clearly seeing their physical flaws as well. Some individuals intentionally wear glasses to distract from another area of their face. Sunglasses are often used to conceal supposed wrinkles, bags, or dark circles under the eyes, or generally to divert attention from other areas of the face.

Make-up is also often utilized to camouflage facial features. Some individuals report that they don't bother wearing make-up because "they already look horrendous and make-up can't even help," and then there are other BDD patients who cannot leave their home without having applied it. I have worked with multiple patients who are so fearful of being seen without their make-up that even their significant others have never seen them without it. Although it is often used to cover up supposed skin imperfections, make-up is also utilized to distract from areas of the face considered flawed.

Case Study: Avery

Avery really disliked the shape of her eyes. She perceived them as too small and "popping" out of her face and was convinced that unless she could alter them by wearing make-up, then everyone would see how offensive she looked. She would spend hours at a time putting on her eye-mascara until she felt that her eyes looked larger and would "fit better in context with her other facial features." Avery also believed that her nose was too crooked and was disproportionally large for her face. In a desperate attempt to divert attention away from her nose she would use excessive blush on her cheeks to emphasize her cheekbones.

Physical Activities and Avoidance of the Elements

Weather conditions that are perceived as detrimental to the body area of concern often lead to avoidance behaviors. Individuals with concerns about their skin, and most commonly their facial skin, may take extraordinary steps to avoid sun exposure. This might include wearing hats that shade their face any time that they are outside, not participating in physical activities that might expose them to the sun, or in extreme cases, not even going outside at all until after the sun has set. Not all individuals with skin preoccupations are apprehensive about sun damage, but the ones that have this concern usually partake in behaviors that eliminate direct sun contact with their epidermis. These individuals may or may not use sunscreen as part of their avoidance regimen; many individuals with skin preoccupations avoid using products on their face out of concern that the product will either damage their skin or clog their pores and cause blemishes. Some individuals avoid athletic activities altogether because they fear that perspiring will increase the possibility of their skin breaking-out.

Individuals who are worried about the symmetry, density, or overall appearance of their hair may make attempts to avoid the wind or rain.

These elements can rapidly dismantle a precisely groomed coiffure that may have taken hours to perfect. Individuals who are preoccupied with thinning hair may avoid the rain or any situation in which their hair can get wet. BDD sufferers with hair loss concerns are often very troubled about their scalp becoming exposed and the subsequent shame they would experience if others were to notice this. These individuals often voice the concern that their hair looks more sparse when it is wet and that their scalp becomes much more conspicuous. I have worked with avid swimmers and surfers with BDD who have discontinued the sport that they love out of the concern that someone else will see what they perceive as thinning hair or a receding hairline. Skin and hair are the areas of the body that BDD patients most frequently worry will be altered by the elements or damaged during physical activities, but any area of the body can become the recipient of similar themes.

Sometimes individuals with body dysmorphic disorder may avoid participating in athletic activities because they do not want to be seen. I worked with an individual who was an avid runner in high school but chose to participate in cross-country running rather than track because to participate in the latter would entail him constantly being observed by people as he circled the track. He believed that running cross-country significantly decreased the number of people who could view him and observe his supposed defect. He admitted that his BDD symptoms would still affect him even while running cross-country races: During the point in a race where there would be spectators, he would intentionally hide in the middle of the running pack even if they were his competitors. His BDD influenced rationale for this was that if he blended in with the other runners, it would be more difficult for the spectators to observe his bodily defects. He acknowledged that this BDD compulsion would significantly impact his race times and on one occasion probably cost him winning the competition.

Mental Compulsions

Many individuals with body dysmorphic disorder partake in mental compulsions. These are not profoundly different from physical BDD compulsions except for the fact that mental compulsions are done internally rather than externally. These are not obsessions: Obsessions are repetitive, unwanted, intrusive, and negative automatic thoughts. Like physical compulsions, mental compulsions are done as a response to the obsessions in an attempt to ward off feelings of shame, disgust, and anxiety, and simultaneously to serve as a mechanism of self-soothing and to provide relief. The content of body dysmorphic disorder mental compulsions will almost always involve the body area that the person is preoccupied with.

I treated a patient who was engrossed by the obsession that her nose made her "look like a chicken." Throughout the day she would participate in multiple physical compulsions such as mirror checking, touching her nose, and studying other women's noses. When she was not doing physical compulsions, she would be performing mental compulsions by doing mental "reviews" of all the noses she had analyzed during the day and mentally compare her nose to the noses she had seen. This mental review-compulsion also entailed "ordering" the noses she had observed into categories of "good noses," "bad noses," and noses that looked like her "chicken nose."

Another BDD patient that I treated, and who was preoccupied with losing his hair, would do mental calculations of how long it would take for him to become completely bald if he lost a certain number of hairs each hour, each day, each week, and every year. The obsession entailed his fear of hair loss, and the mental compulsion was the intentional act of doing constant mental computations. An additional mental compulsion that many BDD patients perform is attempting to get the perfect "snap shot" in their mind of how they think their supposed defective body part should look. If they do not get the perfect mental "snap shot" they report not feeling right or feeling imperfect and they continue the mental rituals until they feel that the "proper mental image" of the body part has been achieved. This frequently entails magical thinking in which the individual believes that unless they get the mental image "just right" that the particular body area of concern will always remain defective and that all hope for aesthetic change will be lost.

It is important for the treating clinician to inquire about mental compulsions and to explain to the patient the difference between an obsession and a mental compulsion. Many body dysmorphic disorder patients are so inundated by unpleasant obsessions and have become so used to doing mental compulsions that they are completely unaware of this behavior. Like physical compulsions, mental compulsions do reinforce obsessions and keep the BDD sufferer hyper-focused on the body area of concern.

Skin Picking

Skin picking, also referred to as neurotic excoriation or dermatillomania, can be a symptom of body dysmorphic disorder, but also commonly occurs with individuals who have impulse control disorders. When skin picking is associated with BDD, the individual usually does so in an attempt to make an aspect of their skin look better, or a least less unattractive. The urge to pick at their skin may be initiated by visual cues, such as viewing what are perceived to be blemishes, moles, unevenness, or any other dermatological feature that is experienced as unappealing. It can also begin with tactile cues such as feeling "the pressure of a blemish" under the skin or feeling an area of the skin that is not smooth. Not all BDD patients with skin concerns pick at their skin. Many intentionally do not do so out of the concern that either it will make their skin appear worse or perhaps even cause permanent scarring to their epidermis.

When a patient with a skin picking compulsion enters treatment, I always attempt to discern the etiology of the behavior. An individual may self-diagnose as having body dysmorphic disorder because they are preoccupied with their skin, act on compulsive skin picking rituals, and spend many hours a day consumed with the thoughts and compulsions related to their skin. They might have body dysmorphic disorder, but there is also the possibility that a BDD diagnosis could be incomplete or incorrect.

Having worked with a multitude of individuals that pick at their skin, I have found that quite a few have what may appear to be body dysmorphic disorder, but actually have a diathesis for borderline personality disorder or at least borderline personality traits. These individuals are usually less concerned with the actual aesthetic appearance of their skin, but are highly sensitive to features of their skin that do not "feel right" to them. They often impulsively pick or dig into their skin in an attempt to remove any "bad or yucky" material from their pores. They frequently describe this process as "mesmerizing" and "self-soothing" as they clean out the imperfections from their skin. Some individuals even describe the experience of skin picking as a form of punishing themselves: Physically damaging the exterior of their body as the most accessible method of destroying what Bateman and Fonagy refer to as the "bad" or "alien" self (2006).

I have observed that individuals with borderline personality disorder who pick at their skin are often unsuccessful in applying habit reversal, exposure and response prevention, or other behavioral therapy techniques. I have found that patients with skin related body dysmorphic disorder symptoms have a greater capacity to refrain from skin related compulsions and are much more able to follow through with behavioral recommendations. It is important for the clinician to properly identify the source of the skin picking behavior in order to commence with the appropriate course of therapy.

Avoidance: Safety-Seeking Behaviors

Almost all body dysmorphic disorder patients at some point avoid situations that exacerbate their intense feelings of shame and disgust about their appearance. Avoidance can be as subtle as not making eye contact with someone in public and as extreme as not leaving one's home. Avoidance is usually connected to not wanting other people to observe the body part that is considered defective, but I have worked with individuals who do not want to offend others by what they describe as their horrendous or monstrous appearance. Unlike a compulsion that is performed to undo a negative experience, the avoidance serves to prevent a negative consequence (Veale and Neziroglu 2010). But similar to compulsions, the safety-seeking behavior of avoidance is a choice that is made resulting from a body related, negative intrusive thought. The intentional choice not to do a behavior in order to not experience unpleasant emotions reinforces the BDD symptoms because the individual never has the opportunity to have a corrective experience; in other words, the shame that has been so closely associated with a body part cannot be unlearned if the person never places themselves in a curative position.

Avoidance behaviors are usually associated with the possibility of interpersonal interactions. Examples of avoidance behaviors include, but are not limited to: Only leaving one's home in the evening so details of the defect cannot be seen in daylight; not participating in any social or public situations in which the individual with BDD feels as if their body flaw will be observed and judged negatively by other people; the avoidance of being "front-lit" when speaking with people and intentionally being "back-lit" so others will not be able to see the body defect in detail; avoiding work or school because the body area is looking defective on a particular day, such as a skin "break-out" or hair that is having a "too frizzy or too curly" day.

Avoidance themes also transcend the therapy process. It is not unusual for a body dysmorphic disorder patient to intentionally arrive late for therapy sessions. Sitting in the waiting room of a clinician's office suite can be very anxiety provoking because of the concern that other people in the waiting area may observe the supposed defects. This referential thinking and correlated behavior can interfere with the patient getting as much therapy time as possible. Most patients are aware that treatment sessions begin on the hour or half hour, thus arriving late diminishes the chance of being seen by other people.

Some patients will only attend evening therapy sessions for the same reason, believing there will be fewer patients in the clinician's waiting room. It is also not uncommon, especially with very severe cases of body dysmorphic disorder, that the individual will only attend evening sessions because it is dark outside and they are avoiding being seen outside of their home in daylight. It is true that sometimes patients are late because they are stuck in traffic, and it is also true that sometimes the person can only come to therapy in the evening because they work during the day. This being stated, if the psychotherapist observes a pattern of possible avoidance in regards to treatment, it should be openly discussed with the patient so that the therapy process is not compromised.

Avoidance compulsions are very insidious. Not only do these interfere with the BDD sufferer having corrective experiences that can challenge the erroneous beliefs about their appearance, but also avoidance soon leads to isolation. As the patient isolates they are deprived of feedback from the outside world and remain besieged by body related negative intrusive thoughts, thoughts that are usually very tainted with cognitive errors. Isolation only perpetuates a cycle of avoidance and related behaviors as the individual remains a captive in the world of body dysmorphic disorder thoughts.

Internet Compulsions

The Internet serves as the perfect forum for body dysmorphic disorder compulsions. As humans invent new and innovative ways to communicate and research data, the symptoms of body dysmorphic disorder simultaneously follow and rapidly morph to accommodate the sufferers' body related rituals. Individuals with BDD tend to avoid unnecessary contact with people because they believe that others will observe their supposed aesthetic defect. Many of these individuals also have social anxiety, often directly related to their body image symptoms and sometimes as a separate, comorbid diagnosis. Because of this, the World-Wide-Web is an ideal method by which to interact with the world while not being seen.

Many of the previously described body dysmorphic disorder compulsions are also accomplished by way of the Internet. Extensive research on cosmetic procedures and the surgeons that perform them can easily be carried out in the solitude of one's home. The privacy of the Internet almost invites the very common compulsion of scrutinizing and comparing other people's body features without having someone staring back. The use of the Internet is not only very conducive to discretely participating in BDD compulsions, but in itself can quickly become an avoidance compulsion, contributing to not having to interact with actual people.

Online Internet forums can easily be utilized for reassurance seeking compulsions where anonymous users post pictures of themselves, seeking feedback from other nameless participants about specific body parts or about general attractiveness. A very common question asked by those with untreated body dysmorphic disorder is whether they actually have BDD or if they are just unattractive. They usually do not believe their clinician when it is explained to them that they are asking this question because they have body dysmorphic disorder: It is the BDD that causes them to view themselves inaccurately. Posting their pictures on online forums can become the method by which they can receive a constant stream of reassurance, whether this is reassurance confirming that they look acceptable or negative opinions that solidify their already rigid beliefs that they are unattractive. Unfortunately, many of the individuals who participate in these online forums have not received sufficient treatment for their own body related symptoms. Although the opinions expressed may provide temporary reassurance relief, the participants in the online forums are partaking in a body dysmorphic disorder compulsion and to some degree are contributing to each others' body image symptoms.

One of the most common Internet body dysmorphic disorder compulsions is that of searching for body related side effects caused by the medications, often the same medications that have been specifically prescribed to assist with minimizing the BDD symptoms. For example, if an individual is preoccupied by the shape and definition of his jawline, he may be excessively concerned that a particular medication will induce weight gain and in turn will negatively alter the appearance of the jawline. Between running a Google search and posting questions in online forums, he will very likely eventually find something that confirms his fears that the medication might cause weight gain. This statistic may be the only one he finds after extensive searches on the Internet, but often this single piece of information sways the individual to not comply with medication recommendations. Ironically, it is sometimes the correct medication supplementation that is necessary in order to improve insight and contribute to the reduction of BDD compulsions (Phillips and Hollander 2008), including the compulsion of excessive Internet checking and reassurance seeking. I always recommend to my patients that they directly consult a psychiatrist regarding concerns about medication side effects rather than drawing conclusions from random information they find on the Internet.

Miscellaneous Compulsions

Some other common body dysmorphic disorder compulsions not previously mentioned include the measuring of a specific body part in order to compare it to the proportions of another physical feature; the studying of one's shadow if a reflective surface is not available; and the avoidance of individuals who the BDD sufferer perceives as attractive. These compulsions and the others mentioned earlier are some of the more common BDD ritualistic behaviors. Clinicians should remain open-minded to exploring any compulsive behaviors that the body dysmorphic disorder patient utilizes in an attempt to reduce uncomfortable feelings and to minimize negative intrusive thoughts about their appearance.

The measuring of areas of the body is not always carried out by conventional methods such as with a tape measure or ruler. The hands and fingers are frequently used in an attempt to compare the proportions of one body part with that of another. For instance, an individual who believes their face is not symmetrical might use their fingers as an improvised tape measure in an attempt to discern if their facial features are proportional. Another example of this is using a finger to determine the length of one's nose and using this "finger data" to compare their nose length with that of other people.

Some individuals with BDD observe and scrutinize their shadow, particularly the areas of the shadow that coincide with their supposed bodily defect. For instance, an individual who does not like the shape or perceived protrusion of their ears may alter their body so that they are backlit to the sun and that their shadow is cast in front of them so that they can observe how their ears appear in relation to their head. Someone who does not like the size or shape of their nose may alter their posture so that a shadow is cast that shows the shape of their nose. This particular body dysmorphic disorder compulsion is similar to that of reflective surface checking in that the individual is seeking an external source by which to observe if their appearance is acceptable. Unlike the use of many reflective surfaces, a shadow's image is highly prone to being very disproportional to the person's actual physical features; but, untreated BDD sufferers who participate in this compulsion often interpret their shadow as an absolute image of how they must appear to other people. Unfortunately this information is often interpreted at face value and only contributes to their belief that they are misshapen, physically defective, or ugly.

A body dysmorphic disorder behavior that could be classified as an avoidance compulsion or safety-seeking mechanism is worthy of special attention: Sometimes individuals with BDD avoid individuals who they perceive as attractive or as having a specific body feature that they themselves wish they had. I have worked with numerous body image patients who have confided to me that they distanced themselves from friendships or avoided becoming friends with someone they truly liked because of the person's physical appearance. Already feeling as if their own appearance is flawed, to be in proximity with someone they perceive as attractive can make the individual with BDD feel even that much more physically defective, thus they avoid these situations. Patients who have reported that they avoid interacting with attractive individuals usually state that they are very ashamed to admit this and feel very badly about it. They also admit that they only feel that much worse about their own appearance when in the presence of someone they feel is attractive, thus this BDD avoidance compulsion trumps the possibility of maintaining or starting a new friendship.

The following is an example of a not-otherwise-specified miscellaneous body dysmorphic disorder compulsion:

Case Study: David

David was extremely preoccupied with the possibility that he might be losing his hair, especially on the crown of his head. Not only was he preoccupied, he was terrified that even if it was not already happening it would only be a matter of time until his scalp would be exposed. David participated in many of the usual BDD compulsions including taking cellphone photos of the top of his head and examining his hair in the mirror.

He would also regularly stand underneath air conditioning vents in order to experience whether or not he could feel the cool air on his scalp. Living most of the year in Southern Florida, air conditioning is a necessity with the thick humidity that exists in that region. If when standing under the air conditioning vent he did not feel that his scalp was getting cold, he would interpret this as he must not be losing hair. On the other hand, if he felt more cool air on his scalp he would experience a feeling of dread because to him this meant there must be less hair on his head. This is a body dysmorphic disorder compulsion because David would intentionally go out of his way to stand under air vents in an attempt to discern if hair loss was occurring.

Another BDD compulsion that David would engage in was placing the top of his head on "cool" objects in order to see if he could feel the object touching his scalp. When sitting at his desk in his office, he would swivel his chair so that he could place the top of his head against the wall. If he could not feel the "coolness" of the wall against his scalp he would be elated because this must mean the crown of his head had enough hair to sufficiently cover his scalp. But when he did this and perceived that he did feel the wall on his scalp, he would become depressed because to him this was absolute evidence that the hair on his head was becoming sparse.

* * *

I always inquire with my body dysmorphic disorder patients about specific compulsions in which they are engaging. Although I intentionally do not emphasize the body as the focal point of treatment, it is important for both the therapist and patient to understand the behaviors they are using to ward off shame and other uncomfortable emotions. Many patients in the beginning of treatment are not able to distinguish which are compulsions because these behaviors have become such an integral aspect of their lives. Years and years of performing these rituals have become the norm as other healthy behaviors have decreased or disappeared altogether. It is the responsibility of the therapist to make the patient aware of these maladaptive behaviors. Even after a patient becomes mindful of these BDD compulsions, they may not have the self-efficacy to begin minimizing them. This is not unusual and often comes with the terrain when working with this patient population. Patients with less severe symptoms and fewer comorbid conditions may be able to attempt to begin decreasing some of these behaviors.

The process of having a patient reduce their body dysmorphic disorder compulsions can be considered behavioral therapy, but is not supposed to be exposure and response prevention therapy. More often than not the BDD sufferer will be unable to significantly reduce their compulsive behaviors early in treatment. The patient's ability to control their BDD compulsions can also serve as an indicator to the treating psychotherapist of the severity of the patient's symptoms, their level of insight, and their emotional development and fragility.

A patient that does not have the capacity to reduce BDD rituals outside of the therapy office should not be considered a difficult case; rather, this should be a cue to the therapist that early treatment needs to take another path. The patient may have delusional symptoms and does not have the insight regarding the importance of reducing compulsions; the patient may not trust the therapist and will need time before beginning to reduce the behaviors that have maintained the status quo, albeit maladaptive; the individual may report he is reducing compulsions to seek approval from the therapist while continuing to employ these behaviors outside of the therapy session. Regardless of why the patient does not reduce these behaviors, the therapist needs to identify this and adapt to the patient. The more comfortable the therapist is with delving into other therapeutic modalities, the better suited they will be to adapt to patients with very inflexible body image disturbances.

Whether or not the patient has the capacity to reduce or refrain from body image compulsive behaviors, therapy has to proceed. It is not uncommon that some patients who have initial difficulty with compulsion reduction to have success later in the therapeutic process. This is often after they have a trusting attachment with the clinician and after they have been stabilized on the appropriate medications. Certain patients never respond when given direction to reduce BDD compulsions. When this is the case I would strongly advise the treating clinician to accept that these behaviors have long served a function to regulate feelings and that removing them may cause the patient to emotionally fragment. As mentioned previously, this is when the therapist needs to view the bigger picture and adapt to the BDD patient's inflexibility. Remember: Body dysmorphic disorder patients are so hyper-focused on details about their appearance that they miss the bigger picture of their life. The therapist needs to be wary of not falling into a similar paradigm and has to remain mindful to view treatment from a very flexible vantage point.

For the patient who does have the capacity to begin reducing body dysmorphic disorder compulsions, it is imperative to educate them that they should not replace these compulsions with new ones. Anything can serve as a replacement behavior, whether it is a different body part, a compulsive or addictive behavior, or even focusing on a different disorder. It is important that the clinician informs the patient that replacement behaviors only serve as another means of regulating emotions and impedes him from directly experiencing feelings that have been buried beneath habitual body image rituals.

I once worked with a patient who, within the first few months of therapy, was able to reduce the majority of BDD compulsions that consisted mostly of mirror checking and reassurance seeking. Although this was quite conducive to the therapeutic process, he concurrently began to study women's reactions to him and interpreted these as evidence of whether or not he was attractive. If a woman looked at him in passing, he would use this as confirmation that he looked acceptable; if they did not look at him, the interpretation was that he must look hideous. The patient's conclusions were very absolute with no room for alternative explanations. Fortunately, the patient's insight was sufficient enough to understand my explanation that he was replacing one compulsion for another and that in both of these behaviors he was seeking external approbation in order to validate his appearance and similarly his self-worth.

As all compulsions are reduced, it is inevitable that the individual will begin to experience thoughts and feelings that have been suppressed since the commencement of the particular behavior. The therapist should be supportive of the patient expressing these uncomfortable emotions and encourage him to openly process them rather than conceal them behind a smoke screen of avoidant behaviors. From my experience it is at this juncture of treatment that the clinician should become fully engaged in an interpersonal therapeutic modality. As the patient's focus shifts away from the body or other external distractions, the therapist needs to be engaged in the interpersonal attachment process. The interactions between two human beings in the room will begin to replace the patient's habitual response to attach to an inanimate body part.

6 Comorbidity and Misdiagnoses

Body dysmorphic disorder is most frequently accompanied by comorbid diagnoses. In fact, it is unusual to see body dysmorphic disorder without at least one other psychiatric diagnosis. The most commonly occurring comorbid diagnoses are described in this chapter.

Obsessive-Compulsive Disorder

It is not unusual for body dysmorphic disorder to be accompanied by a comorbid diagnosis of obsessive-compulsive disorder (OCD). It is also not uncommon for an individual to have been misdiagnosed with and treated for OCD when they actually suffer from body dysmorphic disorder. Similar to OCD, patients with body image disturbances participate in repetitive ritualistic behaviors, but in the case of BDD, these behaviors revolve around body related themes.

Whether or not the patient fully discloses the motive behind the behavior is another issue: Body dysmorphic disorder patients will frequently avoid revealing that they are preoccupied with an aspect of their appearance due to the extreme shame associated with it. An example of this would be the individual who compulsively washes his hands because he does not want them to feel dirty. He discloses to the clinician that he repeatedly washes his hands throughout the day and that this behavior is impacting his daily activities. What he does not divulge is that he is washing his hands excessively because he is preoccupied with his complexion: He believes that if his hands are dirty and he accidently touches his face, then his facial pores might get clogged with the dirt that subsequently could cause a break-out of facial blemishes. This individual's primary preoccupation is with how his skin appears and whether or not it is clear of perceived defects. If this information is shared with the clinician, it becomes much easier to make the diagnosis of body dysmorphic disorder. But, if the patient does not want to draw attention to his skin and does not share his concerns about his complexion, he may very well receive a diagnosis of obsessive-compulsive disorder.

The reverse scenario can occur as well, where a patient reports that he is preoccupied by an aspect of his appearance and that he participates in compulsive behaviors as a result of this preoccupation. For example, take an individual who is very obsessive about having his hair groomed a certain way: He reports that if his hair is not "just right" then he must fix it before he can proceed with his day. With this initial information, the diagnosis would most certainly sound like body dysmorphic disorder, but this may not necessarily be the case. In this example, I base the diagnosis upon the genesis of the patient's need to have his hair perfect. If he is very concerned that other people may judge his hair negatively, he is embarrassed or has shame associated with his hair, or if his identity is profoundly linked to his hair, I will begin to suspect body dysmorphic disorder. If he is indifferent about what other people think about his hair, is not ashamed about it, and just needs to get it right so that he feels in control or less anxious, I lean in the direction of an OCD diagnosis. In other words, an individual can have obsessive-compulsive disorder surrounding an aspect of their body and not necessarily have BDD.

Both obsessive-compulsive disorder patients and individuals with body dysmorphic disorder experience anxiety. Also, both participate in ritualistic, compulsive behaviors in an attempt to reduce the anxiety. The source of the anxiety differs between the two diagnoses: In OCD, anxiety is often correlated with the need for control whereas in BDD the anxiety is not the primary driving emotion. Individuals with body dysmorphic disorder experience anxiety as the by-product of perceived impending shame; the anxiety is a warning signal that they may be shamed, humiliated, or exposed as inherently defective.

With the 2013 publication of DSM-5, body dysmorphic disorder was classified under Obsessive-Compulsive and Related Disorders and is no longer classified as a somatoform disorder (American Psychiatric Association 2013). BDD definitely has similarities with the obsessive-compulsive spectrum, but it also has similarities to other psychiatric conditions as well. The possible downside of placing BDD on the obsessive-compulsive spectrum may be that clinicians interpret that the treatment for body dysmorphic disorder is verbatim to that of OCD. There are similarities in the treatment between the two disorders, but in my opinion, the cognitive-behavioral model utilized with obsessive-compulsive disorder is insufficient for treating body dysmorphic disorder.

Eating Disorders

Body dysmorphic disorder is not an eating disorder (American Psychiatric Association 2013). Comorbidity can occur, but BDD by itself is not and should not be classified as a condition of disordered eating. It is not uncommon that individuals with body dysmorphic disorder are steered toward eating disorder programs even though they are not concerned about their weight or body fat percentage. What can occur with certain BDD patients is that they might restrict food intake or may exercise excessively, and to the eating disorder specialist these appear as red flags for a possible eating disorder.

Individuals with body dysmorphic disorder who do alter their diet or exercise regimen will often do so in an attempt to alter a feature on their face. Examples of this include wanting to lose weight in their face so that their cheek bones are more prominent, their jawline is better defined, their head appears smaller, or that their face will look less round. The concern is rarely about fat and very much involves the preoccupation with the facial feature that they consider to be unattractive. Because there is such profound shame surrounding the body areas deemed ugly, these individuals will not disclose this information to a clinician during an initial intake. But if they are asked if they restrict their diet or exercise compulsively, they will often answer affirmatively because their shame does not involve weight. This is where the eating disorder misdiagnosis often occurs: The nature of BDD is such that the patient does not disclose all pertinent information, so even the most discerning clinicians will not be able to formulate a fully accurate diagnosis.

Body dysmorphic disorder patients who have initially ended up in eating disorder programs almost always report that they feel as if they did not fit in. This only accentuates the BDD experience that somehow they are different from all other human beings: Even in a program that treats body image issues, they still feel very different which further confirms their belief that no one can truly understand their experience. These individuals often do not share their most shameful body related preoccupations even when they are in an eating disorder program. As a result, the treatment staff will never know that disordered eating is not what is tormenting the individual. They would rather be misdiagnosed than to draw attention to their face or an aspect of their body that they are so ashamed about.

Individuals with body dysmorphic disorder can be preoccupied with an area of their body that is not their head or face. If this is the case and the individual is restricting food, the clinician needs to better understand the thought process supporting this behavior. The questions I ask are usually straightforward and may sound something like the following: "You have said that you are very cautious about what you eat and that you exercise a lot because you are trying to lose weight. Are you trying to lose weight because you are very concerned about body fat, the size of your body, how your clothes fit, or the number on the scale? Or, is your main concern about an aspect of your appearance, particularly a facial feature, and you are trying to lose weight in order so that it looks different? Or, are both of these examples applicable to you?"

If the diagnosing clinician asks these questions, the individual with BDD will often admit that they do have a preoccupation with a specific area of their appearance. If these inquiries are not made, the individual with BDD will very possibly avoid providing the information that is shrouded in shame and the primary diagnosis will go undetected. Regardless, the clinician will need to do some detective work because what might appear as obvious signs of an eating disorder may or may not be the case.

Muscle Dysmorphia

Muscle dysmorphia, also referred to as bigorexia, is a variant of body dysmorphic disorder. Individuals with muscle dysmorphia believe that their physical stature is too small or is not muscular enough (Pope, Phillips, and Olivardia 2002) and they participate in compulsive behaviors in an attempt to change this. These behaviors include excessive exercise routines, especially exercises that build muscle, and often a preoccupation with their diet in order to maximize these results. Body building supplements, legal and illegal, are frequently utilized in order to expedite the process of muscle growth. Sometimes these individuals undergo cosmetic procedures, for instance getting calf or chest implants, in order to enhance the body area that they perceive is too small or inadequate.

There are individuals with body dysmorphic disorder who may appear to have muscle dysmorphia but actually do not. Although a comorbid diagnosis is always possible, it is not uncommon that BDD patients are very concerned about their physique because the body from below the neck can serve as a distraction from other bodily regions that they perceive as defective: Often these areas are from the neck upward, especially facial features. The BDD patient may disclose to the clinician that they are preoccupied with the build of their body, while not elaborating that they are very ashamed about another aspect of their appearance.

For the individual with BDD who believes an aspect of their face is misshapen or unattractive, the body from the neck downward is the only area they feel that they can control (unless they receive cosmetic procedures on facial features). These individuals express that there is nothing they can do about how their face looks, but that if their body is in very good shape then other people will focus on this and not what they perceive as their unattractive facial features. Usually the preoccupation with muscles and fitness is secondary to a primary concern about another physical feature that cannot be altered via exercise. In these cases, the anxiety surrounding losing or not maintaining a certain body physique derives from the concern that their body will no longer provide a distraction. They fear that more attention will be directed toward their face and this is often associated with intense shame.

Clinicians who are working with a patient with muscle dysmorphia should also inquire if there are other areas of the body that they dislike or are ashamed to discuss. By inquiring, the clinician can begin to rule out if the patient's exercise regimen solely involves their physique, or if the body is acting as a decoy for other bodily features that the patient is too ashamed to disclose.

Major Depressive Disorder

A very high percentage of body dysmorphic disorder patients experience major clinical depression (Gunstad and Phillips 2003). It is not unusual that depressive episodes occur in conjunction with how they perceive their appearance or supposed defect: If on a particular day they are feeling as if it is not too defective, their mood may be euthymic. In contrast to this, if they are experiencing severe BDD symptoms it is very likely that this would correlate with their mood spiraling into a depression.

I have worked with several body dysmorphic disorder patients who had been misdiagnosed with bipolar I or bipolar II disorders because of the rapid fluctuations in their mood. Having worked with these patients at length I was able to discern that none of these individuals were bipolar, although the mood shifts that they had described to their treating psychiatrists must have very much appeared as bipolar disorder. What they never mentioned to their doctors was that they were preoccupied with their appearance and at any given moment their mood could shift based upon how they perceived their supposed defect. If they perceived the body part as ugly or disfigured, their mood would rapidly plummet. On the rare occasion that they were satisfied with the supposed defect, they could present with a highly elated affect. Once again, shame associated with a perceived defect in appearance prevented the patient from disclosing all relevant information to the treating psychiatrist. To the doctors, the physical appearance of these patients look perfectly normal thus it would never have occurred to them to ask questions related to appearance in the first place.

Patients with body dysmorphic disorder can also experience a depression that is separate from the depressive symptoms that are directly associated with the body image material. In order to better discern the etiology of the depression, I often ask the following question, "Is your mood determined by what you see when you look in reflective surfaces or when you view photographs of yourself, or, do you feel your depressed mood is caused by other factors?" BDD patients will frequently respond affirmatively that how they feel about their appearance frequently correlates with their mood state. It is of course imperative to address the body image symptoms that are at the source of the depression, but it is also important to determine if mood symptoms exist separately from the body dysmorphic disorder diagnosis.

Social Anxiety Disorder

Many individuals with body dysmorphic disorder also have what appears to be social anxiety disorder. They frequently become very anxious in public, especially in the context of social interactions. Their social anxiety derives from the possibility that the supposed bodily defect will be observed by others and that they will experience shame. Shame is the driving emotion behind the anxiety, and this is associated with the concern that somehow they will be exposed as inherently defective and this will be discovered by way of the flaws in their appearance.

A misdiagnosis of social anxiety disorder rather than BDD can occur if the patient only shares the surface facts, that he becomes very anxious in social and interpersonal situations. If he has body dysmorphic disorder, he may not share his primary concern because there is so much shame attached to the body and he may not want to draw attention to it because it is perceived as defective. Unless the clinician asks more in depth questions regarding what specifically makes the patient anxious in social situations, it is likely that the BDD will go undetected and that social anxiety disorder will become the focus of treatment.

Comorbidity of social anxiety disorder and body dysmorphic disorder does occur. In order to discern if the social anxiety stems from body related material I ask the question, "Does your social anxiety only occur in interpersonal situations because of your body image concerns, or, are you worried that other people will judge you based on themes unrelated to the body such as if you are articulate, competent, or smart enough?" It is not uncommon that the patient with BDD also has some social anxiety surrounding how others will judge their social acumen, but the anxiety deriving from the fear that they will be shamed is usually the primary source behind the angst in social situations.

During the course of treatment, social anxiety symptoms that are a product of the body dysmorphic disorder will gradually decrease as the BDD symptoms lessen. If there are social anxiety disorder symptoms that are unrelated to the body image themes, these may need to be addressed separately. Behavioral therapy for BDD should emphasize interpersonal interactions, so regardless of its etiology the social anxiety and body dysmorphic disorder can often be addressed simultaneously.

Substance Related and Addictive Disorders

It is not uncommon that body dysmorphic disorder is concurrent with a substance related disorder (Grant et al. 2005). Although significant substance dependence should not be ruled out, most BDD patients that I have worked with and who have had substance related disorders have reported that they began to abuse substances as a consequence of their body image disturbance. I have yet to work with a BDD patient who has reported that abusing a substance caused their symptoms, but body dysmorphic disorder patients frequently report that substance abuse often increases their pre-existing body image symptoms during the days after usage.

Many report that the only way they could quiet the self-deprecating, negative intrusive thoughts about their appearance was by self-medicating. Others report that their substance abuse began because it was the only way they could feel comfortable interacting with people; for some, being under the influence of a substance was the only time they were able to leave the confines of their home. Over the years I have observed that alcohol and cannabis are the two substances most commonly abused by my body dysmorphic disorder patients, but patients have reported abusing stimulants, opioids, and hallucinogens.

Substance abuse is not compatible with the treatment of body dysmorphic disorder. If a patient seeks treatment for BDD and is also actively abusing a substance, it is recommended that the individual seek treatment for the substance abuse prior to commencing therapy for body dysmorphic disorder. If the substance abuse is only situational and secondary to the BDD symptoms, it is appropriate to begin treatment for the body image disturbance with the condition that the patient remains clean and sober.

Although a recommendation to attend a 12-Step recovery program may seem indicated, many individuals with untreated body dysmorphic disorder are unable to attend these meetings because of the severity of their body image symptoms. After all, they are abusing the substance because this is the only way they feel comfortable interacting with people. This can quickly create a paradox for the clinician: If the patient's substance abuse is significant to the point that it would greatly hinder therapy, the substance abuse needs to be addressed first. But, if the BDD symptoms are extreme and the patient is unable to attend a substance abuse program, then the continued use of the substance will interfere with therapy. The clinician will need to discern to what extent the substance abuse is intertwined with the body image symptoms and decide whether or not the patient can benefit from therapy without having received professional care for the substance related disorder.

Excoriation Disorder

Skin picking, also called excoriation disorder or dermatillomania, is currently classified in the *Diagnostic and Statistical Manual of Mental Disorders*, DSM-5, among the Obsessive-Compulsive and Related Disorders. According to the DSM-5, one of the criteria for a diagnosis of excoriation disorder is that it is not better explained by symptoms of another mental disorder such as body dysmorphic disorder (American Psychiatric Association 2013). Skin picking as it relates to body dysmorphic disorder differs from the DSM-5 classification: Individuals with BDD who pick at their skin mostly do so in an attempt to fix a perceived imperfection. Ironically this often leads to the creation of a blemish, or if a slight skin imperfection does exist, it may be made worse by the picking behavior. Facial skin is one of the most common areas of the body that BDD patients are preoccupied with; not all individuals who have skin concerns pick at their epidermis. Some individuals who are preoccupied with their skin intentionally do not pick at it because they fear creating an infection that might permanently damage or scar their skin.

Sometimes it is quite obvious that an individual has been engaging in skin picking compulsions as evidenced by lesions and scars. Other times these are covered up with make-up or are less obvious and cannot necessarily be observed. When a patient shares that they repeatedly pick at their skin, I inquire regarding the motivation behind the behavior. Just because a patient picks at their skin does not necessarily determine that they have BDD. I have observed that body dysmorphic disorder patients who do pick at their skin have much more of a capacity to refrain from this behavior compared to individuals diagnosed with excoriation disorder.

Somatic Symptom Disorder

Individuals with somatic symptom disorder experience various specific and non-specific somatic symptoms (American Psychiatric Association 2013). Although somatic symptom disorder is a separate diagnosis from body dysmorphic disorder, I have treated numerous BDD patients who report physical sensations and concerns that are not appearance related. I have also observed that it is not uncommon that once the body dysmorphic disorder symptoms begin to dissipate, other body related symptoms may replace the preoccupation with perceived aesthetic defects. These symptoms manifest as internal physical experiences such as nausea, stiffness, dizziness, pain, or an overall hyper-vigilance about physical health. Just as body dysmorphic disorder symptoms can morph from one area of the body to the next, they can also shift to a preoccupation focusing on the internal functioning of the body. It is important for the treating clinician to observe and address this mutation in symptoms because it may be emblematic of underlying emotional material that has yet to be properly processed.

Panic Disorders and Panic Attacks

The *Diagnostic and Statistical Manual of Mental Disorders*, DSM-5, defines panic disorder as recurrent unexpected panic attacks. Panic attacks are defined as an abrupt surge of intense fear that reaches a peak within minutes. Within the duration of the panic attack, the individual experiences symptoms that may include accelerated heart rate, sensations of shortness of breath, sweating, trembling, nausea, numbness, and fear of losing control or dying. The DSM-5 also specifies that panic disorder can be diagnosed if not better explained by another mental disorder (American Psychiatric Association 2013).

It is not uncommon for individuals with untreated body dysmorphic disorder to describe that they are feeling as if they are having a panic attack. These individuals do sometimes experience intense rushes of anxiety that could very well fit the DSM-5 definition of a panic attack. It is possible that an individual could have a comorbid diagnosis of panic disorder, but often what is occurring is that they experience sudden, intense anxiety after viewing an area of their body that they perceive is defective. An example of this would be the individual who has profound shame and anxiety related to hair loss. If they are viewing themselves in a mirror and believe that they see an area of their scalp where their hair is thinning, this situational trigger might very well be the catalyst that activates intense anxiety.

If the clinician discerns that the patient's panic attacks are directly linked to an area of their body that they deem as defective, it is likely that body dysmorphic disorder is the primary diagnosis and that a diagnosis of panic disorder should not be made. But, if the individual also experiences sudden bouts of anxiety that stem from non-body related sources, the therapist will need to gather further evidence to determine if a comorbid diagnosis of panic disorder is valid.

Olfactory Reference Syndrome

The preoccupation that one emits an undesirable odor defines Olfactory Reference Syndrome (ORS). Individuals who experience this syndrome are preoccupied with the belief that they smell or that an area of their body disseminates an odor (Bizamcer, Dubin, and Hayburn 2008). They are also very concerned that other people will experience them as odoriferous and that they will offend others as a result.

I had erroneously assumed that ORS was one of those rare disorders that might appear only once or twice in an entire clinical career; that is before I began asking my patients if they were concerned if they smelled or if other people might smell them. Although it cannot be concluded that ORS and body dysmorphic disorder are frequent co-occurring disorders, I have had multiple BDD patients disclose that yes, they are very preoccupied with their body odor and are excessively concerned that everyone else might perceive them as smelling nauseous.

Similar to BDD symptoms, they had never brought this information up to their previous treating clinicians because it was too shameful to do so; they also did not want to draw attention to the possibility that they might have putrid body odor. Also similar to body dysmorphic disorder, they participate in many compulsive rituals in an attempt to "smell neutral or normal." Some of these compulsions include excessive showering and teeth-brushing, purchasing a wide array of soaps and body washes, asking for reassurance, and frequently wearing perfume or cologne to mask what they perceive as their unsavory scent. Both body dysmorphic disorder and olfactory reference syndrome sufferers share the theme of profound shame, that somehow they must be fundamentally defective and that others will discern this either through observing an aesthetic defect in appearance or by smelling supposed emanating bodily odors.

7 Behavioral Therapy for Body Dysmorphic Disorder

When I began working with individuals with body dysmorphic disorder in the 1990s there was limited information available about the subject, so like many clinicians at the time I assumed that it was just a variant of obsessive-compulsive disorder. There had been only one book published on the topic and that was *The Broken Mirror* by Dr. Katharine Phillips. Experts in the treatment of obsessive-compulsive disorder had taken notice that there were similarities between BDD and OCD: Individuals with these conditions both have repetitive, intrusive, negative thoughts that will not dissipate and that provoke significant psychological and emotional distress. Also, individuals with these psychiatric conditions both participate in compulsions: These are behavioral rituals that are performed in an attempt to reduce the emotional distress caused by the negative intrusive thoughts. Although at this time body dysmorphic disorder was classified in the DSM-IV as a somatoform disorder, clinicians who worked with OCD preferred to describe it as an obsessive-compulsive spectrum disorder because of the similarities between the two syndromes (Saxena et al. 2001).

Because body dysmorphic disorder and obsessive-compulsive disorder shared several common characteristics, it was assumed that the treatment for these disorders should also be similar. The majority of OCD researchers and clinicians in the 1990s were proponents of utilizing cognitive-behavioral therapy (CBT) as the primary treatment for obsessive-compulsive disorder, specifically using a variation of behavioral therapy called exposure and response prevention (ERP). This entails gradually exposing the patient to situations or objects that elicit anxiety, and having them experience the anxiety until they gradually habituate, or acclimate, to the discomfort.

A plethora of research data demonstrated that individuals suffering from obsessive-compulsive disorder exhibited a reduction in obsessions and anxiety after participating in adequate trials of cognitive-behavioral therapy. Many OCD sufferers who had previously not experienced relief by way of other therapeutic modalities were now reporting a mitigation of symptoms and even symptom remission. It had been concluded that

since cognitive-behavioral therapy with exposure and response prevention techniques was proving to be so successful for obsessive-compulsive
disorder, then logically it made sense to apply these therapeutic methods to other obsessive-compulsive spectrum disorders including body
dysmorphic disorder.

At the end of the twentieth century there were very few body dysmorphic disorder experts and even fewer facilities that had enough knowledge of the disorder to provide treatment. Individuals with BDD would
gravitate toward obsessive-compulsive disorder treatment programs
because there were so few other options; OCD treatment appeared to
be the closest match for those with symptoms of BDD. Another reason
why many body dysmorphic disorder patients would end up in OCD
programs is because they would initially be diagnosed with obsessive-
compulsive disorder. The misdiagnosis of body dysmorphic disorder as
OCD was and remains very common: The extreme shame and secrecy
internalized by BDD sufferers is such that many do not disclose their
body image concerns to mental health practitioners. These individuals
often fear they will be judged as vain or narcissistic thus frequently only
disclose other symptoms that they are experiencing such as social anxiety, obsessive-compulsive, or depressive symptoms.

I have worked with individuals who had previously been in psychotherapy for years and never divulged to their clinician that they viewed
themselves as physically unattractive, ugly, or deformed. This oversight
is not necessarily a blunder by the treating practitioner, rather a result
of the abstruse nature of body dysmorphic disorder. Since many BDD
patients also present with symptoms of OCD, this frequently became the
focus of treatment. As a result, many patients whose primary diagnosis
was BDD would end up in clinical programs specializing in the treatment
of obsessive-compulsive disorder.

The treatment of obsessive-compulsive disorder with cognitive-behavioral
therapy, specifically exposure and response prevention, consists of two major
components: The behavioral component entails creating an exposure
hierarchy (McGrath 2007). The hierarchy consists of situations, places,
or things that elicit anxiety and is created such that the patient gradually
works from the least anxiety provoking scenarios to the items that make
them the most uncomfortable. Not only is the patient exposed to situations that will intentionally produce anxiety, but also they need to follow
through with response prevention which entails experiencing the anxiety
rather than doing a compulsion in an attempt to reduce the discomfort.
If the individual does not act on the compulsions, they will gradually
habituate to the uncomfortable feelings and subsequently the intensity
of the obsessive thoughts will also steadily decrease. The second component to cognitive-behavioral therapy is the cognitive content that consists of identifying erroneous thoughts and restructuring these thoughts
(Foa 2010). Many clinicians and researchers who specialize in treating

OCD have observed and even proven that there is a significant decrease in overall symptoms when patients with obsessive-compulsive disorder actively participate in cognitive-behavioral treatment.

In my early years of working with body dysmorphic disorder I recall hearing several OCD experts vent their frustrations regarding patients that presented with BDD features. I remember one proficient OCD practitioner stating, "All body dysmorphic patients are borderlines," referring to the frustration that many mental health practitioners experience when working with individuals with borderline personality disorder. The frustration was not unfounded; this patient population did not seem to respond as quickly or as significantly as patients with obsessive-compulsive disorder. It was not uncommon, and to this day is often still the case, that cognitive-behavioral therapists attempt to apply the techniques that work so well with OCD patients directly to patients with body image disturbances. Obsessive-compulsive disorder patients are exposed to the situations that make them the most uncomfortable, and this treatment template was applied verbatim to individuals with body dysmorphic disorder.

Because body dysmorphic disorder patients despise areas of their bodies, it seemed quite rational to do exposure and response prevention exercises following the methodology that worked so efficiently with treating obsessive-compulsive disorder. The BDD patients would report that they did not like a particular aspect of their appearance and this supposed defect would then become the focus of the treatment regimen. Following cognitive-behavioral protocol, the patient was exposed to what made them most uncomfortable, and this was usually their reflection. Patients were, and often still are, told to "stare at the body part in the mirror" until they habituate to the discomfort.

A method that worked so well with individuals without BDD symptoms was not producing similar results with patients with body image issues. The reputation of body dysmorphic disorder patients soon became that of a very difficult and frustrating patient population to treat. In the cognitive-behavioral therapy establishment, BDD was reputed to be the equivalent of "treatment refractory obsessive-compulsive disorder." It was not uncommon that purist cognitive-behavioral practitioners would choose not to work with patients with body dysmorphic disorder: This was because of the erratic compliance with cognitive-behavioral techniques, poor insight into symptoms, and the negative countertransference the practitioner would experience when their therapeutic tools that worked so well with other patient populations often proved insufficient when applied to BDD sufferers.

I was one of these cognitive-behavioral therapists. My early psychotherapy training consisted of an emphasis on behavioral techniques with cognitive therapy used as an adjunct. I was very interested in this therapeutic modality and soon became a believer that this was the treatment of choice when working with patients who existed on the obsessive-compulsive spectrum. I witnessed patients with severe obsessive-compulsive disorder symptoms respond positively to exposure and response prevention therapy and this reinforced my conviction that this was how one was to treat OCD. But the cognitive-behavioral techniques that seemed to work so well for obsessive-compulsive disorder patients did not render the same outcome when working with BDD clientele. I was soon to endure the same frustration that my psychotherapist peers were experiencing when attempting to apply a cognitive-behavioral modality to a disorder that appeared so similar to obsessive-compulsive disorder.

Patients with body dysmorphic disorder are much less likely to engage in the process of behavioral therapy. They are much more apt to avoid situations that elicit shame and are also less likely to openly discuss the extent and severity of their body image symptoms. Many patients with body dysmorphic disorder have what is referred to as overvalued ideation (Cororve and Gleaves 2001). These are rigid beliefs that hold significant value to the individual. Overvalued ideation is considered to be less inflexible than pure delusional thinking: Delusions are firmly entrenched thoughts and beliefs that do not waiver even with evidence to the contrary. With overvalued ideation there is slightly more insight and flexibility in regards to the possibility that a thought may be erroneous. This makes it very difficult to do cognitive restructuring with these patients. Also, since such a high percentage of these individuals have minimal insight into their symptoms, they regularly present first to dermatologists and cosmetic surgeons. They often believe that they do not suffer from a psychiatric, emotional, or psychological condition so have no reason to attend psychotherapy in the first place. A patient who firmly believes that their appearance is the problem may not fully participate in behavioral therapy, often opting to follow the route of aesthetic procedures.

Like all psychiatric disorders, severity of body dysmorphic disorder exists on a continuum. Not all BDD sufferers have overvalued ideation or are delusional. Some do have insight that perhaps they have a psychiatric condition, but often also believe that their appearance is problematic as well. BDD patients with better insight have more ability to do cognitive therapy and also are more inclined, although still hesitant, to partake in behavioral therapy exercises. Although the group of body dysmorphic disorder patients who have less severe symptoms are more likely to agree to cognitive-behavioral therapy, I have found that compared to OCD patients they are much less likely to complete treatment, and if they do, are much more likely to relapse. After several years of attempting to replicate OCD treatment techniques with BDD patients, I began to question if my skills as a cognitive-behavioral therapist were inadequate; I also began to question if perhaps cognitive-behavioral therapy by itself was insufficient when working with the body dysmorphic disorder patient population.

In the DSM-IV, the fourth edition of the *Diagnostic and Statistical Manual of Mental Disorders* published by the American Psychiatric Association, body dysmorphic disorder was classified under somatoform disorders. These are mental disorders characterized by physical illness or injury with symptoms that cannot be fully explained by a general medical condition or attributable to another mental disorder (American Psychiatric Association 1994). BDD had not been categorized with the DSM-IV anxiety disorders that obsessive-compulsive disorder was affiliated with. This decision was not at all unreasonable because even though BDD and OCD shared the emblematic features of obsessions, individuals with BDD do not primarily suffer from anxiety. They do experience anxiety resulting from intrusive thoughts that they look ugly or misshapen, but shame and self-disgust tend to be the most pervasive feelings that BDD sufferers endure. Body dysmorphic disorder also shares features with hypochondriasis, another disorder classified under somatoform disorders in which an individual experiences excessive preoccupation and worry about having a serious disease. Whereas the body dysmorphic disorder sufferer is preoccupied with an external area of their body that they believe is defective, the hypochondriac obsesses about the internal functioning of their body.

With the publication of the *Diagnostic and Statistical Manual of Mental Disorders*, fifth edition (American Psychiatric Association 2013), body dysmorphic disorder was moved from the updated category called Somatic Symptom and Related Disorders and reclassified under Obsessive-Compulsive and Related Disorders. In doing so, the authors and contributors to the DSM-5 were emphasizing that, based upon their research, body dysmorphic disorder was much more closely related to OCD and other obsessive-compulsive spectrum disorders. As of the publication of this book, body dysmorphic disorder shares this category with obsessive-compulsive disorder, hoarding disorder, trichotillomania (hair pulling disorder), excoriation (skin picking) disorder, substance/medication induced obsessive-compulsive and related disorders, and obsessive-compulsive and related disorders due to another medical condition.

Body dysmorphic disorder also shares characteristics with anorexia nervosa that is classified in the DSM-5 under Feeding and Eating Disorders (American Psychiatric Association 2013). Both patient populations are extremely hyper-focused on specific aspects of their body and appearance and are usually unable to visualize themselves as other people see them. The anorectic patient will restrict food consumption, abuse laxatives, compulsively exercise, and participate in related behaviors in order to control their weight and maintain what they perceive to be an appropriate body image. Although the majority of body dysmorphic disorder patients do not meet DSM-5 criteria for anorexia nervosa, it is not unusual that a BDD patient may rigidly control their diet in order to make a physical feature look less defective.

I was once referred a patient by a psychiatrist who had recently begun treating an individual, and had been informed by the patient's previous clinician that she suffered from anorexia nervosa. The patient openly admitted that she restricted food and sometimes purged because she did not want to gain weight, and actually wanted to lose weight. It was not until I pried further that I discovered that it was not actually her body from the neck down that bothered her, but that she felt her face was too fat. She timidly explained to me that the truth was that she was very, very ashamed about her nose, that she believed looked too small. She disclosed that if her face looked too fat, then this would proportionally only make her nose look smaller, thus she wanted to make sure her face was as small as possible. She divulged that she was indifferent about the shape, size, and weight of her body from the neck down, but it was crucial that her face did not look fat so that her nose would not appear as tiny.

This patient had repetitive and intrusive negative thoughts as experienced by individuals with obsessive-compulsive disorder. She had symptoms that could point toward an eating disorder diagnosis such as being extremely diligent, restrictive, and rigidly preoccupied with her diet in order to make sure she did not gain weight. Because the patient had not disclosed to her previous doctors that it was actually the size of her nose that was her main focus, making an accurate and complete diagnosis was impossible; both OCD and anorexia nervosa would have been reasonable diagnoses with the information available. This example is not an anomaly, rather a common occurrence with body dysmorphic disorder. The BDD sufferer experiences so much shame attached to a perceived physical defect that they may not disclose crucial information unless the clinician asks the correct questions; even if a clinician is asking precise questions there is still no guarantee that the individual will feel comfortable disclosing their bodily secrets.

The ambiguity of making a body dysmorphic disorder diagnosis inevitably affects the treatment process. BDD has overlapping characteristics with multiple psychiatric disorders, some of which are not obsessive-compulsive spectrum disorders. If BDD was mostly similar to obsessive-compulsive disorder, then we would probably observe comparable positive treatment outcomes as is the case when utilizing cognitive-behavioral therapy for OCD. Because BDD appears to transcend other diagnoses that are not necessarily treated with cognitive-behavioral therapy, perhaps other therapeutic modalities should also be utilized when working with a disorder as complex and inflexible as body dysmorphic disorder.

There is a behavioral component to all realms of therapy, including even the most traditional psychoanalytical modalities that emphasize interpretation rather than behavior as the catalyst for change. In order for an individual to even begin the therapeutic process they have to make the choice to attend an initial therapy session, and this act in itself is a behavior. Behaviorists believe that internal psychological and emotional changes will inevitably occur after a person changes their external behaviors (Wolpe 1990). Behavioral therapy is very conducive to the treatment of simple phobias and can also be quite effective when utilized with high functioning, neurotic patients. Patients who lack motivation, have little insight into their symptoms, or who are personality disordered usually do not respond to behavioral therapy as would a patient in the neurotic level of functioning who can easily follow direction from the clinician, complete behavioral assignments, and tolerate uncomfortable emotions. Behavioral therapy can involve anything from directly challenging the symptoms of a psychiatric disorder with exposure and response prevention methods, to making basic behavioral changes in one's life such as altering exercise and eating habits.

There are body dysmorphic disorder patients that can and do benefit from behavioral therapies, including exposure and response prevention therapy. I never begin the therapeutic process with behavioral exercises because many patients with body image disturbances will not be able to tolerate the emotions generated by behavioral changes and consequently may bolt from therapy. It may take many therapy sessions to determine if a patient has the capacity and impetus to participate in and benefit from being exposed to experiences that produce discomfort: Utilizing behavioral exercises prematurely may destabilize the early relational foundation between patient and therapist, especially with patients who have an inflexible personality structure.

Establishing a trusting relationship with the BDD patient should take priority in the initial stages of treatment rather than rushing to resolve overt symptoms with behavioral techniques. The therapist should not attempt to place each BDD patient into the same behavioral therapy template because one mold does not fit all. Instead, the clinician should adapt to the patient and emphasize the attachment with this individual; it is this connection with the patient that will make it easier to discern the optimal time to introduce behavioral therapy.

As explained earlier, exposure and response prevention therapy (ERP) involves the patient being exposed to situations that they previously would have avoided. The perpetual avoidance never allows the individual to habituate to the uncomfortable feelings associated with the situation. Avoidance also never allows the individual to gain evidence that perhaps the circumstance is not as dire as they had anticipated (Krypotos et al. 2015). The exposure component entails a gradual introduction to the avoided situations, and the response prevention necessitates sitting with and experiencing the emotional discomfort rather than doing a compulsion to reduce the negative feelings.

Exposure therapy exercises are intentionally designed to activate uncomfortable emotions. These are the antithesis of the avoidant behaviors that the patient has engaged in and that have subsequently reinforced the beliefs that the event or situation is unsafe. If the patient chooses to experience the feelings and not act on the urge to do a compulsion, they will eventually habituate as the unpleasant feelings gradually subside. If an exposure exercise is attempted but the individual does not follow through with response prevention, this will further reinforce the association between the stimulus and the negative emotions. Thus educating the patient about proper exposure and response prevention protocol is recommended prior to them actually beginning the exercises themselves.

I make a point of working with the body dysmorphic disorder patient to design exposure exercises that directly involve contact with other people. Exposure therapy with BDD patients is utilized for multiple reasons, the most obvious being to minimize the symptoms of the disorder. Exposure exercises can also assist an individual in learning how to self-soothe because they have to tolerate discomfort when experiencing negative emotions. This can also contribute to the building of self-efficacy because it is the patient, not the clinician, who is making the internal changes. Exposure exercises that involve social interactions can provide corrective experiences: Many BDD patients report that their symptoms exacerbate when in the presence of others because they erroneously believe that other people are taking special notice of their supposed defects, thus avoidance of many social interactions leaves the patient isolated.

Exposure exercises geared toward human interactions also sends the message to the patient that the body is not the epicenter of treatment and that interpersonal interactions take priority. The body area of concern is not completely ignored during exposure therapy since it is incorporated into the behavioral exercises that include people. Similar to exposure and response prevention therapy with obsessive-compulsive disorder, a hierarchy is created of situations that are ranked in order from the least to the most provoking of emotional discomfort.

The BDD Exposure and Response Prevention Hierarchy

Case Study: Angela

Angela, a 24-year-old single woman, presented with body dysmorphic disorder symptoms that involved a preoccupation with her facial skin, which she described as looking like "pale sandpaper." She stated that in high school she had a minor case of acne and that some of her peers had teased her about this. It was during this time that she began wearing make-up so that she could cover up her skin. Putting on make-up gave her a sense of relief and security that she would not be ridiculed about her appearance. Throughout the school year her morning make-up routine gradually increased in length; she started skipping breakfast so that she would have more time for her make-up ritual, and she was often late for school because she did not want to be seen by her peers unless her make-up was perfect. Angela admitted that she failed physical education her junior year of high school because she did not want to sweat during class and risk that her "real face" would be revealed to her peers. She also confessed that she was very ashamed to admit this out of concern that she would be judged as superficial.

Angela disclosed that her make-up routine became more and more intense once she went to college and it was during this time that the pre-occupation with her skin began to affect her functioning. She stated that if her make-up was not absolutely perfect, she would be too ashamed to be seen by anyone including her boyfriend. She would avoid any activity that might involve her make-up washing off even if this meant missing out on many activities with friends. On sunny days she would carry a fold-up umbrella to make sure that she would never be caught in the rain, and on rainy days she would often not leave home.

It was difficult for Angela to maintain friends because they would eventually become tired of her constant excuses of why she was not able to get together. When she did commit to meet a friend, she was often very late because she would become stuck in her bathroom mirror doing her make-up over and over in a desperate attempt to get it right. Eventually her college boyfriend also left her: Not knowing that Angela suffered from body dysmorphic disorder, he became weary of the hours she would spend alone in her bathroom and finally told her that he felt that her make-up took priority over him and that he could no longer tolerate it.

Angela was devastated by this rejection. She loved her boyfriend and truly hated her arduous make-up routine, but she was too ashamed to be seen without it because she felt she looked too horrendous when her skin was exposed. It was after her boyfriend left her that she also became preoccupied with the profile of her nose as well as her smile that she perceived as crooked. Although her boyfriend had stated he was break-ing up with her because of the preoccupation with her make-up, Angela believed that "she had been found out as a fraud" and that he had really left her because he must have known she was unsightly underneath the make-up mask.

Angela would do her best not to go outside during daylight hours because she felt that natural light would expose the bumpy texture of her skin. The avoidance of going out during the day was not conducive to attending her college classes. She would always skip large classes that were in lecture halls, and for the classes that she did attend, she would take a circuitous route around her college campus so that she would not run into many people. She would always sit at the very back of the class-room so that other students could not see her complexion.

Along with the preoccupation with her appearance Angela also experienced major depression. On the days that she felt her skin looked less disfigured, her mood would mildly improve because she would have a glimpse of hope that perhaps her skin would someday look normal. But the majority of the time she believed her skin looked disgusting, a belief that would activate an internal feeling of despair that would subsequently lead to a deep sense of sorrow. Between avoiding more than half of her classes and suffering from severe depression, she barely graduated from college.

Angela moved back in with her parents who soon realized that she was not doing well: She was sleeping a lot during the day and was usually in the bathroom for hours at a time at night. Angela eventually disclosed to them that she was extremely ashamed of her appearance and that she did not see the point of continuing to live if she had to look like this. Her parents had no idea that she thought she looked so ugly, in fact they were shocked because this was the last thing that they would have assumed was the problem. They told her that her skin looked just fine, but Angela could not believe this, stating, "they have to tell me this as my parents, and they really know that I'm unattractive, but just don't want to hurt my feelings by telling the truth." Realizing that their daughter needed outside assistance, Angela's parents reached out for help and catalyzed the process of Angela receiving treatment for what she now understands is body dysmorphic disorder.

The following is Angela's exposure and response prevention (ERP) hierarchy utilized after she had been in psychotherapy for several months. When she entered therapy she was very depressed and had limited insight into her symptoms. A rapid entry into behavioral therapy was not indicated because she would probably not have been able to tolerate the exposure exercises and likely would have discontinued treatment.

Note:

- The clinician and patient should work together to create the BDD ERP hierarchy.
- By no means does the hierarchy have to be precisely followed. Sometimes the patient is ready to work toward more difficult ERP exercises and this is acceptable as long as they are capable of following through with response prevention after the therapy session is over.
- The numbers used are referred to as standard units of distress (SUD) and simply indicate how uncomfortable the patient might feel when participating in a particular exposure exercise. Unlike with anxiety disorders where SUD usually refers to anxiety, with BDD exposure and response prevention the SUD should include the entire spectrum of emotions. The SUD number allows the clinician to gauge the patient's level of emotional distress.

Angela's BDD Exposure and Response Prevention Hierarchy

- 100++ Going out in public during *daylight hours without* wearing make-up and interacting with men that are her age.
- 100+ Going out in public during *daylight hours without* wearing make-up and interacting with people.
- 100 Going out in public during *daylight hours without* wearing make-up but not interacting with anyone.
- 100 Going out in public at *night without* wearing any make-up.
- 100 "Staring exposure" in the therapy session *without* wearing any make-up.
- 99 Driving her car during *daylight hours without* wearing any make-up.
- 98 Going out in public wearing make-up but *without* wearing foundation and interacting with people.
- 97 Going out in public wearing make-up but *without* wearing foundation and *not* interacting with people.
- 95 Attending therapy *without* wearing any make-up.
- 94 Attending therapy *without* wearing foundation but with the rest of her make-up intact.
- 90 Attending therapy *without* wearing eye-shadow or eyeliner.
- 87 Attending therapy *without* wearing lipstick, eye-shadow or eyeliner (but while still wearing foundation).
- 85 Walking in the hallway outside of the therapy office under the florescent ceiling lights (but wearing full make-up).
- 70 Attending therapy *without* wearing lipstick.
- 60 "Staring exposure" in the therapy session while wearing full make-up.
- 55 Writing and then reading a worst-case scenario flooding script.
- 40 Intentionally having the thought that her skin might "always be ugly" and sitting with the feelings of shame that arise.

Exposure and Response Prevention: Imaginary Flooding Scripts

A body dysmorphic disorder exposure therapy exercise that can easily be done in the office setting is a flooding script exposure. I find these to be a very appropriate exercise to transition into more difficult exposure and response prevention work because the patient can do it in the obscurity of the therapy office and they are also aware that it is based on imaginary information; this in itself automatically reduces the fear that their perceived defect will be unmasked. I often utilize these before all other exposures because the imaginary component serves to mollify excessive feelings of shame and anxiety while they can still learn how the process of exposure and response prevention is done correctly. I explain to the patient that the goal of the imaginary flooding script is to write a worst-case scenario fictional story about everything that *they would not want to happen* in regards to an aspect of their appearance that they dislike. This exercise is beneficial not only because it is an introduction to exposure and response prevention therapy, but it also allows the individual to begin experiencing the negative feelings associated with the body. This is the opposite of what the patient had previously been doing, performing compulsions in an attempt to manage body related thoughts and feelings.

Example: BDD Imaginary Flooding Script

The following is an example of an imaginary flooding script exposure exercise based upon Angela's body dysmorphic disorder symptoms. The objective of creating this fictional script is for the patient to intentionally produce disconcerting body related thoughts that in turn will activate very uncomfortable emotions. The script should usually include scenarios that otherwise cannot be replicated in person.

- It is not unusual that the patient will express concern that they will have to do exposure exercises that mimic the actual flooding script. It is acceptable to reassure them that the script is only meant to be an initial exposure exercise and is fictional. This reassurance should be given prior to the start of the exposure exercise and should only be stated one time.
- The worst-case scenario flooding script should be written in the first person and in present tense.
- The script should not include statements such as "this is a fictional story" or "I am writing this as an exercise for therapy." Statements such as these undermine the efficacy of the script, which is meant to specifically activate uncomfortable feelings.
- The purpose of creating the script is not to create the perfect, grammatically correct essay. Emphasis should be on the content of the script. This may be an exposure in itself for perfectionist patients who feel uncomfortable doing anything that is not flawless.
- After the exposure script has been written, the patient should be instructed to read it to the clinician over and over again until they begin to habituate to the exercise. If there is access to an audio recorder, the therapist can record the patient narrating the

(continued)

(continued)

imaginary script; the patient can then listen to it continuously until they experience habituation.

- The patient should be reminded that while they are reading the flooding script, the focus should be on experiencing the uncomfortable feelings while not participating in mental compulsions. An example of a common mental compulsion in this scenario would be if the patient were constantly having the thought "this is only a fictional story and that it isn't true." Like all compulsions, this mental compulsion will interfere with the patient naturally habituating to the negative emotions.

Angela's Worse-Case-Scenario Flooding Script

After leaving my therapy appointment, I start driving to school because I have to give a presentation in front of my entire class. As I drive I see the sky becoming grey and rain clouds beginning to drift overhead. It begins to drizzle, and soon the rain begins to pour down. I pull into the parking lot of my university and find that all the underground parking spaces have been taken and the only available spots left are at the far end of the parking lot. Already running late, I park my car and reach into the back seat to grab my umbrella. Nothing. I realize that I must have put the umbrella in the trunk, so I get out of the car and attempt to open the trunk as I begin to get soaking wet. I open the trunk of my car to find that the umbrella is not there either! I do not have a choice but to make a run for the nearest entrance—about 200 meters away.

I am drenched as I enter the lecture hall. I realize that the make-up that I meticulously put on earlier in the day had been smeared all over my face by the rain; I had intentionally made a point of doing my make-up perfectly because I knew I would be speaking in front of people and I did not want them to see my blotchy skin, pale complexion, acne scars, and huge pores. I sit down next to an acquaintance—a woman with a flawless complexion. We exchange pleasantries before the class begins, and I see her eyes examining my skin. She says to me, "I don't mean to be intrusive, but I know a really good dermatologist that could really help you. I used to have blotchy skin with big pores just like yours." As she said this, the professor called my name and requested that I come to the front of the lecture hall to present.

I walk up to the front of the lecture hall and as I turn around I see hundreds of pairs of eyes staring at me. There was not one empty seat, and even worse, the podium on which I am standing is directly under a bright florescent light exposing all of my skin defects. I begin to feel sweat dripping down from my forehead and onto my cheeks, only exaggerating the make-up mess that had begun when I stepped out of the car and into the pouring rain. As I begin to speak, I notice that the acquaintance who had made the comment about my skin was chatting with a woman sitting on the other side of her. I can hear them giggling as they keep looking at one another and then at me. The acquaintance then points to her cheek as if she is trying to make me aware of something; I proceed with my talk as I continue to sweat profusely. I then notice that another pair of women in the lecture hall are giggling, and then even another pair.

After I finish giving the talk, I walk back to my seat and sit down next to the acquaintance. She leans over to me and remarks, "the talk was really good, but have you looked in the mirror today?" I reach into my purse for my compact mirror, open it, and see the reflection of what can be best described as a cross between a clown and Marilyn Manson: Ultra pale skin exposed through streaky lines in my blush where the rain and sweat had dripped down my face. My acne scars and pores appear massive. I look horrendous! I begin to rush out of the lecture hall to the women's room to clean up the mess, but before I get to the double-door exit of the lecture hall, the professor asks, "Where are you going? I have some questions for you, so please come back to the podium!" I return to the podium and stand under the ultra-bright florescent light shining down from directly above. As I answer questions from the audience all I can think about is that everyone in the lecture hall is scrutinizing my pale skin, smeared make-up, and crater-sized pores.

After I answer the final question I make a B-line to the exit. As I open the door to leave the lecture hall I am horrified to see that the entire hallway is packed with students who are waiting for their next class. I turn around in order to go out the exit on the other end of the lecture hall, but by this time everyone is behind me on their way out. I am surrounded by my peers and there is nowhere to go but to slowly follow the crowd down the hallway. The hallway is lit with florescent lighting and my face is within inches of a cute guy to my left. With my periphery vision I see him staring at my skin: Being so close to me and standing under florescent lights he must notice my pale, sandpaper-like skin and my smeared make-up. I am so nervous that he is going to see how bad my skin looks that I begin to sweat. As the sweat dribbles down my face, the make-up continues to smear as my skin becomes even more exposed to the people all around me.

Exposure and Response Prevention: "Staring Exposures"

An exposure exercise that I often do with my patients in the therapy office is what I call a *staring exposure*. I prefer to begin exposure and response prevention (ERP) exercises in the office so that the patient can concentrate on learning how to do it correctly. Starting these exercises outside of the office is not necessarily bad, but I find that the familiarity of the office provides a safe place with fewer stimuli to distract the patient. I explain to the patient that during this exercise I will stare at the body part(s) that they believe are defective. I allow the patient to decide how far away I will sit from them; some patients are ready for me to sit at arms length while others may only feel comfortable if I am on the opposite side of the room.

Before the exercise begins I explain that even though staring at each other is socially uncomfortable, we do not want to talk during the exercise because talking will distract them from experiencing the uncomfortable feelings that are activated. They are instructed not to do mental compulsions during the exercise, such as attempting to figure out what I might be thinking about their appearance. They are to sit with the emotional discomfort as well as the body related thoughts that will be activated during the exercise. For example, if they are having the thought that I may be thinking that "their skin looks blotchy or their nose is too big," they are to go with this thought rather than challenge it. Cognitive restructuring is contraindicated during the exercise because to do so can distract from the patient experiencing emotional discomfort. Also, there is the possibility that cognitive restructuring may actually turn into a mental compulsion if done over and over again.

The patient needs to be reminded that if during the exercise they are scrutinizing body area(s) of the clinician, especially the body parts that they dislike about themselves, that this too is a compulsion and will undermine the ERP exercise. Although I do not expect the patient to stare into my eyes during the entire exercise, it is important that they do make some eye contact. Individuals with body dysmorphic disorder will often avoid eye contact with others because they feel as if seeing this person looking at them is equivalent to them viewing their own physical flaws. Thus not making any eye contact during a staring exposure is avoidance and may reduce the efficacy of the exercise.

I ask the patient to point out to me the area of the body—usually the face—that they dislike and to do so without touching it. I ask them to describe in their own words what they believe is wrong with that particular body part. When the exercise begins I repeat the exact phrases and descriptions used by the patient, for instance, if the patient states, "I feel my forehead looks too furrowed and crinkly," I will use this narrative verbatim when telling the patient what I am staring at. I always allow the patient to point out to me what areas of the body he feels are defective and I give him the opportunity to describe why he believes it looks flawed.

Body dysmorphic disorder patients are highly sensitive and are prone to misinterpreting even neutral comments, thus the clinician runs the risk of contributing to an increased or new bodily obsession if their description differs from that of the patient. So during the exposure exercise I might say to the patient, "I am staring at your forehead that *you* have described as too furrowed and crinkly" rather than saying something to the degree of, "I am staring at your wrinkled forehead that has a lot of furrows in it and makes you look old." By restating the patient's description you are sending the message that this is how *they* view this body part, not how you view it. This also provides for the patient a mirroring experience from another human being rather than from a reflective surface.

Once the patient has been given instructions regarding how the staring exposure exercise works, the exposure and response prevention protocol continues the same as if treating obsessive-compulsive disorder or phobias. As the clinician stares at the patient's perceived defect, he will remind the patient to breathe, not to talk, and to experience any uncomfortable thoughts and feelings. The clinician will occasionally check in with the patient to monitor his SUD, usually on a scale of 1 to 10. The goal is for the SUD level to decrease at least 50% before ending the exposure exercise. I usually continue the exercise even after a 50% decrease in order to make sure that the patient has completely habituated to the particular exercise. After the exposure has been completed, I check in with the patient to find out what feelings were activated and what it was like to experience these emotions.

It is important to remind the patient that the exposure is only half of the exercise and that doing the response prevention is imperative to get the most out of the therapy. I explain to the patient that if he goes and checks his appearance in a reflective surface immediately after the exposure exercise, he is doing so to make sure that everything looks acceptable. Because exposure exercises for BDD can activate deep feelings of shame, the patient may have the urge to check the supposed defect after the exercise because they want to make sure that other people did not see what they believe is so unattractive about their appearance. The response prevention is very important because the patient needs to experience the discomfort associated with the perceived defect in order that they can habituate to these feelings.

After the patient has habituated to the initial staring exposure, the therapist will then increase the difficulty of the exposure. This might include moving closer to the patient, having the patient's supposed defect front-lit during the exercise, verbalizing the patient's explanation of the flaw, or a combination of these. The patient will gradually work toward more difficult staring exposures, the top of the hierarchy consisting of the patient sitting within arms length of the therapist under a bright light. Once they have habituated to this scenario, they are usually ready to begin exposure exercises outside of the therapy office.

I previously recommended not making the body part the epicenter of the therapy regimen. I want to clarify that even though staring exposures involve the area of the body that causes the patient distress, the patient is not staring at their own body. They are observing the therapist view what they have a mental representation of as being defective, but they are not looking at their own reflection. The exercise allows the patient to habituate to the discomfort that they experience when in the presence of another person. So even though the patient may believe that the exercise is designed for them to become more comfortable with the supposed defect, it is actually about allowing them to begin socially interacting with people. If they can habituate to a person staring at them at close range, they will have less of an adverse reaction during normalized interactions with people outside of the therapy office.

If the patient is not ready to do a staring exposure, I explain to them that it is completely up to them when we begin, if at all. Not all exposure and response prevention exercises are compatible for every patient, so the clinician needs to adjust each ERP hierarchy to match the needs of the individual. For individuals who have experienced physical or sexual trauma in their past and are especially uncomfortable with another person staring at them, I would not recommend this exercise. Although many body dysmorphic disorder patients have concerns involving their face and head, features of the body below the neck can also be the source of distress. I never do staring exposures with areas of the body such as the groin, the buttocks, breasts, or any other area that may have sexual connotations. I feel that this is inappropriate for the realm of the therapy office and may be misconstrued by certain patients, especially those with a very fragile sense of self or those who have difficulty with socially appropriate boundaries. If the patient does not feel comfortable with you, it is best not to engage in staring exposures until they feel much more safe in your presence.

Exposure and Response Prevention: Interpersonal Exposures

The majority of behavioral therapy exercises for body dysmorphic disorder should involve people. After the patient has habituated to exposure exercises within the therapy office, I recommend incorporating exposure and response prevention exercises that involve people outside the office. As is the case with all exposure exercises that I recommend to my patients, I always do the exercise with them in session before I give them homework assignments to do on their own. An example might be to have the patient speak to a clerk in a store and ask a question that would be reasonable for that particular venue. The patient is to concentrate on making eye contact with the person who they are speaking with rather than scrutinizing the person's appearance.

Individuals with BDD are often so distracted by studying the body parts of another person—especially those that they do not like about themselves—that they miss basic facial expressions that are important social cues for nonverbal communication. The patient is to stand at approximately arms length from the person they are interacting with: They may have previously spoken to people at a further distance so that their supposed defects could not as easily be observed. Keeping regular eye contact and standing within arms length of the other person may seem obvious to us, but many individuals with BDD need to be reminded or even taught these basic skills.

As is the case with any other exposure exercise, the patient will begin with situations that are less shameful and anxiety producing; as they habituate to these they will gradually engage in more difficult exercises. Body dysmorphic disorder patients often report that they feel inferior to and uncomfortable in the presence of individuals who have physical features that they consider attractive. For instance, a patient who considers his teeth "too crooked, too yellow, and having too many gaps" might feel inadequate when interacting with a person who they perceive to have "shiny, straight, white teeth." So a beginning social interaction exposure exercise might involve practicing normalized interactions with a person who the patient considers not to have attractive teeth and working toward exposure scenarios with individuals who the patient considers to have beautiful teeth.

The patient participating in the social interaction exposure exercise should be reminded not to partake in compulsions while speaking to the person. This includes, but is not limited to, the avoidance of being front-lit by lights or the sun, changing posture to avoid showing their "bad side," camouflaging the supposed defect, or cutting the conversation short in order to remove themselves from the situation. As is the case with all BDD exposure exercises, the patient is to not utilize reflective surfaces after the social interaction. In fact, they may even be encouraged to accept the thought that the other person possibly observed the "defect" in their appearance.

As the patient habituates to the more uncomfortable social exposures, they may be amenable to exaggerating these exercises to elicit even further discomfort. I explain to them that I realize in their day-to-day interactions with people they will probably never do some of these exposure exercises; but, if they can habituate to more extreme versions of daily interpersonal interactions, then everyday contact with people will not generate the same discomfort that it did for them in the past.

An example of this is to embellish the body part that they already feel is defective; for instance, with an individual who believes his skin is defective, purposely creating "blemishes" with make-up or body paint and then having them interact with the public. Although the patient and the therapist are aware that the blemishes are fabricated, other people do not know this and will assume it is acne. If the BDD patient can habituate to this, then it is likely they will be less uncomfortable when interacting with others once the painted-on blemishes have been removed. As with the staring exposures previously described, the exercise does involve the body but it does not necessitate the patient monitoring his own appearance. Even though areas of the body may be utilized to provoke uncomfortable feelings, the emphasis of the exercise revolves around the patient experiencing and tolerating discomfort when in the presence of other people.

Interpersonal behavioral exposure exercises outside of the therapy office can be very valuable for several reasons. Beyond the immediate goal of unlearning body dysmorphic disorder compulsions and related maladaptive behaviors, is the process of learning how to appropriately give and receive mirroring to other people. One of the most common BDD compulsions is the observing and scrutinizing of other peoples' appearances, especially the specific body areas that they most dislike about themselves. The person whose appearance is being scrutinized becomes a human mirror for the individual with BDD: This is problematic because these people have unknowingly become the source of the BDD sufferer's sense of self, whereas under other conditions they would provide an opportunity for learning healthy attachments.

One of the main objectives of interpersonal behavioral exposures is to foster improved reciprocal interpersonal relationships with other human beings. I explain to the BDD patient that healthy relationships with other people involve reciprocity, and that avoidance of human contact or interpersonal interactions that are wrought with self-comparison compulsions will significantly interfere with a two-way discourse. Needless to say, a unilateral relationship cannot nourish a healthy relationship or secure attachment with another person.

Another purpose of interpersonal exposure exercises is for *the patient to become the human mirror* for other people rather than the other way around. It is normal that the individual with BDD will experience elevated intrusive thoughts and increased uncomfortable emotions when interacting with other people: This is because they erroneously believe that other people scrutinize appearances as much as they do. I explain to them that even though they are experiencing these very distressing feelings, they want to try their best to make the other person feel comfortable. I call this "flipping the script on BDD." Rather than using another person as a human mirror, the patient is to become the mirror for this person while focusing on making them feel safe, relaxed, and connected.

This is not easy for the BDD patient to do because it can be very difficult for them to override the intense, vivid emotions that remind them of how unattractive they physically feel. That being said, this process needs to begin somewhere and it will include initial emotional discomfort. Please note, however, that patients with very poor insight or delusional levels of body dysmorphic disorder symptoms, those with borderline personality disorder, as well as patients with a history of severe interpersonal trauma may not have the capacity to tolerate this particular exposure exercise.

Locations such as shopping malls or college campuses provide ample opportunities for the patient and therapist to practice these particular exposure exercises. Examples of this might include having the patient go into a retail store and asking the clerk appropriate questions that might be asked by any random customer. The goal of these questions are to give the patient the opportunity to experience a new paradigm of being the mirror for another person and practicing reciprocal interpersonal interactions. Although in general I do not encourage excessive talking between the therapist and patient during exposure exercises (because this can distract from the patient experiencing the uncomfortable feelings), I often check in with the patient to inquire about the emotions being generated.

The feedback that I usually receive from patients who are just beginning this exercise is that they find it difficult to not gauge the other person's facial expressions, which they often interpret as negative. I validate their experience while also giving them positive feedback for trying something that may be a completely new concept for them. We repeat the exercise multiple times, changing locations and interacting with different people, not only to provide fresh exposure scenarios but also to maintain the patient's confidentiality.

On our return to the therapy office, I usually spend some time with the patient reviewing their experience as well as identifying possible cognitive errors that they may have had during the interpersonal interactions. As previously stated, I feel it is contraindicated to overly discuss or process information with the patient while they are actively participating in the exposure exercise: To do so detracts from them experiencing uncomfortable emotions, something that has to occur so they learn that they have the capacity to tolerate these feelings. Common cognitive errors include mind reading and emotional reasoning: Mind reading that the other person must have been thinking how ugly they are, and, emotional reasoning because since they feel so "yucky" or disgusting, then the person they were interacting with must also have felt this way about them. I feel it is acceptable to do cognitive restructuring at the very end of the exposure therapy session so that the patient can get feedback from me regarding how I experienced their interactions with other people. Usually their interpersonal interactions appear quite normal from an objective vantage point, even though the patient will often report feeling the complete opposite of this.

I ask the patient to make a point of intentionally practicing interactions with people in this manner, focusing on how they can make the other person feel calm, heard, and relaxed. I explain that, along with not participating in the classic BDD compulsion of scrutinizing other people in order to calculate their appearance and self-value, they are creating a completely new paradigm of how they interact with the world. The short-term goal of interpersonal exposure exercises is to reduce overt body dysmorphic disorder symptoms. The long-term goal is to begin creating a new template for how the patient interacts with people while simultaneously catalyzing healthy human mirroring based upon mutual, reciprocal interactions. This inevitably can only lead to an increase in secure attachments with people while simultaneously challenging the BDD belief system that the body must look a certain way in order to connect with and be loved by others.

Reducing Camouflaging Behaviors versus Exposure Exercises

The majority of individuals with body dysmorphic disorder engage in behaviors to camouflage the area of their appearance that they consider to be flawed. As discussed in Chapter 5, there are a myriad of camouflaging rituals that are utilized to ward off feelings of shame and inadequacy. Because these are BDD compulsions, they eventually need to be reduced, as do all other compulsions that fuel the cycle of intrusive thoughts and negative emotions. This can become an area of confusion for the clinician who is first attempting to reduce the patient's BDD compulsions prior to commencing exposure and response prevention exercises. The confusion occurs because the reduction of the compulsive behaviors can also rapidly become an intense exposure exercise. Take the following example:

Adeline would constantly wear fake eyelashes and would never let anyone, including her family, see her without them. She stated that without these covering her natural eyelashes, "she looks disgusting, like a rat or a very unattractive boy." Adeline wears the imitation eyelashes in order to disguise what she perceives as disgusting, and this is a body dysmorphic disorder compulsion. To have her take off the fake eyelashes would not only be removing a BDD compulsion but would simultaneously be creating a significant exposure exercise. So from a behavioral therapy standpoint, is this a reduction of a compulsion, an exposure exercise, or a combination of both?

When a patient begins to refrain from BDD compulsions such as excessively checking reflective surfaces or constantly touching the body area deemed defective, uncomfortable feelings will be experienced because the compulsion is being removed. During exposure exercises the patient is intentionally engaging in a behavior that will elicit negative emotions opposed to eliminating a behavior that has served to reduce their discomfort. But, certain compulsions may provide so much cover for intense shame that to reduce these too early in treatment may produce an experience equivalent to the patient doing a very a difficult exposure exercise. If removing a particular body related compulsion will activate too much distress, it is best advised to postpone addressing these particular behaviors; at least until after the patient has successfully reduced the majority of other compulsions and has had some success engaging in less difficult exposure exercises.

Behavioral Exercises: Contraindicated for BDD

Something that I do not recommend as a behavioral exercise is to have the patient ask random people to "rate" their appearance, whether this is in person or by showing them pictures. I can speculate that clinicians do this to impress upon the patient that other people do not see them as unattractive as they see themselves, or to impress upon them that everyone has a different subjective viewpoint of attractiveness. The problems with doing this are multifold: Even though asking for an external viewpoint may temporarily serve as reassurance to the BDD patient that they are not as unattractive as they assumed, it is a version of reassurance seeking and this makes it a compulsion. Inevitably there will be someone who "rates" the patient's pictures less favorably than the patient would desire. The concern is that individuals with body dysmorphic disorder tend to hyper-focus on details while missing the bigger picture, and these details often tend to be the information that validates the narrative that they are unattractive. So even if multiple people may have responded positively to the patient's pictures, the patient may very well dismiss the vast majority of feedback and begin to obsess over the less positive responses.

I feel that this exercise is contraindicated even if all the feedback that the patient receives is positive. In fact, exclusively positive feedback may be more precarious than a less perfect scenario because of the value associated with attractiveness that is reinforced by numerous people. The patient may feel even more pressure to remain flawless to continue receiving positive reactions from others, fearing the one less stellar comment as evidence of their imperfection. Irrespective of whether people respond positively, neutrally, or negatively to the patient's pictures, the inflexible and all-or-nothing thinking of the body dysmorphic disorder patient can swiftly turn a well-intentioned therapeutic exercise into fodder for an exacerbation of BDD symptoms.

Another behavioral intervention that I do not recommend is the clinician examining the supposed body defect in order to see if it is actually defective. Having the perceived defect examined will make the patient feel very uncomfortable because of the fear that they will receive confirmation that it is flawed. We are already aware that the patient believes the body part is unattractive and inspecting it will only open Pandora's body dysmorphic box: This leads to the very ambiguous terrain of disputing what is or is not defective and what is considered normal. The BDD patient already has a fixed belief of what is aesthetically acceptable and any opinion that does not match their criteria will be misconstrued as further evidence of physical imperfection. Rather than getting stuck in the quagmire of disputing what defines physical attractiveness, it is best to sympathize with the individual and communicate to them that you believe they are having the tormenting thoughts and feelings that they have described.

Exposures With Mirrors: Contraindicated

I do believe that there is a time and a place in the therapeutic process in which cognitive-behavioral therapy, and more specifically exposure and response prevention, can and should be employed with the BDD patient. I also believe that a major error that psychotherapists make when doing behavioral therapy with BDD patients is that of using the mirror for exposure and response prevention. I can only assume that because BDD patients dislike their reflection, behavioral therapists must conclude that the mirror should be the epicenter of treatment. I am guessing that their reasoning is that if an individual is ashamed and anxious about a body part, then it makes sense to apply the same techniques that are successful for anxiety based and OCD related disorders. If one concludes that BDD is extremely similar to obsessive-compulsive disorder, then this thinking is logical. The problem is that body dysmorphic disorder is not OCD, and in my opinion it has more differences than similarities to obsessive-compulsive disorder. From many years of working with body dysmorphic disorder patients I have observed that using the mirror as an exposure and response prevention technique actually contributes to BDD symptoms rather than reducing them.

If the focal point of treatment revolves around the reflection of one's body, the psychotherapist is explicitly conveying to the patient that the body must be the problem, thus needs to be fixed. The patient entering treatment is already convinced that their body is defective and needs to be corrected in order for them to move forward in life. If the treating clinician even unintentionally communicates that the body is the problem, this reinforces the already rigidly held belief that they are physically unacceptable. Mirror centered exposure exercises not only send the wrong message to the patient but also can easily become a BDD compulsion.

To have a body dysmorphic disorder patient stare in the mirror at their perceived defect might seem indicated if using the logic behind exposure and response prevention for treating obsessive-compulsive disorder. But what might appear to be an exposure exercise to the treating clinician may quickly become a compulsion for the patient receiving BDD treatment: The clinician is assuming that if the patient stares at the despised bodily feature they will eventually habituate to the negative emotions associated with it. What actually occurs is that the clinician is participating in a body dysmorphic disorder compulsion while attempting to fix the patient. Many BDD patients already spend numerous hours a day gazing at their supposed defect, one of the more common BDD compulsions. For the clinician to instruct the patient to do the same is only perpetuating a behavior that has already contributed to the development of severe body image symptoms.

Individuals with body dysmorphic disorder do not solely utilize mirrors to determine how they appear. In fact, many BDD patients avoid mirrors altogether because they are so disturbed and tormented by their reflection that they perceive as so unattractive. Many BDD sufferers touch the body parts that they consider to be defective. Examples of this include rubbing their nose to feel if it is too large, too small, or too bumpy; feeling their hair to examine if it is too thin, too thick, or the "wrong" texture; or touching their jawline to make sure it is has sufficient definition. In fact, any body part can be the recipient of touching compulsions.

Another behavior that BDD patients engage in which is not related to gazing at their reflection is scrutinizing other peoples' body parts, especially the areas that they detest about themselves. Mirror checking is only one of a plethora of compulsive behaviors that BDD patients employ in an attempt to reduce duress, thus many other exposure exercises can be productively utilized during the course of treatment rather than just having the patient stare at his reflection in the mirror.

Mirror Hygiene

Mirrors and other reflective surfaces will always exist in our environment, thus it is important for the individual with body dysmorphic disorder to relearn how and when to use mirrors. I refer to using reflective surfaces in a healthy, normalized way as *mirror hygiene*. For individuals with BDD who are constantly checking their perceived defects in mirrors, psychosocial education needs to include explaining that this is a BDD compulsion that has to be significantly reduced. This bodes the question, when is it acceptable to use the mirror?

The 6 p.m. Rule

Although the majority of BDD patients dislike what they see in the mirror at any given time of the day, the morning and evening are especially difficult times. Having to get ready to leave home for school or work in the morning means having to utilize the mirror, and this can often become an exhausting, tormenting process for individuals suffering from body dysmorphic disorder. The thought of leaving home and having other people view their supposed flaw can elicit extreme feelings of shame and anxiety, thus it is not unusual that the morning grooming rituals can become very arduous and time consuming.

The evening is also a difficult time for those with body dysmorphic disorder. The average person would naturally feel tired at the end of a long day, and when we are fatigued we are much more susceptible to negative thoughts and emotions; those who have thoughts and feelings fueled by BDD are not an exception. Many patients have reported to me that their BDD symptoms tend to exacerbate when they are tired, especially in the evening. Being tired also decreases an individual's ability to identify the BDD symptoms and to resist from acting on body related compulsions. Thus it is not uncommon that those with BDD get stuck in the mirror or other reflective surfaces when they are tired late at night.

The 6 p.m. rule refers to evening mirror hygiene. If the individual with BDD is at home at the end of the day and does not plan to leave later in the evening for a social event, there is no reason to utilize reflective surfaces. Teeth can be brushed, showers can be taken, and the face can be washed without using the mirror. For those individuals who have untreated BDD or who are in the beginning of their recovery, they are much more likely to be lured into mirror related checking compulsions in the evening, so choosing not to use mirrors is the preferable option. Although this might appear as avoidance, I explain that this is about understanding one's BDD symptoms and being aware of when they are most vulnerable to engage in mirror checking compulsions. This does not mean avoiding the mirror altogether, rather it is about the BDD sufferer having insight into when they are least likely to partake in excessive body related mirror checking compulsions.

The Arm's Length Rule

Many individuals with body dysmorphic disorder get very close to the mirror when they are participating in grooming activities. Although this behavior can occur with any area of the body, patients who are preoccupied with their facial skin frequently report that this is how they use the mirror. They believe that it is necessary to be in extremely close proximity to the mirror so that they may observe their skin as other people view it. They are not taking into consideration that people without BDD are probably not even thinking about their skin and also do not stand centimeters away during interpersonal interactions.

In Western Society, arm's length is an acceptable distance from which to stand when speaking with another person. I recommend to my BDD patients that they stand no closer than an arm's length from the mirror when using it for normal grooming activities. This is mirror hygiene. The purpose of this is twofold: These individuals already tend to hyper-focus on appearance related details, thus getting even closer to the mirror only interferes with them seeing themselves as one entity rather than as multiple, separate defective bodily features. Using the arm as a measuring apparatus gives them an immediate tool that they can use to discern if they are getting too close to the mirror. The arm's length rule also allows the individual to practice standing within an arm's length while interacting with people: Many individuals with BDD intentionally put more distance between themselves and others so that the supposed aesthetic defects cannot be detected.

8   In My Own Words
Miquel's Story

I was born and raised in a small, rural town in Northern New Mexico. I come from a traditional Roman Catholic Hispanic family of five. My father was an educator, and before him, his father was also an educator. My mother was a homemaker. We were a very close knit family growing up; I never experienced any trauma and I never witnessed domestic violence or anything like that. I would say that I had a very good childhood. I remember that when I was around 8-years-old I used to have the habit of washing my hands repeatedly. I also remember that around the same time I often used to look in the mirror at my face. I would examine the symmetry of my face as well as my profile to see if it was pleasant or to see if there were things wrong with it. This was the first manifestation of body dysmorphic disorder that I remember.

From about eighth grade until my sophomore year in high school I was really affected by obsessive-compulsive disorder. I learned how to manage it very well, although sometimes it would get out of control and I would wash my hands too much or would focus on organizing things or being very clean. But for the most part I learned how to manage obsessive-compulsive disorder quite effectively. Body dysmorphic disorder really began to surface when I was 16-years-old and this is when I really began to focus on my face. It was also around this age that I went to see an optometrist where I was fitted with glasses and with contact lenses. It was amazing how bad my vision must have been because it was like a whole new world opened up and for the first time I could see things in detail. I think this must have exacerbated my focusing on details because when I was looking in the mirror with clearer vision I would see more subtle imperfections in my face.

I had very bad acne in high school. I remember going to a dermatologist who put me on medication for my acne, but she also mentioned that I had some acne scars and said that in the future I might want to consider receiving treatment for this. She also emphasized that I needed to take care of the acne now before the acne scars got out of control. Just this one comment triggered a whole new set of obsessions and compulsions: This was the point in time when I began always having to examine my skin in the mirror. This comment by the dermatologist, along with the fact that I was now wearing contact lenses, contributed to me spending a lot more time looking in the mirror. This started a snowball effect of me looking in the mirror and constantly analyzing myself.

It was also during this time that when I looked in the mirror I began to wonder if I had a big head and if my head was too big for my body. Even though my body dysmorphic disorder was still primarily focused on acne scars, I also began to believe that my nose was too big for my face, and this continued, jumping from one physical trait to the next. Now when I look at it, I have a more objective perspective: Like all people I have some minor imperfections in my skin, but back then when looking at it I felt there were deep pits and craters in my face. I would spend my time focusing on these pits in the mirror and they would only seem to get worse and worse. I was focusing so much on my face and I thought I was so ugly; I believed that my nose and head were too big and felt that my acne scars appeared really, really bad. This went on for about two years and became so severe that for several months during my senior year in high school I contemplated suicide. Looking back on it, I was in a lot of despair and I felt so ugly that I questioned the point of living; this is how far the BDD had taken me. In any reflective surface that I viewed myself I would see facial imperfections.

One day during my senior year of high school I broke down crying. My parents noticed and tried to figure out what was going on with me and they took me to a primary care physician. The doctor recommended a Selective Serotonin Reuptake Inhibitor (SSRI) anti-depressant medication and, combined with the support I was getting from my family, I was able to get control of things—for a while. I graduated from high school and had been accepted to the University of California, Los Angeles (UCLA) so was able to put a positive attitude together and this helped muffle a lot of my worries. I went to UCLA for undergrad and things were looking up: I had a positive attitude and I thought that I could deal with my symptoms. University life was very intense, and because there were so many things that I had to do for school I was temporarily able to remove myself from the constant focus on the BDD. The first two or three months at UCLA were a good experience for me because I was not thinking too much about my skin or the size of my head.

However, my body dysmorphic disorder symptoms began to resurface. When I would be in a lecture hall full of hundreds of other students, I started thinking about my appearance and the body dysmorphic disorder fears starting coming back. I again started to feel that I had really bad acne scars and so I began to wear hoods, hats, and sweatshirts. I distinctly remember that the happiest days for me would be on gloomy days when there were a lot of clouds and sunlight was not able to shine on my face. Because I was not in direct sunlight I felt that other students on campus would not notice that I had acne scars. Again, when I say acne scars, I felt that these were like huge dents in my face. I have always done well in school and have always liked school, and ironically the BDD helped me even more with my academics. I would focus more intensely on academics because I was only concerned about going to school, going to lectures, doing my reading, and getting back to my dormitory room and avoiding people because I felt that I was so ugly. My BDD had such an effect on me that it convinced me that I needed to stay away from people, especially during the daytime.

My body dysmorphic disorder had ways of being very intense at times, but then at other times it would decrease for a while. I would have moments where I would go out partying with friends and was able to socialize normally, but then there would be episodes of two or three months of intense BDD symptoms and I would have to isolate myself. I developed some very bad habits and remember developing a very intense, negative feeling about my face and about myself. I continued to wear hoodies and hats, I would avoid people, and I would sit at the back of lecture halls. It got really, really bad to the point that by the end of the year I began to consider suicide again. This continued into the beginning of my second year at UCLA. During this time I began to see a psychiatrist who identified that I had body dysmorphic disorder and that is when I began to learn more about BDD. The psychiatrist prescribed another SSRI for me; I am not sure if it was a placebo effect, but in my second year at UCLA my body dysmorphic disorder symptoms got a little bit better. I got a job at a local diner and I noticed that it was a little easier to deal with the day-to-day grind of campus life.

My third and fourth years at UCLA went okay, but it was just before I graduated that my BDD symptoms began to flare-up again. It was after I graduated from UCLA and took my first job as a teacher that things really got bad. Because of this I sought out individual therapy and also joined a body dysmorphic disorder support group. It was at the BDD group that for the first time I was able to see other people who had similar symptoms to what I had, and I was able to look at them and see how normal they appeared. They did not have any physical imperfections, but they imagined things on themselves that were worse than anyone could ever think of. This group started to change my mindset about body dysmorphic disorder.

It was also during this time that I started worrying about my voice; this shows how BDD can jump around. I started getting a feeling that my voice was weak. Someday I wanted to be a teacher and I worried that students might sense that I was nervous. I remember this time period as one that I learned many new tools of how to deal with body dysmorphic disorder, but I was not necessarily as invested in treatment as I should have been. I would practice the behavioral therapy, but I would not practice it on a daily basis and I thought that I could do this casually and still be alright. I did not take body dysmorphic disorder seriously: I knew that I had something like body dysmorphic disorder, but I did not realize what was to come.

I finally got a teaching job but it was also during this time that I stopped attending therapy, and this is when all hell broke lose. I grew a lot in my first year as a teacher: It was very helpful for me to be in front of students but I also remember that some of my old body dysmorphic disorder symptoms began to reappear. I began checking my face in the mirror during work hours. I remember for about a period of a month I would see hair in places that I thought I should not have hair, for instance, above my cheeks. Focusing so much on this only triggered me to think that it was worse than it was and I began to research hair removal treatments. I would go to the store and buy waxing kits and I would spend time in the mirror trying to get rid of the hair. My BDD symptoms continued to worsen.

The teaching was going okay and I did not have any major problems besides the body dysmorphic disorder. Since I was so busy as a teacher, I was not able to complete all the required classes necessary to continue teaching the following school year. I was not fired, but I could not be rehired until I had completed these classes in order to continue with my teacher certification. This is when everything began to spiral out of control because I was unemployed and I had all day to start thinking about things, and this is when the body dysmorphic disorder took control.

I would spend all day in my apartment doing the face and skin checking. I would also go to plastic surgeons to see if they could help me with what I thought was hair in the wrong places on my face. Other body dysmorphic disorder issues began to appear, such as wondering if I could do something about my nose. My BDD started to get worse, and worse, and worse and this went on for about a year where I was not doing anything but focusing on my appearance. I was not going to therapy and I was not doing anything to counter the body dysmorphic disorder. I began to contemplate suicide, and soon afterwards was when my first suicide attempt occured.

The body dysmorphic disorder filled me with such despair, and because it continued over and over for a period of months I got to the point where I could not take it any more. I remember that I went to the store and I bought four containers of extra strength sleeping pills. I went home and took them all: My breathing started to get very short, I was stumbling around my apartment, and I realized that this was not going to be a pleasant experience. I think it is important to talk about this because for those people who are out there who are thinking about suicide, it is not a pleasant experience. It is most definitely not. I remember thinking that this was not going to go well and I freaked out and, if I remember correctly, I called 911. The next thing I remember is waking up and there were police officers and paramedics in my apartment. They put me in an ambulance and brought me to the emergency room at a hospital in downtown Los Angeles.

I spent three days in the hospital's intensive care unit. It was a scary experience but it was sadly not enough to make me deal with the body dysmorphic disorder once and for all. When I was in the intensive care unit my parents came to visit me and they ended up staying with me for a while after that. Eventually they went back to New Mexico because they did not realize how serious my BDD was, and I did not even realize how serious it was either. I continued to try to get back into teaching, but it turned into another year of the same thing; being alone in my apartment focusing on the body dysmorphic disorder symptoms while experiencing extreme despair. My next suicide attempt was preceded by two or three months of the worst depression that I have ever experienced. This was a horrible depression that persisted all day, every day. I could not sleep at night and I was crying nonstop during waking hours.

I ended up living like a hermit. I would go out at night to get food because I did not want to be seen or to have people look at me. Then I would go back to my apartment, sleep all day, and then the next day was the same thing all over again. My depression got so bad that I was not thinking clearly at all; my thinking was off and I did not even realize I was in such a severe quagmire. This is another thing that I want people to understand about BDD, that it can lead to some terrible, severe depression that creates an environment where you cannot think clearly. I remember that I was so depressed that every day I was thinking about how I could kill myself. This is how bad my depression became.

I remember that it was the 4th of July, I was out of it and was not thinking clearly and this was obvious through my behavior: I got in my car and drove to a hardware store where I went inside looking for charcoal grills. Looking back, this is absurd to me because I do not know what I was thinking. I had a plan that I could use charcoal in my apartment to gas myself to death by carbon monoxide poisoning. I bought two mini-grills and to this day I still do not know why I purchased two. I then went to a grocery store and bought four or five bags of charcoal briquettes and went home. I want to emphasize that during this I was crying nonstop. I remember while driving to the hardware store there were people on the side of the road who were very excited about the 4th of July and who were on their way to celebrations. I could not look to my left or right because I did not want people to see that I was sobbing.

When I returned to my apartment I put the charcoal briquettes in the bathtub. I believed that if I put all the briquettes in the tub, lit it, and then sealed myself in the bathroom that I would be dead in five minutes. I was not thinking about possible danger to other people because I thought that the charcoal briquettes would be contained in the bathtub. I wrote notes to warn other people not to come into my apartment; again, I was not thinking clearly. The reason why I am telling the details of this is because I want people to know what body dysmorphic disorder does to you and your thinking if you do not deal with it. If it is allowed to fester and grow, this cycle will just continue. I went from a clear thinking individual who was able to make lesson plans for students, to an individual who, three years later, was thinking about throwing charcoal briquettes in a bathtub to gas himself.

My plan was to take several Xanax pills about 10 minutes before I attempted suicide so that I would relax and pass out. I sealed the door to my apartment and took the Xanax and within 10 minutes I started to get woozy. I went into the bathroom, threw a match on the charcoal briquettes, and immediately the flames rose to the roof. Maybe it was the primitive fight or flight response that is in me that signaled danger, but I quickly realized that this was going to be a catastrophe. I remember that one of the flames from the fire burned me on the neck, and to this day I have a scar from this. I closed the bathroom door and I ran to the telephone and dialed 911, and after that I vaguely remember being outside in front of my apartment in my underwear. I remember hearing the sirens and the horns of fire trucks: This has always been hard for me to deal with because I went from being an overachiever in life, straight As all through high school and a UCLA student, to this guy standing in front of other people on the lawn in my underwear. A failed suicide attempt. Who knows what I said; who knows who saw me. To this day it pisses me off that this is where body dysmorphic disorder took me.

The next thing that I remember is that I woke up in a hospital room and there was a nurse who was checking my pulse. Two Los Angeles Police Department detectives arrived and handcuffed me in my hospital gown. I was still drugged from taking the Xanax pills and I vaguely remember asking why I was being arrested. I recall saying something to the police officer about not trying to hurt anybody. He responded, and rightly so, "Yea, you're not trying to hurt anybody but you almost burned a building down." I remember the tone of his voice was just another shot to my self-esteem because here is a police officer who did not know anything about my life but was very angry at me. I understand because I know if I had been in the building, I would have been angry if a neighbor did something like this. The police detectives took me to Los Angeles County Jail where I was stripped down and given LA County Blues—a pair of pants and a shirt—and this was the beginning of a new life for me. As awful as it is to remember this, it is what saved my life because that was the beginning of an intense three months of a remaking of who I am as a person.

I was a humiliated, demoralized 24-year-old man. For the next eight or nine hours that I was in the Los Angeles County Jail I was handcuffed to a bench. The Xanax had begun to wear off and I soon became aware that I was being exposed to an entirely new world. I remember being shackled differently from everyone else; since I was a danger to myself they had me handcuffed with a chain around my hip so that I could not even move my hands. The deputies were not friendly at all. I had asked a deputy to loosen the handcuffs because I could not feel my hands, and I remember him saying, "If you make any sudden moves I'm going to put you face first on the ground and knock your teeth out."

I was eventually taken to a room in the psychiatric ward of the jail. After two or three days I was moved to another room with three other inmates, one who had really bad schizophrenia and would spend the whole day and night talking to himself and punching the walls. The other guy—I do not know what he had—spent the whole day and night just staring at me. This was my new world. I went from being in a UCLA lecture hall to sitting in a room with very mentally ill people. These were probably the worst days of my life: I would keep waking up throughout the night wondering if I had killed anyone, and if I did, it would mean my life was over. Fortunately, I received news that my parents were coming to see me, and one of the jail psychologists told me that no one had died in the apartment fire that I had been responsible for starting. I was also told that I was being charged with felony arson, and it was this information that made me feel that my life was over. I believed that I would never be a teacher again.

After about two weeks I was moved out of the psychiatric ward to the regular part of the jail. The first time they moved me I was really scared. Everybody in the first pod was really mentally ill and doing crazy things. Every five minutes someone would come up to me and threaten me, usually a mentally ill person who thought I was talking to them when I was not. I had to sleep on the floor because there were not enough beds for everyone. It was a very scary situation. I was eventually moved to another pod that had less mentally ill people, but the trade-off was that this pod had gang members and career criminals, people that were able to actually contemplate what they wanted to do to you. I was to spend the next three months in this pod.

The three months that I spent in F-pod was the greatest learning experience of my entire life. It was intense behavioral, exposure therapy for my body dysmorphic disorder. The truth is that I learned a lot from those inmates. There were people in F-pod that were going to be sentenced to life without parole, and rather than brooding over it they would spend their days on what they called "programs." They would do their exercises, then their reading, and structure their entire day. This was something positive that I learned, but I think the most important thing I learned pertaining to BDD was that I learned how to start dealing with my physical appearance. In jail you do not have a mirror; there are steel mirrors but these are imperfect and are often scratched-up by inmates so I was not able to see the details of my face. I could see the general image of my face, but was unable to look at specific things. I went from concentrating nonstop on my appearance to focusing on how to survive in jail.

In jail you do not have control over anything. Being in jail was behavioral therapy for me; rather than starting at the lowest exposure exercise and moving upward, I was forced to begin with the most intense exposures because I had no choice. There are inmates who are very blunt: They would come up to me, sit down next to me, and sometimes stare at me. I had the scar on my neck from when I was burned during my suicide attempt and inmates would frequently ask "what the hell happened to you?" The fire had also caused some minor burns on my face that had caused scabs and inmates would often stare at these as I passed them going in and out of my jail cell. The Los Angeles County Jail has bright florescent lights everywhere and my face was constantly exposed under these and there was nothing that I could do about it.

There were many times that I had to go to court. I would be marched into the courtroom in front of a whole bunch of people staring straight at me and who would see me in my shackles and uniform, and there was nowhere to hide. Because the jail cell mirrors were not effective, I could not check my skin, hair, or my face. I was in a situation where it was no longer about my physical appearance but it was about how I could survive and out-think inmates who were trying to take advantage of me. My whole primitive focus on surviving left no room for my body dysmorphic disorder concerns.

I remember that I felt very humiliated because this was not what my life was supposed to be. There were several female deputies that were very attractive and I remember feeling humiliated that I was in handcuffs, that I had some burns on my face, and that I was not able to shave or comb my hair. When these female deputies were handcuffing me, I was supposed to look at them directly in their face, and obviously I was in very close proximity to them. This started to break down my self-consciousness and humiliation to a point where they would see me so often that I did not care any more. This helped me when I got out of jail because now whenever someone looks me in the face I do not care because I have been in much worse situations. This humiliating experience was another challenge to my body dysmorphic disorder because this took me all the way to the bottom and I learned how to deal with situations like this. When I would have visitors come, I could not control how I was presented to them and I would be handcuffed and dirty. My time in jail was just one exposure exercise after another at a very intense level and there was absolutely no avoiding these situations.

The most frustrating thing about jail is that there is nothing worse than the feeling of being trapped in a cage. I was considered an inmate that the deputies could trust so at times I was allowed out of my jail cell to mop and do similar work. One day I was mopping the floor: I stopped and I began looking at the three tiers of jail cells with inmates inside of them. What was so revealing to me about this was that there were people in these cells like caged animals and I noticed that everybody was trying to occupy themselves doing something. By doing activities, they were trying to take their mind off the fact that they were in a cage. I saw people doing pushups, people doing situps, people writing, and people reading.

It was a way of taking their mind off whatever horrible predicament they were in and this made me realize that this is kind of like body dysmorphic disorder. There was not one person who was not trying to be productive in an attempt to bring meaning to their lives. I especially noticed this with inmates who were facing serious time and every day they would do their program. This definitely helped me to realize that on the outside, if I was going to deal with BDD, I would have to develop a program every day. This is something that I still do to this day because the more you allow body dysmorphic disorder to take over your idle time, the more it takes control of you.

My lawyer would occasionally visit me in jail, and as much as I wanted to get out I soon realized that the legal system moves very, very slowly. So I had to get used to my time in jail and had to see a lot of horrible things. I was lucky because I was not in what was known as the "Old Los Angeles County Jail" that held the hardcore gang members. My pod level had dangerous people and criminals but I was fortunate because I was always around deputies that could at least see what was going on. My father was able to find a program that he presented to my lawyer who in turn offered it to the district attorney. After some negotiating they came up with a sentence for me and it was presented to the judge. Everything went well and I was released from jail after being locked up for three months. It was strange because I remember when I was let out they gave me some other guy's clothes, a random pair of pants and a shirt, and it felt very symbolic: I went into prison as one person and I came out as somebody completely different wearing another man's clothes. It was very strange to finally be out on the street and to feel sunlight shining on me. Looking back it seems so surreal.

My sentence was eventually reduced from felony arson to what was called unlawful burning of a structure, but I was given five years of probation. Someday I would like to thank whoever the district attorney was because reducing my sentence down from being a felony gave me hope and a chance to rebuild my life. I was required to attend a mental health program where I had to check in once a week. I do think I had post-traumatic stress disorder: I look back at this time and I think I was in shock and it took me about a year to get over this. I had been given five years of probation, but with a criminal record it was difficult to get employment and I still wanted to go back to teaching. After a further four years I went to court and the judge stated that "you've done well and you don't need to be on probation anymore because you've done what you needed to do" and he released me and wished me luck.

I began to slowly rebuild my life which entailed going through all sorts of legal paperwork in order to get the felony expunged from my record and reduced to a misdemeanor. I also had to appeal to the California Board of Education to receive a certificate of clearance to allow me to teach again. After nine months I received clearance and this allowed me to get into a teaching program, to get my teaching credential, and I finally earned a teaching position. I also receive my master's degree and my life has never been better. The strange thing is that I rarely think about my experiences in jail, but I feel like a completely different person because of it. People look at me like I am crazy and do not believe me when I say this, but I think that if I had not gone through jail I would not be the person I am now. I also do not think I would be able to control my body dysmorphic disorder as much as I can today. Jail was the best experience that has ever happened to me because it completely changed my way of thinking, it made me a stronger person, and it made me grow up.

When I was in the throes of my body dysmorphic disorder I never thought that I would be able to get away from this illness. I never thought that I would get to a place where 95% of my life is normal and I can go through daily routines without worrying about my appearance or being self-conscious. I used to think that this would always be a part of me. I currently spend every day on a routine, try to make every day as productive as possible and I get out of my apartment every day. I do not avoid mirrors because to use them is a natural part of grooming oneself, but I no longer get stuck in them. As a teacher I am forced every single day to stand in front of a room of 30 or more kids who look at me and sometimes make comments about my appearance. I have had numerous students ask me about the burn scar on my face and I just tell them the truth, and every single day it is a body dysmorphic disorder exposure. In the past this would have affected me and I would have gone to the restroom to look at my face in the mirror, but I no longer have to do this.

When I take my break in between classes, I have to walk outside directly past all the 9th, 10th, 11th, and 12th year kids while the sun is shining on my face. In the past this would have been a nightmare for me, but now I do this and I do not even think about it anymore. I feel the sun on my face, and sometimes students will come up and talk to me in close proximity. In the past I would have maneuvered in such a way so that the sun would not have been directly on my face. But now I look directly at them and talk to them and I do not even think about my skin or how I look. Prior to my exposure experiences in jail I would not have been able to do this, but again, jail was one intense exposure exercise after another, every single day.

As an inmate, I was often transported from the Twin Towers Correctional Facility to the various different courthouses in Los Angeles County. I remember the last time I was in the dungeon-like cages beneath one of the many courthouses and the last time I spoke with my lawyer from behind jail bars: He came in a suit and tie and explained that the district attorney was offering a deal that would allow me to leave jail, avoid prison time, and possibly have the felony I was charged with eventually reduced to a misdemeanor and expunged from my record. My lawyer was not always the most empathetic man, and he often stated things in a matter-of-fact, black-and-white tone. After I accepted the deal, he said: "This deal will put you on probation for five years, but any violation will put you back in jail with the possibility of prison time. This is a good deal for you, but I want you to know that you will never teach again. No school will take a chance on you."

My lawyer is a good man and this was his way of trying to get me to understand the reality of my future. This was his way of preparing me in what he thought was the best way. After my release, I completed my requirements during my probation, worked diligently to rebuild my life, and petitioned countless agencies and individuals for a second chance. Ten years after my release from jail, I am proud that I have risen once again in the field of education. I am currently the assistant principal at a charter school in Los Angeles. I went from the dungeons of Los Angeles County Jail to an office. On a daily basis, I guide and assist students, teachers, and parents. Through continual practice and usage of behavioral therapy, the body dysmorphic disorder is no longer an intrusion in my life. At most, it exists only as fleeting and infrequent thoughts against the invigorating demands of my newly rebuilt life. I am alive and well.

9 The Cerebral Conundrum
Cognitive Therapy

Cognitive therapy for patients with body dysmorphic disorder can be very challenging for many of the same reasons that make behavioral therapy difficult with this patient population. Because many BDD patients entering treatment have such poor insight into their symptoms, just attempting cognitive techniques can be wearing for even the most skilled cognitive therapists. If a patient has overvalued ideation or delusional thinking regarding an area of their body that they believe is defective, there is very little chance that they have the capacity to engage in a conversation regarding erroneous cognitions about how they may look. Insight into symptoms can fluctuate with BDD patients, thus one day the individual might acknowledge they may have a psychiatric disorder but the next day they are convinced it is solely their appearance that is the problem.

From my experience, I have found that attempting cognitive therapy at the beginning of treatment with a body dysmorphic disorder patient can be interpreted as "another person trying to convince me that I look okay when I know I am ugly." These individuals have often had family members, friends, and doctors tell them they look fine, that it is all in their head, thus they may interpret cognitive restructuring as another attempt to convince them that they do not see themselves accurately. This does not bode well for cultivating rapport with the patient, as he will view you as just another person who really does not understand his experience. If this occurs, I would recommend delaying cognitive therapy until the patient demonstrates improved insight. Sometimes I may intentionally introduce cognitive therapeutic techniques early in treatment as a barometer to discern if the patient I am working with has any insight into their symptoms. If they have restricted insight, I will discontinue cognitive therapy techniques until later in treatment. Many BDD patients with limited insight will need medication management before they demonstrate more cognitive flexibility.

There are those patients who have less severe symptoms and simultaneously have some insight into the fact that perhaps some of their thoughts are erroneous and that psychiatric, psychological, and emotional issues may be at the root of their body image preoccupation. There are also the patients who enter therapy with poor insight, but are amenable to medication management recommendations and subsequently begin to have improved insight into their symptoms. This can be the opportune time to begin utilizing more cognitive therapy techniques as the patient may have less resistance toward examining other possibilities about why they are so preoccupied with their appearance. Cognitive errors that frequently occur with body dysmorphic disorder patients include perfectionism, all-or-nothing (black-and-white) thinking, mind reading and referential thinking, emotional reasoning, and selective bias. These very rigid patterns of thinking not only pertain to their appearance but often to how they interact with the world.

Perfectionism

The need to appear perfect, or at least making sure that a particular area of the body is perfect, is a pervasive theme in body dysmorphic disorder. This extreme prerequisite guarantees that the individual can never be satisfied with how they look, or that the outcome of a cosmetic procedure will never be good enough if they choose to take this drastic step. They usually have a fantasy of what the perfect body part will look like, the problem is that they do not take into account that this perfect image most likely cannot be created, especially if it is based on the physical features of another person. The bar is raised so high that it is impossible to achieve, and this keeps the BDD sufferer trapped in a perpetual quest for aesthetic perfectionism. They usually view the lack of perfectionism as evidence of being flawed, thus in order to defend against fundamental feelings of inferiority, they strive for the opposite extreme.

Perfectionism may temporarily ward off uncomfortable emotions and create a temporary sense of control, but it is never sustainable. If one is perfect, it means that they have no flaws. Flaws are highly subjective to interpretation, especially to the individual who desperately needs to be perfect because at their core they essentially feel so flawed. These same individuals can never be satisfied with themselves, thus even if they reach what they believe is close to perfection, the experience is ephemeral and only lasts until they detect the next imperfection. The majority of perfectionists never get close to reaching their lofty goals, including in the realm of cosmetic procedures. A self-fulfilling prophecy that I have witnessed too many times is the individual with BDD getting a cosmetic procedure, being disappointed with the outcome, and then returning for a second, third, fourth, or even fifth procedure on the exact same body part. Every new surgery is done in a desperate attempt to correct the perceived damage caused by the surgeon who did not perfectly alter the body area as requested by the patient. The BDD patient becomes more and more distraught as they see the body part becoming further removed from their fantasy of aesthetic perfection.

Another example of BDD perfectionism, and another instance of a self-fulfilling prophecy, is the individual who picks at their skin in an attempt to correct perceived flaws. The attempt to correct imperfect skin in order to relieve feelings of shame and disgust often leaves the individual feeling angry at themselves for destroying what they had hoped would someday be perfect. The cruel irony of the desperate need to be perfect is that it drives the individual to impulsively act upon behaviors that ultimately lead to imperfection. This is not only applicable to BDD patients in regards to the appearance of a specific body part, but also can transcend all other areas of their lives.

Throughout the years of working with body dysmorphic disorder, I have had many patients express "until I look a certain way I cannot be loveable and cannot be in a relationship." The perfectionism effectively maintains the status quo of keeping the individual from becoming romantically involved because, inevitably, perfectionism cannot be achieved. The lack of cultivating an intimate relationship serves to fuel the belief that imperfection (physically or otherwise) is the problem: The individual becomes more driven to be perfect and this only makes it more and more difficult to formulate an intimate connection.

I always tell my perfectionist body dysmorphic disorder patients that the only guarantee I will ever make is that perfectionism will ultimately fail: It may temporarily camouflage feelings of inadequacy, inferiority, or a desperate need to be genuinely loved, but it can never be maintained. I also explain to them that the need to be perfect also distracts them from having to feel both good and uncomfortable emotions. If we are constantly struggling to fix the next imperfection, we are not able to experience ourselves in the moment. It is important for the clinician to identify the perfectionism associated with the patient's BDD symptoms and bring this to their attention. For many of these individuals, this is how they have been thinking for years and they do not know any different, thus it is so important that this is explained to them.

Case Study: Jasper

Jasper, a young man from abroad who attended our body dysmorphic disorder intensive outpatient treatment program, arrived with incredibly rigid and perfectionistic thinking. Not only did he need his appearance to be perfect, he believed that if he was not the best at everything he participated in, then there was "no reason to even bother trying in the first place." Jasper would repeatedly attempt to squeeze external life events and situations into the confines of his very narrow and perfectionist paradigm, and inevitably he would always be left feeling hopeless and depressed. Our treatment team pointed out to him that "he was continuously trying to force a triangle shape into a circular pattern, and a circle shape into a square pattern" and even though he would not achieve his desired result, he would continue with the same rigid behaviors. We encouraged him to begin thinking about this differently: Rather than continuing to fit the world into his paradigm, we emphasized responding to life in a malleable manner. This would entail having to experience uncomfortable emotions, notably feelings of not being the best and not having things perfect.

All-or-Nothing Thinking (Black-and-White Thinking)

All-or-nothing thinking is another cognitive error very pervasive within the body dysmorphic disorder population. It is closely related to the erroneous thought pattern of perfectionism in that there are extremes and no middle ground—what I like to refer to as "the grey." Not all individuals who are perfectionists are necessarily all-or-nothing thinkers, but it is not uncommon that these coincide. Like the name implies, the individual who perceives themselves in the context of all-or-nothing can never be satisfied with their appearance because there is never a "good enough" or "okay is acceptable." Unlike the perfectionist who has to be on the precisely perfect end of the spectrum, many individuals with all-or-nothing thought patterns do not even try to be perfect. In fact, they may intentionally fail or put in minimal effort because they feel that reaching their aesthetic goals are so near impossible that by not trying they will avoid having failed.

An example of this in a BDD context is the individual who is preoccupied with their facial complexion and is highly ashamed of what they perceive to be skin imperfections and discoloration. Because they believe that the appearance of their skin is so flawed and that there is no hope of it being corrected, they never seek appropriate dermatological advice. This is the antithesis of the perfectionist who may continuously hound dermatologists in an attempt to correct any perceived flaw. Giving up before there is possible confirmation that nothing can be done about the supposed skin imperfection protects the individual from subsequent depression when they realize that their fantasy of the perfect skin cannot be achieved.

Another very common example of BDD all-or-nothing-thinking is the belief that because a particular body area is (perceived to be) unsightly, then this must be evidence that their entire appearance is unattractive. The rigidity of this thought places excessive pressure on the individual to correct the supposed defect. As the individual focuses further on the body part, thought patterns involving the value associated with the body become more inflexible and more polarized.

This all-or-nothing cognitive error theme frequently exists in many areas of BDD patients' lives, extending beyond aesthetic issues. This makes participating in life wearisome because there is no end to the search for perfection and this often results in the opposite extreme, that being avoidance. I tell my body dysmorphic disorder patients that I would much rather them try to do something fairly well then to attempt to do it perfectly or to avoid it altogether: Avoidance will eventually result in the experience of being stuck in life.

Being "stuck" leaves a person feeling extremely hopeless and can often be directly traced to all-or-nothing thought patterns. When an individual who is predisposed to body image disturbances becomes stuck, the default is usually to turn to their body as the justification for what is not working in their lives. It is the responsibility of the treating clinician to point out the all-or-nothing thought patterns and to explain how these ultimately interfere with quality of life. Although learning how to tolerate failure, rejection, and imperfection may initially feel disconcerting, it is much better than the alternative of feeling constantly stuck because of the fear of not being perfect.

Mind Reading and Referential Thinking

Making assumptions about what other people are thinking without concrete evidence that they are having these thoughts defines the cognitive error of mind reading. The majority of body dysmorphic disorder patients mind read, specifically in regards to how they believe people perceive an aesthetic aspect of their appearance. They incorrectly assume that everyone is as consumed with appearance as they are, thus they leap to the automatic conclusion that other people are scrutinizing their physical features. The conviction of this cognitive error will vary based on the level of insight of the individual; those with extremely poor insight and excessive overvalued ideation might be better defined as having delusional symptoms as opposed to merely cognitive errors. Regardless of the intensity of the belief, there may be some basis of truth to these assumptions. For example, if we walk into an elevator that is already occupied, the people in the elevator will see us entering. Unless one of the people in the elevator is blind, it is very unlikely that we will not be looked at as we enter. The BDD sufferer might misinterpret this situation as the people in the elevator are taking special notice of them and their "defect." This is called referential thinking.

A former patient of mine had been preoccupied with the size, shape, and profile of his nose. He was very ashamed about how his nose appeared and would describe it as "looking like a chicken beak." He had already undergone one rhinoplasty but had not been satisfied with the result. When he entered treatment he had already begun contemplating going under the knife for a second cosmetic procedure on his nose. When having conversations with people he would conclude that they could not look him in the eyes because his misshapen nose was too distracting. Whenever he heard someone use the word "knows" he would experience a wave of shame because he would instantaneously interpret it as someone was commenting on the nose on his face. This is an example of a mind reading cognitive error and referential thinking, respectively.

Individuals with body dysmorphic disorder assume that other people are noticing their aesthetic features because this is exactly the behavior that they regularly engage in. The majority of BDD sufferers are constantly comparing themselves and their supposed defects to that of other people, and they erroneously conclude that everyone else is doing the same. They are often very surprised when it is explained to them that the majority of people do not continuously ruminate about appearance and also do not constantly examine the physical features of others.

Sometimes they do not believe this because they are adamant that they saw another person looking at them. Along with studying other peoples' appearances, they are often looking at a person's eyes to see if this person is staring at the supposed defect. I explain that yes, this person is looking at you, and it is probably because they are wondering why you are scrutinizing them! I point out that we absolutely have no factual evidence that another person is examining their appearance; to conclude otherwise is solely based upon a mind reading cognitive error that has been heavily biased by the body dysmorphic disorder belief system.

Emotional Reasoning

Many patients with body dysmorphic disorder will state that they feel as if something is wrong with either a particular body area or that their face "just feels ugly or feels that something is wrong with it." This experience has been reported to me by hundreds of patients with BDD thus I have to believe that they are experiencing visceral and tormenting feelings within the body area of concern. Sometimes the individual can describe the feeling in detail, for example, "I feel that my eyebrows are too thick and heavy and it feels as if they are drooping" or "I feel there is too much air between my ears and head and it feels as if my ears stick out too far." They often experience an ambiguous sensation that something about the body part just does not feel "right." When patients tell me about these experiences, I always make sure to let them know that I believe them: Too many times they have been told that they are imagining it and that it cannot be true.

With a neurotic patient who does not have body dysmorphic disorder, the restructuring of emotional-reasoning cognitive errors may be straightforward. This is often not the case with body dysmorphic disorder patients who regularly report that "they feel the body part is defective" even if they have fairly good insight into their symptoms. It can be very difficult for someone to believe that a thought or feeling is erroneous if they are actively experiencing such a lucid feeling connected with their body. They might intellectually be able to understand that just because they feel a certain way does not mean that it is a fact, but this still does not lessen the somatic sensations.

The feelings attached to the area of body preoccupation can occur anywhere and at anytime, and definitely is not limited to when they see their reflection. It is not unusual that this experience exacerbates when they are in the presence of people or when they are forming closer interpersonal relationships. The result is a constant agonizing reminder that something must be so wrong with how they look.

It can definitely be pointed out and explained to the patient that the emotions they attribute to their body are not necessarily facts. But, it is important that the therapist remains mindful that what might appear as an obvious cognitive error to the outside observer is certainly not the case for the BDD patient: If the clinician focuses too much on this particular cognitive error, it may be inadvertently interpreted by the patient as invalidating their experience.

Confirmation Bias

Individuals with body dysmorphic disorder hyper-focus on the area of their body that they have deemed defective. This is similar to how they selectively attend to certain thoughts about their appearance while dismissing any evidence to the contrary. Information regarding their appearance that they have accumulated throughout their life becomes the platform from which the body dysmorphic disorder thrives. The firmly held beliefs that are synonymous with this condition evolve from the amalgamation of very biased, self-deprecating thoughts. In turn, these beliefs are strengthened, become more entrenched, and will inevitably influence future thinking with an even more unbalanced bias.

Body dysmorphic disorder patients often remember exact details about when they received negative feedback about their appearance. They frequently remember the exact location, year, and usually the name of the person who made the derogatory comment. Whether this external incident was an isolated example or a reoccurring event, it is rapidly metabolized into fodder for an already biased belief system. Even if the negative comments were received many years previously, they are fiercely retained as solid evidence that there must be something wrong with their appearance. These same individuals have difficulty absorbing any comments about appearance that are positive, rapidly dismissing them as impossible.

Case Study: Ashleigh

As an adult in her late twenties, Ashleigh would regularly receive compliments about her appearance. She would intellectually understand that she was receiving positive feedback about how she looked, but emotionally she would feel ashamed because this was so incongruent with how she felt about herself. It was difficult for her to comprehend the discrepancy between how other people could find her attractive and how this was not apparent to her. Ashleigh had not received any negative comments in recent memory, but this had not always been the case.

As a child she had been an avid gymnast. This is something that she enjoyed and excelled in and she eventually progressed to doing gymnastics with an advanced group of girls. As the new member of the team Ashleigh did her best to fit in, but she was not received kindly because her peers viewed her as competition. One of her teammates would frequently refer to her as "ugly Ashleigh" while her peers would often laugh when they heard this comment. Ashleigh internalized these mean statements as facts. All she wanted to do was fit in and be a part of the team, but she was not able to do so and she associated this with the belief that she was not being accepted because of how she looked. Prior to this experience Ashleigh had never been teased about her appearance.

Many years later, as an adult in treatment for body dysmorphic disorder, she would find it difficult to reconcile how she could be called ugly as a child and now be complimented for being an attractive woman. She understood that people grow up and change physically, but her confirmation bias was such that she would continue to refer to the teasing incidents as proof that something must be wrong with her appearance. Ashleigh would still refer to the nasty comments from years ago as facts, whereas current compliments did not readily fit into the negative narrative about her appearance.

Cognitive therapy focuses on erroneous thoughts and the restructuring of inaccurate thought patterns (Beck 1976). Individuals with body dysmorphic disorder most certainly have their share of inaccurate cognitions, but I do not recommend that cognitive therapy be implemented as the nucleus of the treatment process. It can definitely be used as one of multiple tools that a therapist utilizes when treating BDD, but to only employ cognitive therapy can be disadvantageous. BDD patients are usually very cerebral: They intellectualize, ruminate, analyze, and obsess. Many are also extremely disconnected from their emotions, something that often occurs with individuals who are excessively analytical.

Years of filtering emotions through a supposed body defect as well as attempting to analyze their way out of the torment only leaves them more emotionally disconnected. For an individual who is significantly disconnected from their feelings, learning how to experience feelings without having to quantify them is often a foreign concept. I explain to them that they are attempting to figure out something that should be experienced rather than solved. This is counter to the internal BDD process of needing to fix the body, the seemingly overt origin of the emotional pain.

Most body dysmorphic disorder patients partake in some form of mental compulsions revolving around thoughts about their appearance. These often entail figuring out what is wrong or what needs to be fixed aesthetically, and this endless stream of analysis leaves the individual more disconnected from their feelings. Utilizing cognitive restructuring techniques runs the risk of morphing into mental compulsions, thus a clinician with the best intentions might unknowingly be contributing to further mental compulsions. If cognitive therapy techniques are used, it is recommended that only one cognitive restructure be applied per thought or situation.

Case Study: Stacy

Stacy, a woman in her mid-thirties who recently had begun psychotherapy with me, would easily become stuck on a thought about the definition of body dysmorphic disorder. She would obsess over the wording of the academic description of BDD: "A perceived flaw might be nonexistent, but if the perceived flaw is actual, it is minor or the perception of its significance is severely exaggerated." Stacy was preoccupied by the belief that her eyes were not symmetrical, that her chin was "too pointy," and a general feeling that her face was unattractive. Like most BDD patients, Stacy experienced her perceived physical defect as an actual physical problem that needed to be corrected.

One of her primary compulsions was the mental compulsion of analyzing the academic definition of body dysmorphic disorder. She would ruminate over and over again whether she had a nonexistent perceived flaw or an actual perceived flaw. Stacy hoped that she actually had BDD with a nonexistent flaw because to her this meant that she really wasn't unattractive and that it "was just her brain wiring sending her faulty messages." But her experience of her reflection was that of someone who had uneven eyes and an elongated chin. Thus her mental compulsion involved dissecting the definition of BDD over and over in an attempt to convince herself that she did not look unsightly.

Stacy would also ask for reassurance about the definition of body dysmorphic disorder. She would ask me numerous times "whether or not a person could have BDD and not actually have anything wrong with their appearance." This question is frequently asked by BDD patients because they so badly want reassurance that they are not ugly, misshaped, or repulsive. I would explain to Stacy that for me to answer that question would be indirectly giving her reassurance and partaking in a BDD compulsion.

In the case of Stacy, utilizing cognitive therapy might look like the following:

- Asking the patient to identify the possible cognitive errors (assuming that this has already been previously discussed). For example, this might look like labeling the thought as a very absolute, all-or-nothing BDD thought that needs to be perfectly understood in order to ward off the uncomfortable beliefs and feelings that something might be wrong with how the patient looks.
- Allowing the patient to attempt a cognitive restructure of the cognitive error on their own, without assistance from the clinician.
- Assisting the patient with the cognitive restructure. With Stacy, examples of cognitive restructuring might sound something like, "I am attempting to perfectly figure out a definition of BDD and this can never happen because even if I get close to a perfect understanding of the wording, it will never be good enough." Or, "Might it be possible that the need to exactly understand this definition is actually a symptom of my BDD?" Or, "I am not really sure if there is something wrong with my appearance or not, but figuring out the precise definition of BDD will not alter my actual physical appearance for better or worse."
- Reminding the patient that the cognitive restructure should only be done once per situation. If the intrusive thought returns in the same scenario, the patient is to go directly into behavioral therapy (see Chapter 7).

The reason why I prefer not to over-utilize cognitive therapy with body dysmorphic disorder patients is because I feel it is important to get them out of a very analytical space and to move toward being more connected with their emotions. Most BDD sufferers have spent many lonely years mulling over tormenting thoughts and this does not contribute to improved interpersonal relationships or being in touch with feelings. There is definitely a time and a place where cognitive therapy is useful and should be applied, but over-emphasizing cognitive therapy techniques and correcting erroneous thoughts can easily push the patient back into an internalized and isolated mode. This is the antithesis of the larger picture of BDD recovery that emphasizes emotionally secure attachments with other people rather than relationships with body parts.

Cognitive therapy is also not compatible with working through the profound feelings of shame that so many body dysmorphic disorder patients experience. The "core beliefs" that are referred to in cognitive therapy may possibly be the source of the shame, but more often than not the core belief exists *because of the shame*. The process of working through shame in psychotherapy is not about fixing, changing, or restructuring the emotion. It actually entails the opposite of cognitive restructuring, to intentionally communicate very shameful feelings to the psychotherapist and to process them in the presence of another human being who can bare witness. Shame is usually the emotion that fuels body dysmorphic disorder: To overly emphasize the cognitive restructuring of the thoughts, many of which have evolved because of shameful experiences, misses the mark on truly attuning with these individuals.

For body dysmorphic disorder patients with overvalued ideation, cognitive therapy is hardly ever effective. The overvalued ideation belief system can be so absolute that even the most logical, quality cognitive restructuring will not make a dent in the patient's conviction about their supposed bodily defect. I compare overvalued ideation in BDD to that of ideological extremism: Attempting to convince a political or religious extremist that their beliefs and perspectives are incorrect is not going to happen. Attempting to convince a body dysmorphic disorder patient with overvalued ideation that there is nothing wrong with their appearance is not going to happen. Continued attempts at cognitively reframing the beliefs about the perceived aesthetic flaws will soon leave the patient and the clinician very frustrated.

There are mental health practitioners who utilize cognitive therapy as a primary modality when treating body dysmorphic disorder because it is evidenced based. Evidence based means that something can be measured, precisely defined, and that there is concrete data that the treatment method reduces symptoms. There is no dispute that cognitive therapy can assist in the reduction of overt BDD symptoms; evidence based means that there is proof of symptom reduction, but then what? How much are symptoms reduced? Does this symptom reduction include moderate, severe, and extreme cases of BDD, or is it only from clinical samples of individuals with mild body dysmorphic disorder? Are comorbid conditions reduced simultaneously? Does a reduction in symptoms mean that the patient will go into remission or does this mean that symptoms are only temporarily diminished? Is this evidence based treatment applicable to BDD patients with personality disorders? The reduction of blatant body image symptoms may or may not imply that the patient is well on their way to rehabilitation: Often, the reduction of the overt symptoms only mark the beginning of the recovery process.

I believe that an over-emphasis on measuring the reduction of BDD symptoms solely through concrete evidence based modalities misses the bigger picture of the BDD sufferer's experience. A reduction in body related symptoms can be measured, but what is very difficult to quantify is the emotional material that is always percolating below the surface. The dilemma with over-emphasizing symptom focused techniques such as cognitive therapy is that this can begin to actually mimic the essence of body dysmorphic disorder with the hyper-focus on concrete symptoms.

The symptoms obviously exist and of course cannot be ignored because every patient seeks treatment so that they do not have to suffer. But, if too much importance is placed on short-term symptom reduction then this might distract from the exploration of pertinent emotional themes that may have contributed to the development of the symptoms in the first place.

10 Medication Management

Many independent research studies have demonstrated that medication management can be very effective in the treatment of body dysmorphic disorder. SSRIs are often the first medications utilized when treating body dysmorphic disorder (Phillips and Hollander 2008) since they are efficacious in the reduction of body related negative intrusive thoughts. Examples of SSRIs include Lexapro (Escitalopram), Zoloft (Sertraline), Prozac (Fluoxetine), Celexa (Citalopram), Luvox (Fluvoxamine), and Paxil (Paroxetine). I have worked with many individuals with body dysmorphic disorder who have reported experiencing a reduction in BDD symptoms after following the proper medication protocol designed by their psychiatrist. Psychiatrists may sometimes need to augment a SSRI with other medications depending on the severity of a patient's symptoms as well as if there are comorbid diagnoses that need to be treated (Phillips and Hollander 2008).

SSRIs may take upward of 12 weeks to become fully efficacious (Veale and Neziroglu 2010). SSRIs do not provide instant relief from BDD symptoms, and it should be understood that utilizing an SSRI does not work like taking an aspirin or Xanax where relief is experienced shortly after consuming the medication. The utilization of an SSRI should be monitored specifically by a psychiatrist, not a general practitioner. I understand that sometimes individuals want to have their general medical practitioner prescribe their medications because their insurance network covers these doctor visits, but I do not recommend this: It is likely that the general practitioner has never worked with body dysmorphic disorder, and possibly has never even heard of BDD. Although they might be prescribing the same SSRI that a psychiatrist would prescribe, they probably do not understand that the proper psychiatric treatment for BDD is not the same as prescribing medication for other psychiatric conditions. They may also not be cognizant of the gravity of body dysmorphic disorder symptoms.

Medication management by itself is not sufficient in adequately treating body dysmorphic disorder. There is no doubt that proper medication usage can significantly contribute to the recovery process, but medication alone is usually inadequate to achieve the best long-term prognosis. There are times where patients only want to do medication management and are not willing to participate in therapy. Participating in psychotherapy is a commitment: It takes time and can be very emotionally painful for the patient who will need to address many archaic themes that have been ignored for years. Individuals who decide not to do therapy for their BDD symptoms and only follow through with medication management can experience some relief, but they are also leaving themselves very vulnerable to a major relapse in the future. The etiology behind body dysmorphic disorder derives from more than just brain chemistry, and a multitude of issues need to be processed and worked through to achieve the best prognosis.

There are instances when BDD patients do not want to be prescribed psychiatric medications and only want to partake in the therapy process. One of the main reasons for this is that they are very concerned that possible medication side effects will impact the body part they are preoccupied with. They may utilize Google to search for SSRI side effects, or go online into chat rooms seeking information that confirms their worries that the prescribed medication will damage the body area that they already believe is defective. If they search long and hard enough they will inevitably find something on the Internet that confirms their fears, even if the possibility of the medication side effect is incredibly rare. Because the individual is so hyper-preoccupied and experiences so much shame with their perceived defect, they will often refuse to take the prescribed medication. These individuals often have overvalued ideation surrounding their supposed flaw and have limited insight, thus are very susceptible to choosing the safety of their body part over taking a medication that might be very conducive to them not obsessing about the physical feature.

Sometimes individuals with BDD are hesitant about taking medications because they are concerned that they might stop worrying about the perceived defect. They agonize over the possibility that if they actually stop worrying about the supposed defect, other people will see how defective it looks and that they will be shamed while being oblivious to this shame. Their level of insight will determine the flexibility of their thinking: If they take the prescribed medication, not only will they experience far fewer obsessive thoughts about the supposed defect, but they also will not be thinking that other people are paying special attention to what they perceive is unattractive.

Case Study: Devon

Devon, a married man in his early thirties, was preoccupied with his facial skin and had been so ever since high school. He reported that when he was a teenager he never experienced having acne, in fact he always had clear skin and people would often make comments to him about how lucky he was that he did not have to experience teenage acne. One of his best friends in high school did have very severe acne and was often the butt of jokes because of his complexion. Devon remembers worrying that if he did get a pimple then his peers might start teasing him and treat him differently. It was in high school that he became hyper-focused on his skin, and it was also during this time that he began participating in elaborate compulsions in order to make sure that his skin remained free of blemishes.

As with almost all untreated body dysmorphic disorder cases, Devon's preoccupation with his skin gradually worsened over time. His body related compulsions became much more extensive and time consuming, and the obsessions about his skin became a constant, endless stream of intrusive negative thoughts. It was not until these symptoms began to affect his marriage that Devon agreed to seek outside help. His wife had suggested to him multiple times in the past that he might want to consider going to therapy for his concerns about his skin; for several years she had recognized that he was tormented by the preoccupation with his complexion. She had done some research and initially thought he had obsessive-compulsive disorder because he would wash his face over and over and carry out other skin related ritualistic behaviors, but her own psychotherapist mentioned that perhaps Devon had body dysmorphic disorder.

Devon had never been in any kind of therapy before. He was raised by a father who emphasized "pulling yourself up by your boot-straps" and "needing to look after yourself because no one else could be trusted." Devon believed that going to a psychologist or psychotherapist meant he was weak because he could not figure out his own problems. This changed when his wife explained to him that his symptoms were significantly affecting their relationship and marriage and that there were three entities in their relationship: Him, her, and his skin. Although Devon was initially stubborn about the idea of going to someone else to help him with his problems, he did acknowledge that his way had not been working for many years, so perhaps it was time to seek outside guidance.

Although Devon was initially resistant to his wife's suggestion of going to treatment, he entered therapy fairly receptive to the possibility that he had something called body dysmorphic disorder and that someone else could help him overcome the preoccupation with his skin. He presented with very typical body dysmorphic disorder symptoms, and also had overvalued ideation: He understood that it was likely that he had BDD, but was also unconvinced that his skin wasn't the main issue. He committed to the therapy process and attended sessions on a weekly basis. Although he was making progress, it soon became evident that his thought process was very rigid and absolute and that some of his convictions regarding his skin may have been bordering on a delusional level.

From the very beginning of therapy Devon made it clear that he did not want to take medications. He stated that he was willing to commit to the therapy process for as long as it would take, but that he did not believe in psychiatric medications. When it became evident that some of his thoughts about his skin were absolute and would probably not become more flexible with therapy alone, he was asked if he would consider having a medication consultation. It was explained to him that, although he was doing well in therapy, there are occasions where therapy itself cannot touch the neurobiological components of a disorder and that taking the correct medications might contribute to his recovery. This suggestion was met with extreme resistance: Devon explained that it was a massive step for him trusting another person with his deepest, most shameful thoughts and feelings and that he did not think that medications were necessary to make him better. He stated that, with the help of the therapist he could do this himself, even if not following through with the medication recommendations meant it was a lengthier process.

The resistance that Devon had to medications became part of the process work that commenced in his therapy. In his family of origin, Devon had received the message that counting on other people for assistance was a sign of weakness. He explained that if he took the medication recommendation, he would feel as if something must be inherently defective about his character if he needed to "put a pill in his body" to feel better. He also eventually admitted that he was extremely fearful that consuming a psychiatric medication would somehow affect his skin or even cause him to break-out. He had undertaken research on medications and had read on a random online message board that acne could be a possible side effect with certain medications.

The rigidity of Devon's thinking involving skin related themes also affected how he interpreted and searched for information: Although he had found some random information online stating that acne might be a side effect, he did not acknowledge all the cases and examples where complexion was never impacted. His absolute thinking, fear, and profound shame associated with his skin determined how he would search for facts that would support his BDD skin belief system. To not follow a medication recommendation might only perpetuate the extremely inflexible thoughts about his skin, as well as the thoughts about how medications might affect his skin. Thus a BDD paradox had evolved: Not taking medications meant that Devon might remain stuck with his strongly held convictions, while to follow a medication management recommendation might mean he would have to risk the miniscule possibility that somehow his facial skin would not remain perfect.

Although Devon was very skeptical and fearful about taking a medication prescribed for his condition, he did have very good rapport with his psychotherapist. In fact, he even trusted his therapist, which was something of a revelation to him because, growing up, he had always been taught that people outside of the family should not be trusted and that he needed to count on himself to solve problems. Devon disclosed to his therapist that his main concern was the "big unknown," which was if the psychiatric medication would affect his facial complexion. He eventually agreed to meet with a psychiatrist for a medication consultation, but stated that he was not committing to following through with taking prescribed psychiatric medications. He did not follow through with the psychiatrist's initial recommendations, but at his second appointment he decided to "accept the risk" of taking the medications.

What Devon had considered to be a massive risk turned out to significantly impact his treatment. The therapy component had been in place for a while, but the rigidity of his thinking had been preventing him from truly turning the corner in his recovery. Following through with the proper medication management blatantly made his thinking process much more flexible and this in turn significantly boosted his progress in therapy. Devon became much more capable of examining his body dysmorphic symptoms in an objective manner, and simultaneously he found it much easier to follow through with behavioral exercises that he had previously avoided.

I have observed over the years that the best prognosis for body dysmorphic disorder patients includes a combination of therapy and medication management. I have worked with individuals on the mild end of the BDD continuum who were able to make significant advances without taking medication, but these individuals are the exception rather than the norm. I have observed that most individuals with moderate to severe body dysmorphic disorder are usually limited in how far they can go in their recovery without the assistance of proper medication management. For individuals with delusional body dysmorphic disorder symptoms, the utilization of medication is imperative.

A psychotherapist and a psychiatrist working with a mutual body dysmorphic disorder client need to have open communication because of the multitude of issues that may arise. The psychotherapist needs the assistance of the psychiatrist in order to assist with rigidly held body related thoughts; the psychiatrist may need the psychotherapist to assist in processing with the patient why it is that they are so resistant to medication management. The symbiotic relationship between mental health practitioners is often essential, especially when working with very complex body dysmorphic disorder cases. Even if the patient is amenable to the idea of medication management, a communicative relationship between the psychotherapist and psychiatrist can only benefit and streamline the process of the BDD patient's recovery.

11 Intimacy and Interpersonal Relationships

Individuals who suffer from body dysmorphic disorder continuously seek feedback about their appearance from reflective surfaces and other external sources. What becomes lost in this cyclical pattern is genuine connectivity with other people. For many, giving up years of BDD behaviors and trusting the therapist with alternative strategies may or may not be a smooth process. Although some patients crave this connection with another human being, others are unknowingly very anxious and even fearful about having a true authentic connection with another person. The rational is often as follows: "If I only looked better and my bodily defect was fixed, then I would be loveable and could have quality relationships." Ironically what occurs is that the constant inward focus and the relationship with a body part prevents the individual from ever truly connecting with another person; they remain stuck in the cycle of holding their appearance as the answer to the quagmire of life. I always point out to my body dysmorphic disorder patients that there is no room for another human in a relationship when you are having an affair with a body part.

The intimate relationship that body dysmorphic disorder patients have with their appearance impairs their ability to cultivate sincere and trusting relationships with people. Here exists the origin of the BDD paradox: The belief that one cannot be truly loveable unless they look more attractive (or less unattractive), and that the only way to obtain love would necessitate correcting aesthetic defects. Desperate attempts to gain reassurance from the object of desire, the body part, will consistently leave the individual disappointed and ultimately angry at themselves. Somewhere during the person's development, basic human needs such as nurture, love, and attachment became associated with the body, a physical entity that is much more of a tangible object than the former. With some individuals, especially with those who have experienced childhood trauma surrounding a body part, the emotions connected to the body may be disgust, shame, and fear.

I conceptualize body dysmorphic disorder as a tangible concept that defines the ambivalence arising from the simultaneous experience of coveting intimacy while also fearing it. Human beings are hardwired to connect with others; if we have a deficit of interpersonal connections we often experience feelings of loneliness or sadness. The individual with BDD often interprets loneliness as a signal that there must be something wrong with their appearance. This keeps them focused on how they look because they believe improved relationships are correlated with improved appearance. They truly want to love and to be loved, but this is constantly stifled by their belief that this cannot happen unless the supposed defect is fixed.

Body dysmorphic disorder wedges itself between the sufferer's desperation to connect and the fear that they might be rejected while attempting to do so. This serves the purpose of preventing rejection; if one is constantly dismissing oneself it becomes much more difficult to be rejected by another human being. For many highly sensitive body dysmorphic disorder patients, rejection is experienced as the ultimate proof that something must be inherently defective about them. For this to be the case is often interpreted as absolute confirmation that they can never be loved. Taking the risk of possible rejection might mean experiencing these dire consequences, and to most, the benefits do not out-weigh the consequences. Thus body dysmorphic disorder exists in the space of relational ambivalence, completely changing the focus from fears of intimacy and fundamental feelings of inadequacy to excessive attention toward perceptible physical features.

Identifying this BDD paradox is necessary in order to begin the process of unraveling the connection between a body part and the genuine needs of the patient. I have observed that this process is often more streamlined with patients who covet intimacy but who have not been able to achieve it because of their body image symptoms. This is usually not the case with patients who have experienced shame or trauma associated with their bodies. This does not necessarily mean that they do not want to have intimate relationships, but that the process of emotionally connecting with others will be much more uncomfortable and possibly more chaotic than it is for individuals who have not had negative experiences associated with their appearance.

When a patient reaches the juncture in the therapeutic process where excessive focus on the body begins to wane, the opportunity arises for the clinician to explore all other material that has been concealed beneath the body image preoccupation. This can be the ideal time for the therapist to place himself in a position to become the transitional animate object in the patient's life. The intent is to gradually replace the inanimate features of the body with that of human connectivity. This may be the first time in years, if not ever, that the individual has experienced a genuine connection with another person. Without a body part serving as a barrier, there becomes the increased possibility that a living, breathing person—in this case the therapist—might begin to displace the relationship with an inanimate body object. Thus the therapist becomes the transitional object who provides everything that the patient was desperately attempting to obtain through their appearance: Nurture, warmth, mirroring, safety, consistency, unconditional positive regard, trust, and being heard and understood.

Something that I always tell my patients is that, "I completely believe you are having all of these thoughts and feelings about your body. In fact, I know you are having this experience." I say this for two reasons: First, I am fully aware that I am not going to convince them that they look fine, nor do I want to convince them. Second, I want them to feel heard and understood. They have had enough people tell them that there is nothing wrong with their appearance—a comment that highly frustrates them—and this only contributes to them feeling more isolated and misunderstood. The patient is experiencing the symptoms that they describe and challenging this is not conducive to the development of a secure attachment with the therapist. Individuals who have experienced childhood body related trauma may be much more guarded during this stage of treatment as well as less trusting of the clinician.

This process of attachment to the patient does not mean fixing the patient or the body image disorder. The individual has arrived in therapy because their attempts to fix the supposed problem, the body, has not only exacerbated the preoccupation but has ultimately interfered with them getting basic human needs met. Chances are that doing more fixing will only perpetuate a cycle of concentrating on concrete, external objects that will never fully furnish the absence of genuine human attachment.

Because individuals with body dysmorphic disorder are often avoidant of interpersonal relationships, they end up doing many things alone including attempting to solve their body image worries. The poor insight and significant shame associated with BDD symptoms only contributes to the avoidance of seeking help from a mental health practitioner. I always emphasize to my patients that it is impossible to recover from BDD alone; to do so would be accessing the same information that was behind the development of the body image disturbance in the first place. Many individuals with body dysmorphic disorder have felt emotionally alone for years, thus the therapeutic relationship between the clinician and patient provides a more objective template from which self-reflection can occur.

There are definitely aspects of treatment that the patient can practice alone, for instance exposure and response prevention homework assignments. Much of the therapeutic work (that which is not based around behavioral therapy techniques) exists in the office with the psychotherapist, another person that can mirror the feelings of the patient so that they no longer have to fight their internal battles alone. We do not know what we don't know, thus body dysmorphic disorder recovery cannot occur without the reflection of another human being.

The therapist should not be surprised if increased resistance occurs during the attachment stage of therapy. Resistance may manifest itself in a multitude of ways including absenteeism, help-reject behaviors, tardiness to sessions, or even a preoccupation with a new area of the body. As the professional in the room, the clinician needs to be mindful of their own countertransference so that an averse reaction to the resistance does not thrust the patient out of therapy and away from the process of attaching to the therapist. It is acceptable to discuss and process the resistance behaviors with the patient so that they may become mindful of how these actions contribute to keeping the therapist at a distance. I am never shy in expressing to my patients what my experience in the room with them is like: In fact, I think it is very important during the phase of interpersonal therapy that the patient receives feedback from the therapist about how their actions might affect another person.

Patients with body image disturbances are so internally focused that they often have a limited capacity to understand that other people have different experiences from their own. The therapist is in an opportune position to make the patient cognizant of such behaviors that may significantly impact interpersonal relationships. The patient is usually not aware that these behaviors keep others at a distance; rarely do they have insight into the possibility that these behaviors may have evolved to serve the purpose of warding of apprehensive feelings of intimate commitments. Although it is acceptable for the therapist to bring this to the patient's attention, I would not recommend spending excessive time on interpretation. More important is the emphasis on the interpersonal connectivity between the therapist and the patient. The content of the therapy session is not irrelevant, but should not become a distraction from the process of attachment.

For individuals who have dealt with body dysmorphic disorder symptoms for years, many basic social and interpersonal skills may never have developed. Patients who have symptoms on the less severe end of the BDD continuum may have much less to learn or relearn. The therapist also needs to be aware of the patient's experience and not assume that just because a particular social cue is obvious to them that it must also be for the patient. The implications of years of obsessing about and gazing at one's appearance can leave an individual extremely socially inept. The process of interpersonal therapy not only allows the patient to better understand another person's experiences and feelings, but allows the patient to observe what appropriate social and interpersonal interactions look like.

Case Study: Gavin

Gavin, a man in his late thirties, was brought to therapy by his mother. For 15 years he had been living at his mother's home. With the exception of several months when he was able to hold a job, he had been stuck in a routine of isolation and endless body dysmorphic disorder compulsions. Although initially timid in articulating his particular body related concerns, he eventually disclosed that he disliked almost every area of his body. He believed that his head was misshapen, that his widow's peak made his hairline look "weird," that his skin was blotchy, that there were dark circles under his eyes, that his hair was uneven, and that he was out of shape, along with many other concerns about his appearance. As is the case with so many of my BDD patients, none of these supposed defects appeared obvious to me.

I was very much aware that almost 15 years of isolation from the world meant that recovery would entail much more than the reduction of body image symptoms. These symptoms had obviously caused a lot of damage to Gavin's psychosocial development. I could not help but ask myself if perhaps the symptoms were in place to guard against something much less concrete and tangible than the external boundaries of the body. Like the majority of my body image patients, he entered treatment fixated on numerous body parts, which he experienced as "disgusting, ugly, and very different from that of anyone else."

Because Gavin had so few social interactions over the years, he never learned the basic interpersonal skills that are imperative for daily functioning. I soon realized that almost his entire existence revolved around the thoughts about how unattractive he perceived himself to be. Because of the intensity of his body dysmorphic disorder obsessions and the resulting isolation, he lacked very basic interpersonal awareness. I want to emphasize that just because an individual with a body image preoccupation is inwardly turned, this does not signify that they are narcissistic. With many body dysmorphic disorder sufferers, the antithesis of narcissism tends to prevail, as was the case with Gavin: He was very kind and caring about the few people in his world. He was also overly concerned about not offending others because he did not want them to feel as badly about themselves as he did himself.

The intensity and conviction of Gavin's belief about his "ugliness" was such that I quickly concluded that he needed expert medication management as an adjunct to psychotherapy. I referred him to my psychiatric colleague who prescribed a medication regimen that stabilized his mood and reduced the acuteness of the body dysmorphic disorder symptoms. This increased his capacity to focus on our conversations during therapy sessions as he was less distracted by the constant deluge of intrusive thoughts about his appearance.

I observed that Gavin interacted with me in a way that mimicked how he had experienced life over the past 15 years: Negatively scrutinizing himself and being self-deprecating. I kindly expressed to him that even though we were in the same room together, I felt as if I might as well have been elsewhere. I explained that I did not feel that he was trying to ignore me, but that there was absolutely no reciprocity in our interaction because he would speak tangentially until I interrupted him or until the therapy session ended. Although in different circumstances this one-directional conversation might point toward that of a self-aggrandizing narcissist, this again was not the case with Gavin. A decade and a half of self-imposed appearance related exile had left him socially desolate and truly unaware that conversations entailed a two-way interaction.

Although Gavin's case presents on the very severe end of the body dysmorphic disorder continuum, deficits in interpersonal functioning occur even with individuals with moderate symptoms. I have worked with individuals with BDD who have managed to function at a very high level despite their symptoms, but still have difficulties navigating certain areas of their lives. It is not unusual that these areas entail the intimate attachment to others. The themes of shame and secrecy that fester at the core of the body image disturbance are not compatible with healthy intimate relationships in which personal disclosure is paramount.

As demonstrated above with the case of Gavin, avoidance behaviors only perpetuate a cycle of increased body image preoccupation and the correlating dearth of social interactions. The individual turns inward, searching for the "defects" that initiated a perceived interpersonal rejection. The continuous internal dissatisfaction and self-deprecation inevitably inhibits any possibility of gaining evidence to the contrary that perhaps it was not appearance alone, if at all, that was the source of the rejection.

Time and time again my body dysmorphic disorder patients have confided to me that their symptoms blatantly increase when in the presence of someone they are physically attracted to. I do not consider it unusual that one becomes giddy or coy in the presence of someone that they have an affinity for; in the case of the person with a body image disturbance, a reaction by another person can be the defining factor influencing their interpretation that they must be unattractive. To be rejected by another human being, especially one they are attracted to, is often interpreted by the BDD patient as steadfast evidence that they must be ugly. Any consideration that there may be numerous other factors resulting in the rejection are often either overlooked or completely discounted. The inflexible interpretation of what is viewed as an interpersonal failure only fortifies the person's fundamental belief that they are physically inadequate. Because the rejection activates such dreadful and shaming feelings, the urge to avoid similar circumstances in the future is only reinforced.

A profound fear of rejection permeates the internal experience of those with body dysmorphic disorder. The terror associated with rejection is frequently experienced psychosomatically: Over the years I have had numerous BDD clients describe a wrenching feeling that occurs in their lower gut during and after a rejection or perceived rejection: They have explained this experience as if the pit of their stomach is "bottoming out" and then "drops into a deep depressive feeling." Many have described this awful feeling as if it is a warning signal that there is something inherently defective about them, and as a result they could never be loved. This gut-wrenching psychosomatic experience is often experienced after a rejection, thus it should come as no surprise that these individuals will do anything in order to avoid rejection.

Many of the body dysmorphic disorder patients that I have worked with have expressed experiencing psychosomatic symptoms at some point during the course of their body image disturbance. The psychosomatic experience usually exists with the body feature that they are preoccupied with. These palpable feelings have been described to me by a multitude of individuals, all of whom report having a physical feeling connected to the point of the body that they believe is defective. These physical manifestations of body dysmorphic disorder are a constant reminder that something must be wrong with the particular body part. These sensations can be experienced so vividly that many patients have difficulty discerning if these are symptoms of a psychiatric disorder or if these are actual physical feelings occurring within the perceived body imperfection.

Patients have described that the body part actually feels as if it is morphing or "shape-shifting." Others have expressed the feeling as if the body part is drooping, pulsating, prickly, or that "it just feels incomplete and wrong." Feelings of warm or cold sensations, pins and needles, burning sensations, and even "the body area molting" have been how many BDD sufferers have described these psychosomatic experiences. Some individuals have conveyed that these tactile symptoms only occur when their BDD is flaring up; sometimes it is situation specific such as during social scenarios where they believe that other people might notice their supposed aesthetic flaw. Other patients have reported that these physical sensations occur continuously and only subside when they are doing body related compulsions or when they are asleep.

Case Study: Regina

Regina, a soft-spoken woman in her early forties, was referred to me by a colleague at a local university. Like many individuals with body dysmorphic disorder, Regina was at first ashamed to disclose to me the area of her appearance that tormented her. I expressed to her that there was absolutely no rush to tell me, and whenever she was ready to elaborate on the details I would not judge her any differently. After several weeks into the therapy process, at the beginning of a session, she stated that she thought I needed to know what was bothering her.

She asked me if I could turn away before she told me about the body part that she believed looked so misshapen. She explained that although I had already seen it, she did not want me to scrutinize it after she told me what it was. I let her know that I wanted her to feel safe and if this entailed having me turn in the opposite direction, it was completely okay with me.

With my back facing her, Regina shared that she felt her face was way too long and because of this her facial features looked "stretched out." She elaborated that she felt as if her face looked like the painting "The Scream" by the expressionist artist Edvard Munch. She believed that the distance between her bottom lip and the bottom of her chin was extremely elongated. She felt as if her nose and forehead were also too long, and as result her face looked abnormally lengthy. To me, Regina's face appeared quite normal.

Regina was born and raised in the San Francisco bay area. Both of her parents were high achieving individuals who had been successful academically and financially and expected the same from both her and her younger brother. Her father worked extremely long hours as a vice-chairman at a Silicon Valley corporation. Her mother managed a flourishing real estate practice from home, so as a child Regina was mainly raised by her mother.

As an adult Regina realized that her mother really did care about her and wanted the best for her and her brother. This realization was not the case when she was a little girl. She recalls that her mother's mood was highly erratic and that at any given time it could fluctuate from being very sweet and nurturing to angry and very irritable. She could never be sure if her mother would give her a hug or give her the cold shoulder. Not only was this very confusing, but her mother's turbulent moods would terrify her.

Regina recollects so badly hoping that her mother would be in a good mood and would approve of her. She explained that she would experience a profound "sinking-rejection feeling" when her mother was angry. Already being a sensitive child, Regina internalized her mother's irritability as meaning she had done something wrong. She attempted to do everything perfectly: She received very good grades in school, completed all of her chores, and was always on time for everything. But despite these external successes, Regina felt her achievements were never good enough for her mother.

Never knowing exactly what mood her mother would be in at any given time, Regina began to focus on her mother's facial expressions in an attempt to predict how she was going to act. She also began to scrutinize the facial expressions of people that her mother would interact with as a barometer to gauge her mother's emotional state. It was during this time that she also began to analyze her own facial features.

Regina vividly remembers the sadness and loneliness she would experience when her mother appeared agitated with her. She recalls withdrawing to her bedroom and hiding underneath her bed covers while feeling the contours and features of her face with her fingers. Sometimes she would get up out of bed and go to the bathroom mirror where she would study her face from different angles. These behaviors began as a child and continued for several decades until she began receiving psychotherapy for severe depression in her late thirties.

Like many body dysmorphic disorder sufferers, Regina never mentioned the negative preoccupation with her face to previous clinicians. She reported that she received quality psychotherapy in the past but was always too ashamed to mention that she felt her face was too oblong shaped. In fact, she was not even aware that there was a diagnosis called

BDD until she came across an advertisement for a research study that was recruiting individuals who were unable to stop obsessing about an aspect of their appearance. Realizing that she was not alone, that other people might also agonize over their appearance, led her to seek out proper care and to open up about what was really tormenting her.

As Regina became more comfortable with me and the process of psychotherapy, she continued to disclose more and more about her body image experiences. I knew when she was about to share very shameful material because she would always commence with "you're going to think I'm completely crazy." Regina was definitely not crazy, but she was extremely tormented by the thoughts, emotions, and psychosomatic reactions that were associated with her face.

During one therapy session she hesitantly divulged that at times she really felt as if her face was becoming longer. She made the analogy that it was as if her face was made of melting clay that would slowly droop downward and pull her facial features with it. She was quick to clarify that she did not really believe this could be happening, but that this is how it truly felt to her. She again stated, "I know you think I must be totally crazy but I'm just being honest with you regarding how it feels." I thanked Regina for her honesty and told her that these sounded like classic body dysmorphic disorder symptoms. Although this was hard for her to believe, she also found my response to be relieving because finally she did not feel so alone.

Throughout the course of psychotherapy, Regina began to notice a pattern of when she would experience the psychosomatic feeling of her face sinking. This very disconcerting facial feeling would most frequently occur whenever she had an interpersonal interaction with someone that did not "feel positive" or when she perceived someone was disapproving of or rejecting her. She would automatically conclude that the other person must not have liked her because of the shape of her face. She would respond to these feelings and thoughts by using a reflective surface to study her face; if a reflective surface was not available she would examine the contours of her face with her fingers.

An actual or perceived rejection was the primary trigger that would activate the very visceral feelings in Regina's face. She had the insight to acknowledge that her actual face could not be suddenly morphing, but this in itself did not prevent the conditioned response between interpersonal rejection and psychosomatic symptoms. The physical facial feelings seemed so real that it would distract her from addressing anything else besides the immediate bodily symptoms.

Regina was an active participant in psychotherapy. She significantly reduced the majority of her BDD compulsions and was soon able to begin exposure and response prevention therapy. It was during the behavioral therapy component of her treatment that she began to make the connection that these feelings were not actually about her face but perhaps might be about something much, much deeper. It was during the course of exposure and response prevention therapy that the association between her facial psychosomatic symptoms and feelings of rejection began to dissipate.

It was also during this period of her recovery that Regina arrived at a significant conclusion: The physical feelings that she experienced in her face were not unique. In fact, it was exactly the same sinking feeling that she would experience as a child every time her mother would reject her. What now seemed like a very obvious explanation of her symptoms had been anything but obvious for many years: The hyper-focus on her face shape and facial features were decisively shrouding archaic emotional wounds. Although this revelation by itself was not the panacea for reducing the psychosomatic BDD symptoms, Regina began to understand that she was not to blame for her inherent feelings of defectiveness.

Regina became increasingly aware of how acting on body dysmorphic disorder compulsions would reinforce the connection between the features of her face and the childhood emotions that had never been processed or even addressed. Not only did the reduction in ritualistic behaviors assist in disconnecting the association between these, it also contributed to her becoming much more insightful, self-reflective, and emotionally attuned. This allowed her to begin directly addressing the fundamental feelings of defectiveness that derived from the childhood experience of having erratic and inconsistent interactions with her primary caregiver.

* * *

It is not uncommon that individuals with body dysmorphic disorder misinterpret social cues and facial expressions. Facial expressions that are interpreted as neutral to most of us may be interpreted as negative or even threatening by those with BDD (Buhlmann, Etcoff, and Wilhelm 2006). Many of these individuals completely avoid social interactions, but for those who do not, there is the likelihood that they may misread the expressions of the people that they are interacting with. It is difficult to imagine sustaining or even initiating a relationship if everyday neutral facial cues are depicted as pejorative. This is the experience of many individuals with BDD who so badly desire an intimate attachment but concurrently find it so difficult to achieve.

I explain to my body dysmorphic disorder patients that, not only is it necessary to reduce body image compulsive behaviors that involve comparisons to other people, formulating a healthy, intimate relationship cannot be about using another person as a mirror to validate self-worth. I point out that this is the antithesis of the foundation of a genuine connection: Attaching to another person should not primarily be about them making us feel adequate, rather, we have to already feel sufficient and want to connect with another individual because we care about and respect them. Although many individuals with BDD desperately utilize other people as a means to monitor their own intrinsic value, this does not come from a place of manipulation but rather from the desperate need to not feel fundamentally defective. The vast majority of these individuals are empathic, kind, and caring people who turn to others to seek some semblance of self-worth to compensate for their deficits in their sense of self.

Friends, family members, or significant others can easily become a sounding board for an individual with BDD who is desperately looking for reassurance. This instant source of feedback can quickly become the ethos of the relationship and this may evolve into dependency upon the other person. The relationship is not reciprocal and the other person becomes just another external object by which the body dysmorphic disorder patient attempts to self-soothe. This may be the only type of connection that they are familiar with; after all, their on-going relationship with their reflection has been a very one-sided affair.

Time and time again I hear body dysmorphic disorder patients stating something to the effect of, "My parents tell me that I am attractive, but the only reason they tell me this is because they are my parents." Or, "They told me I look good, but they are only telling me this because they feel sorry for me that I am so ugly." Even when the feedback is positive, it is either not believed or is misinterpreted. Not only is the patient participating in a BDD reassurance seeking compulsion, they are also setting up a scenario in which they ask for help and then reject the feedback. I explain to them that this dynamic can only negatively affect the relationship: They go to another person for feedback, next they reject the feedback, and this will inevitably make the other person feel discounted. Not only do they not feel reassured, but they leave the other person feeling frustrated and this in turn interferes with the relationship.

The majority of the negative and unfulfilling interpersonal interactions that the BDD patient experiences outside of the therapy office will most likely be re-enacted during the context of therapy itself. This gives the clinician the opportunity to feel what other people might experience when interacting with the patient. I frequently make a point of expressing to the patient how I am feeling during certain interactions with them, and I do so for several reasons. I want to demonstrate that it is acceptable to communicate and express feelings and that it is safe to do so. This allows them to understand that I may be having an experience very different from their own and that the only way to know this is by direct communication. Also, the appropriate emotional self-disclosure by the therapist will inevitably change the focus of therapy from externalized body related issues onto the process of two people connecting. Emotional self-disclosure by the therapist does not entail anything outside of appropriate professional boundaries as the emphasis is on the therapeutic relationship.

Generally, mental health practitioners do not want to be the focus of attention within the therapeutic setting because this may divert the patient from concentrating on their own issues. I do make an exception to this when undertaking interpersonal therapy with my body image patients:

As the therapist I become the animate object attempting to replace the inanimate object, in other words, the perceived physical defect. As the animate object, I model reciprocity, consistency, mirroring, and compassion and serve as a liaison between the patient and their interpersonal relations outside of the therapy office. The therapy does not become about the therapist, rather it takes the emphasis off fixing the disorder and related distractions and permits the patient to exist in a safe and consistent space with another person. In my experience, providing a therapeutic environment that allows the body image patient to attach is more important than the modality in which the clinician chooses to work.

Body dysmorphic disorder symptoms can significantly interfere with the development of intimate relationships. For those with untreated symptoms who are in an intimate relationship, it is likely that these symptoms will eventually create dissention between the couple. The most common theme is that the partner without the BDD symptoms becomes frustrated that many couple oriented interpersonal activities are curtailed because of body related compulsions. Continuous reassurance seeking, constantly being late for events, or missing events altogether because the partner with BDD is doing compulsions, eventually takes its toll on the relationship. As compassionate and empathic as the significant other may be, BDD compulsions will eventually wear down the patience of even the most devout partner.

Individuals with body dysmorphic disorder may also project their symptoms onto a significant other or a loved one, becoming preoccupied with an aspect of the other person's appearance. This displacement of symptoms does not diminish the BDD sufferer's own anguish, but it does begin to significantly interfere with the relationship. The hyper-focus on a significant other's body may involve the same physical feature that the partner with BDD dislikes on their own body; sometimes it may be a completely different physical feature, while other times multiple bodily characteristics may become the focus. The emotions experienced regarding their partner's physical features usually mimic the shame, disgust, anger, frustration, and anxiety that they feel about themselves and their appearance. The preoccupation with a partner's appearance can quickly drive a wedge between a couple.

Individuals with body dysmorphic disorder who project their symptoms onto their partners are often ashamed that they are doing so. The majority of these individuals really do love and care about their loved ones but just cannot stop obsessing about what they perceive as their partner's aesthetic defects. The partner who is on the receiving end of the projected material usually feels objectified and hurt that they cannot be loved unconditionally. As the focus in the relationship shifts toward the partner's supposed defects, intimacy between the couple quickly diminishes. Resentment inevitably begins to build with the non-symptomatic partner who becomes a repository for unresolved body dysmorphic disorder symptoms.

Case Study: Joshua

Joshua entered treatment with moderate symptoms of body dysmorphic disorder. His symptoms involved a primary preoccupation with his facial complexion and a secondary concern that his forehead was too narrow. He admitted that he had decided to get help for his BDD symptoms not only because they were beginning to affect his work, but because his girlfriend had been urging him to go to therapy for a long time. He had met his girlfriend in college during a period when his body image symptoms were bad but still manageable. In the past three years since graduating from university, Joshua had become more preoccupied with both his own appearance as well as that of his girlfriend. He shared that even though he was physically attracted to her, he could not get the thought out of his mind that her ears did not appear to be symmetrical.

Joshua reported that his preoccupation with appearance would alternate back and forth between his own appearance and hers: He would either be focusing on his girlfriend's ears or obsessing about his own complexion. If he was less preoccupied by his skin and forehead, he would find himself hyper-focusing on her appearance. Joshua was very hesitant about disclosing how obsessed he was with his girlfriend's ears out of concern that he would be judged as superficial. Like many individuals with body dysmorphic disorder, he was anything but superficial and was actually a very empathic, caring, and self-reflecting individual. But these qualities still could not quench the negative intrusive thoughts about his own appearance or that of his girlfriend.

Joshua had avoided speaking to her about his obsession with her ears out of concern that she would take this very personally. It was his girlfriend who initially breached the topic: She noticed that he would often seem distracted when they were speaking face to face and that he would glance from her left ear to her right ear, and repeat. The first time she brought this to his attention Joshua experienced a wave of shame and abruptly changed the topic of conversation because he felt as if his secret had been exposed. He had not realized that his scanning of her ears had been so obvious to her. It was only a matter of time until she again observed him scanning her ears, and this time she would not allow him to avoid the conversation.

Joshua's girlfriend was already aware of the preoccupation that he had with his skin because he would often ask for reassurance about it. She was completely unaware that he was equally as preoccupied with her appearance, and learning about this after being in a relationship with him for five years came as a total shock to her. She was angry and confused, but Joshua emphasized that he loved her and that he would do his best to stop prioritizing her ears. This was easier said than done: Although Joshua was able to reduce the compulsion of scrutinizing her ears, he would continue to obsess about how her ears looked wrong and this would always make him question if she was the one for him. He really liked her personality, she was funny and intelligent, and with the exception of her ears, he found her attractive. But this was not enough for him to halt the intrusive thoughts and constant doubt of whether or not he could remain in a relationship with her because of her ears.

As the body dysmorphic disorder symptoms became entangled within the couple's relationship, intimacy began to give way to an undercurrent of dissention. What had been simmering as a seemingly subtle issue eventually surfaced as a massive stressor that interfered with all aspects of the relationship. The breaking point occurred just prior to Joshua entering psychotherapy: He had been having continuous, intrusive thoughts about his girlfriend's ears for several weeks and had been contemplating either breaking up with her or asking her to have her ears pinned back. He chose to ask her if she would consider having surgery to pull her ears back. Not surprisingly, this made her extremely angry. It was at this point that she gave Joshua an ultimatum: Either he sought treatment for his body related issues, or they would have to part ways. As much as her ears bothered him, he was insightful enough to recognize that losing a relationship over a body part was absurd. The realization that he might throw away a five-year relationship over ears, a body part that is used for hearing, served as the impetus for him to seek treatment.

During the process of psychotherapy, Joshua gradually gained insight into his preoccupation with his girlfriend's ears. He had never previously experienced obsessions with another person's appearance. Then again, this was the first time he had been in a long-term intimate relationship. There appeared to be a parallel between him becoming emotionally attached to his girlfriend and an increase in his preoccupation with her appearance. When they were friends prior to dating, Joshua could not recall even noticing her ears. He remembers noticing them for the first time after they had begun dating. As dating progressed into an emotional and physical relationship, the preoccupation with her ears gradually became more pronounced. Joshua expressed that, as they had become more intimate, he had begun to feel more defective: He explained that it was almost as if he was taking on her physical imperfections, something that was difficult for him to tolerate, thus the intrusive thoughts about her ears.

It is quite obvious that Joshua's preoccupation with his girlfriend's ears had begun to cause a significant riff in their relationship. It is difficult to discern which came first: Were the body dysmorphic disorder symptoms the source of tension within the intimate relationship, or, did Joshua already have trepidation about intimately attaching to a woman and this manifested itself through body image symptoms? He had never previously projected his BDD symptoms onto another person until he became involved in an intimate relationship, and it was probably not a coincidence that becoming intimately attached to someone activated uncomfortable emotions. It is likely that both scenarios contributed to his symptoms, also producing the symptoms that he transferred onto his girlfriend. Regardless of the etiology, the interpersonal intimate relationship had been significantly impacted by his preoccupation with the physical features of his significant other.

* * *

Joshua's story is an example of how someone with body dysmorphic disorder can project their symptoms onto another person. As is the case with Joshua, this transferring of symptoms usually occurs with people they are closest to or who they have attached to intimately. This projection process happens much less frequently to individuals who have not entered the inner emotional boundaries of the BDD sufferer. There are occasions where an individual with body dysmorphic disorder has a parent who is overly preoccupied with their child's appearance. This may be a case of a parent who themselves has BDD and is projecting their symptoms onto their child, but there may also be another explanation for this parent-child transference.

There have been numerous occasions that I have worked with a BDD patient who has a narcissistic parent. In these particular cases, the parent did not have body dysmorphic disorder, but as a narcissist they were extremely conscious about image, appearance, performance, and how the outside world viewed them and their offspring (Young, Klosko, and Weishaar 2003). The child of a narcissist often becomes what is called the narcissistic extension, in other words, the child is the mirror by which the narcissistic parents experience themselves. Within the dyad of the narcissistic parent and child, love is highly conditional and the child learns from a very early age that they receive approval from their parent when they meet certain criteria. This criteria could be anything, but it often entails performance and outward external appearances.

The narcissist lacks the capacity to self-reflect, thus the narcissistic parent does not look within but rather looks to their child for mirroring. The identities between the parent and child become fused: The child never has the opportunity to develop their own sense of self because to not mimic the needs of their parent means that they will not receive what is perceived as love. The child comes to understand love as a very conditional response to their parent's wishes, and they also learn that to not comply with these desires will involve love being withheld. Naturally any child will follow the source of a parent's love, and for a child of a narcissistic parent this means never diverging from the path from which the parent wields the highly conditional love. This can significantly interfere with a child developing its own identity and also impairs the process of learning how to emotionally self-soothe.

If a child never has the opportunity to develop their own identity, then they will inevitably have to look elsewhere to discern who they are. Besides looking to the narcissistic parent, they will utilize external cues in order to latch onto something that can give them a sense of self. This external entity can easily become their own physical body because it is part of them, albeit the most exterior boundary of their identity. Even if the narcissistic parent did not particularly emphasize body image as the conditional basis for approval, it is not unusual that the child's appearance becomes at least an aspect of their self-value. If the parent did overly emphasize aesthetic appearance, it is highly likely that the child will have made the association between their parent's love and how their body is viewed by the outside world.

Sometimes the narcissist's preoccupation with their child's appearance disturbs the parent more than the identified patient who is in treatment. The patient may be in treatment for a mild body image disturbance, but what is interfering with their life the most is the parent who will not stop scrutinizing their appearance. As previously stated, this might be a case of a parent who has body dysmorphic disorder and is projecting their experience onto their child. In this situation, the parent with BDD usually has the insight to discern that this is not about their child and is about their own unresolved issues. But, this certainly would not be the case with the narcissistic parent who is incapable of separating their own experience from that of their child, the narcissistic extension.

Because the identity of the narcissistic parent is so fused with that of their child-mirror, it is inconceivable for them to separate their identity with that of their child (Gardner 2004). Thus having a child with a flaw in appearance is experienced by the narcissistic parent as their own defect. For the clinician working with the dyad of a narcissistic parent and their child with a body image disturbance, it is important to discern the etiology of the parent's pathology. How treatment proceeds with the identified patient will often parallel the reactions of the parent: If the parent actually has body dysmorphic disorder and does not have a narcissistic character structure, they can easily be directed toward their own psychotherapy. In the event that the parent is a narcissist, the clinician should expect much more resistance within the dyad as the child-patient becomes more comfortable with their own external appearance. Also, the narcissistic parent is much less likely to follow through with a clinician's recommendation to seek their own psychotherapy: With the incapacity to self-reflect, the narcissist will continuously look outward at their child, their mirror-image, and incessantly focus on how their child needs to be fixed.

Whether it be a parent-child attachment, a bond between a husband and wife, or any other intimate connection, a body image preoccupation can very easily take precedence over a true, genuine, and unconditional loving relationship. Thus it becomes the clinician's role to model how a healthy, trusting, and consistent relationship is supposed to look. This allows the patient to experience the nurture and connectivity that is so necessary for people to thrive. It is commonplace that individuals with body image disturbances have either never experienced unconditional love and nurture or have been too body focused to get these needs met. The psychotherapist becomes a consistent, animate object from where the patient can begin to explore themselves and the world. Regardless of the therapeutic modality from which the clinician operates, it is the modeling of relational consistency that is such a profound catalyst in the process of body dysmorphic disorder recovery.

12 The Trauma Conceptualization Model

Psychotherapy for body dysmorphic disorder is a complex process of navigating between overt symptom reduction while concurrently identifying and unraveling patterns and events in the patient's life that may be at the source of the diagnosis. It is important for the clinician to have an understanding of a patient's life timeline in order to best conceptualize how and why their body image symptoms came into fruition. There is often a series of emotional wounds that have occurred along the life timeline and these are what the discerning psychotherapist needs to identify. These emotional wounds are not always body related, but very frequently the body was the backdrop for the circumstance or series of events that led to emotional scarring. Emotional injuries can also arise from an accumulation of what did not occur, and do not necessarily always have to be directly linked to one identifiable point in time.

Rarely do body dysmorphic disorder patients enter therapy with the intention of addressing trauma and emotional wounds. Most have already been overtly wounded by the insidious, tormenting preoccupation with their bodies and symptom relief is their primary focus. Many of these individuals are either unaware that they have had emotional wounds, or if they are aware, often minimize the impact these may have had on the development of their symptoms. Trauma occurs when an event creates an unresolved impact on an individual (Levine 1997). The term trauma usually summons images of extreme events such as natural disasters, car accidents, or brutal physical abuse, but trauma exists on a continuum and is experienced differently by every individual. An event that is seemingly innocuous to one person may profoundly impact another person.

Outside the realm of psychotherapists and trauma specialists, the term trauma is usually interpreted as an event that is exceptionally devastating and out of the norm. Individuals who are aware that they have experienced a trauma often seek out help specifically to address the event. If a patient has not previously been in psychotherapy, or enters treatment exclusively to address their BDD symptoms, they may not understand what the clinician is referring to if they are asked if they have experienced trauma. As in any psychotherapy patient population, there are body dysmorphic disorder patients who have endured blatant traumas and are very aware that these are significant events. There are also many BDD patients who deny experiencing trauma. This is not usually because they are intentionally withholding the information, but because they have never even considered the possibility that trauma may be applicable to them. Asking the question in a different way may yield different results, for instance, "Growing up, were there any events or situations that left you feeling different, inferior, or bad?"

An example of an emotional wound that may not be perceived as a traumatic event is when someone has been teased by their peers, especially when it has been systematic and reoccurring. Although many individuals with body dysmorphic disorder have never endured excessive teasing, there are those that have experienced emotional or verbal abuse involving their appearance. In my experience, body dysmorphic disorder patients often do not report this unless they are asked specifically if they have ever experienced teasing or bullying. Sometimes they do not disclose that they have endured ridicule about their appearance because of the shame associated with being belittled. More often they do not mention it because they assume that everyone gets taunted in their youth and that their experiences were not out of the ordinary. They are often surprised when they are informed that not all children and adolescents are teased about their appearance because to them verbal abuse by peers had been the norm.

If something does not occur, can it be a trauma? If the basic physical needs of a child such as food, water, clothing, and shelter are neglected, this would certainly be classified as traumatic. If an infant does not receive the basic emotional necessities such as nurture, attunement, and love, should this amalgamation of deficits also be considered trauma? Child Protective Services can observe when a child is lacking the physical basics and will take appropriate measures to insure the child's safety, but it is almost impossible to ascertain emotional neglect. Most healthy parents know that they are supposed to provide the physical basics for their child, but emotional provisions are much more ambiguous. A parent that did not receive sufficient nurture from their own parents will not be able to pass on what they themselves were never given. This deficiency in emotional cognizance is passed on multi-generationally and is not identified as problematic because it is the only paradigm that the family knows.

Emotional neglect is characterized as developmental trauma. There does not have to be one specific event that defines developmental trauma, rather a continuum of a paucity of the emotional nutrients that are imperative for a human being to thrive (Strathearn 2011). A person's perspective on what is adequate emotional sustenance derives from their family of origin. As a result, patients who never received sufficient emotional care are unaware that something crucial was missing during their childhood. It is often difficult for them to initially understand that familial emotional deficits leave a massive gap in their developmental process because they are oblivious that emotional nurture was even supposed to exist. When the clinician brings this to the attention of the patient, it is not unusual that they defend their parents as being very good providers, something that might be accurate. The parents may have been very proficient at providing all physical and material needs, but this does not necessarily include the emotional essentials.

If a child receives ample emotional nourishment, they will be much less susceptible to internalizing negative or traumatic incidences that occur away from their family of origin. If a child is being teased or bullied outside of their home but they come from an emotionally attuned family, they will be much more likely to share these experiences with their parents and be adequately comforted. Children who are bullied and come from homes that are not emotionally affluent are often too ashamed to disclose these events to their parents. The result is a scenario where the world outside of home is not safe and the home environment is not emotionally secure. This leaves a child highly vulnerable to either externalizing or internalizing their experiences because there is nowhere else to turn to explain their emotional states. Sometimes children act out and become the teasers and bullies while other times children internalize the material and blame themselves. The latter group are the individuals who are more vulnerable to developing body dysmorphic disorder.

There are always a multitude of factors that contribute to an individual developing body dysmorphic disorder. There are people who came from emotionally intact families and were never teased about their appearance and still have BDD. But it is not unusual that somewhere on the individual's life timeline there was something that made them more vulnerable to developing a body image disturbance versus another disorder. A particularly potent combination of scenarios that significantly increases the possibility of BDD development is when a child endures emotional developmental trauma and is also teased about their appearance. Because the child has nowhere to turn to process the negative emotions that come from being teased, this material can easily be internalized and interpreted as fact. This differs from the child who endures similar teasing but who is from a family that can freely discuss emotions and who are emotionally attuned with one another: Although these children may be hurt by cruel comments made by peers, the information is not internalized because it is appropriately processed in the family system.

The dyad of emotional developmental trauma and trauma stemming from appearance related verbal abuse provides an ideal climate for the germination of body dysmorphic disorder. The child who is systematically teased about their appearance and who is unable to process these experiences with emotionally available adults will eventually begin to believe their abusers. Body dysmorphic disorder thrives in the very lonely space in between the emotionally empty family and the emotionally abusive outside world. In this space there is often nowhere to go but inward as the negative messages about appearance accumulate and inevitably become an internal dialog. This internal dialog can also be referred to as body dysmorphic disorder: What had begun as external verbal trauma is internalized and the BDD sufferer inadvertently perpetuates the trauma by continuously picking apart their own appearance.

Even after the threat of appearance related verbal abuse subsides, the internalized threat continues to exist as the individual remains on high alert for any future negative evaluations about their body. The emotional wounds that were so closely associated with comments about physical appearance do not heal properly in emotionally disconnected families. Because the child has interpreted that they are being teased because of physical flaws, it is rapidly discerned that they must change their appearance or suffer further abuse. The induced hypersensitivity to physical appearance propagates a pattern of attempting to figure out what is wrong with their appearance and how to fix it: These thoughts can be defined as BDD obsessions. The behaviors that the individual utilizes in an attempt to ward off the obsessive thoughts about their appearance can be defined as body dysmorphic disorder compulsions.

It is these compulsions that provide the emotionally wounded individual with a very temporary sense of relief. This becomes the mechanism by which the overwhelming feelings of shame, disgust, anger, fear, and anxiety are managed. The problem is that a metaphoric scar coagulates over the emotional wounds and the negative emotions are not processed in a healthy manner. Because these emotions are not appropriately processed, they will continuously fester as more and more symbolic scar tissue builds layers of protection over the emotional wounds. The body related compulsions are an adaptive response to danger and initially provide much needed armor from the emotional lacerations. From a trauma model conceptualization, the malady that has been titled body dysmorphic disorder is the mind's response to previous body related emotional injuries. The entity we call body dysmorphic disorder exists once an individual's sense of identity becomes entangled with the futile attempts to mend these wounds.

Emotional traumas involving interpersonal relationships are a common theme with individuals with body dysmorphic disorder. Although teasing or bullying may be the more overt version of interpersonal traumas, these can also include scenarios where the individual was systematically not included in groups, whether this be on the playground, in school events, or even in their own family of origin. The disintegration of a family system, as in the case of a divorce or death of a family member, can also be interpersonally and emotionally traumatic. Many individuals with body dysmorphic disorder report that they feel and have always felt as if somehow they are different from everyone else. This experience of feeling different from the rest of humanity exists on a continuum, but often falls on the more extreme end of the spectrum, for instance "feeling like an alien" or "feeling like no other human being on the planet truly understands me." It is not unusual that somewhere on their life timeline there was either an event or series of circumstances where the individual was left feeling on the far periphery of their family or peers.

Case Study: Patrick

Patrick contacted me in a frantic and desperate state. He communicated that he could not stand all the flaws with his skin and that this was significantly interfering with his work and his social life. When he entered treatment he matched all the classic symptoms of body dysmorphic disorder: A preoccupation surrounding areas of his body that he believed were defective and that caused him impairment in all areas of his life. Although his skin was his foremost concern, he was also worried that his hair was thinning, that his nose was too big, that he had too much body hair, and that he was not fit enough.

As is the case with the majority of body dysmorphic disorder patients that I work with, Patrick entered therapy convinced that these areas of his body were extremely defective and that they needed to be corrected because otherwise he would not be able to function. He was able to work, but admitted that he was severely distracted by the obsessions about his appearance and by the constant compulsive behaviors including checking different reflective surfaces to see if his skin was still flawed. He explained how he would go from examining his skin in the reflective surface of the computer monitor to the screen of his smartphone, and then to the bathroom mirror, as well as using a compact mirror that he would carry around with him in order to study his skin. He would also constantly take pictures of his skin with his smartphone camera to make sure it was not getting worse.

I was amazed that Patrick was even capable of holding employment considering the severity of his symptoms. But outside of work his quality of life was drastically impaired. Patrick stated that he had not been in an intimate relationship with a woman for years: He could barely speak with women because doing so would make him extremely anxious, automatically assuming that they would consider him as unattractive as he viewed himself. His avoidance of women, as well as most social situations, left Patrick with limited human contact outside of his family. He described how he felt very alone because no one could really understand how tormented he was about his skin. Like many individuals with body image disturbances, Patrick felt that nobody could truly relate to his experience and this only contributed to his fundamental feelings of inadequacy.

During the process of therapy, Patrick was eventually able to begin discussing material beyond that of his supposed body flaws. He stated that at the age of seven years he was devastated when his parents divorced. He explained that as a child his father had given him much attention and treated him as if he was special. This ended abruptly once his parents separated. Not only did his parent's marriage dissolve but his father remarried and moved out of state. Patrick explained how this was a double blow to him because, not only did his parents divorce, but also his father, who had previously placed him on a pedestal, was no longer present.

I have observed that individuals who have a diathesis for body dysmorphic disorder and an innately sensitive temperament seem much more susceptible to these circumstances, and Patrick was not an exception. Patrick expressed frustration about how he so desperately wanted to be in a relationship but admitted that he was fearful of women. He explained how being in the presence of a woman that he was attracted to would activate thoughts about how ugly he believed his skin looked. The anxiety and shame was so overwhelming that he would avoid women altogether. His family and close friends would frequently pester him about why he never dated or was never in a relationship, and this only magnified his shame while perpetuating his yearning for a seemingly infeasible relationship.

As the therapeutic process progressed, Patrick began to connect the dots. He gradually began to realize that what was so seemingly problematic, his appearance, was actually only a façade for deeper-rooted issues. For so many years he had firmly held the belief that if he could only fix his skin and other aesthetic imperfections then he could have an intimate relationship. He began to realize how the precipitous divorce of his parents had significantly impacted how he understood and experienced intimate relationships; not only seeing his parent's relationship fragment but also experiencing sudden abandonment from an individual who had doted over him. His reaction to these circumstances had initially manifested itself through attempting to control his environment by way of obsessive-compulsive behaviors. Fixating on his appearance became the mechanism by which he would attempt to control his life and regulate his emotions.

With thorough psychotherapy and proper medication management, Patrick's body dysmorphic disorder symptoms began to dissipate. This of course came as a relief to him, but as is the case with so many BDD patients, Patrick still remained very vulnerable to the unresolved material that festered just beneath the veneer of the body image concerns. As his body image preoccupation decreased he began to date women, something he had not done for years. He explained that he was feeling more comfortable in the presence of women, but he also found himself preoccupied with when or if they were going to contact him and whether or not they were attracted to him. Patrick soon discerned that women were becoming a barometer for how he would measure his self-worth and that this was only replacing the body image preoccupations. Women were analogous to his skin and other body image concerns because both were serving as external objects utilized to validate his sense of self.

It is not unusual that once body image concerns begin to fade that other external objects may serve to substitute for the initial body related preoccupation. This was the case with Patrick, and bringing this to his attention was imperative in order that he did not become further distracted by external objects that could only divert attention away from underlying themes. Even though I did not discourage Patrick from dating, we did thoroughly examine why he was now becoming so absorbed with meeting, talking with, and dating women. Although he was excited about his new prospects of having female relations, there was a not-so-subtle fear of women. As he placed women on a pedestal, he was also unknowingly using them as a source of gauging his sense of value as an individual. I explained to Patrick that this is exactly what we did not want to happen, alternating from using one object to another in order for him to feel fundamentally sufficient. Exchanging one obsession for another interferes with an individual developing self-efficacy and an integrated, solid sense of self.

The external objects that diverted Patrick's attention were only a masquerade for his intense fear of intimate connectivity. We theorized that although he so badly wanted to be in an intimate relationship, this simultaneously conflicted with the very deep-rooted fear of again losing such connections if they were to occur. The experience of the two most meaningful relationships in his childhood promptly disintegrating had traumatized Patrick more than he had ever been aware. He had not thoroughly addressed this because he had been so distracted by attempting to fix what he believed was at the source of a lack of intimacy. Formal psychotherapy was not to end as his body dysmorphic disorder symptoms faded into the background; in fact, it was during this point in therapy that interpersonal relationships became the emphasis of treatment.

* * *

There are individuals with body dysmorphic disorder who have experienced physical trauma to their bodies. Blatant corporeal traumas such as physical and sexual abuse may manifest through the victim's body unless the trauma has been promptly addressed and processed with a mental health practitioner (Herman 1992). With the majority of BDD patients that I have worked with who have been victims of bodily trauma, the trauma had never been adequately processed. The body image disturbance evolved as a response to the physical trauma; sometimes the predisposition for bodily preoccupation had already existed and the traumatic event served as the catalyst for it evolving into a full-blown disorder.

It is not uncommon that BDD patients who have been sexually abused were much too ashamed to disclose the event to even their parents, thus are left having to make sense of the trauma all alone. The individual who may already have a sensitive, introverted temperament and who has experienced sexual trauma will frequently interpret the event as resulting from something that they did wrong rather then placing blame on the perpetrator. The victim may intellectually understand that they were a victim, but emotionally they internalize the trauma and often experience the ambiguous feeling that somehow *they are bad*. Because this feeling is so amorphous and because the source of this inner experience resulted from trauma to the body, it is the body that becomes the repository for all unprocessed emotions.

The nebulous emotions of fundamentally feeling bad or defective often become very pervasive within the victim's life. In a desperate attempt to explain these extremely disconcerting internal experiences, the body can become the repository because it is the most tangible aspect of their existence. It is not unusual that the victim becomes preoccupied with the body part that was physically injured; other times the individual experiences a general sense of their body being defective, bad, or "wrong" (Herman 1992). This leads to the preoccupation of desperately trying to fix the body area that is deemed to be bad. The excessive focus on the body can also serve as a decoy from having to think about the horrendous experience that is likely at the origin of the body image disturbance. It is also not unusual that the individual has become so detached from the trauma that they begin to question if they really were abused or if they are just imagining it (Jaeger et al. 2014).

Regardless of whether a trauma results from physical harm to the body, verbal abuse, or emotional developmental neglect, the body dysmorphic disorder symptoms may serve as the mechanism that allows the victim to function. As previously mentioned, just because someone has a body image disturbance does not mean that they have experienced trauma. But clinicians need to be cognizant that there is always the possibility that the patient who is hyper-focusing on their body may have trauma in their background. Like the majority of BDD patients, they will arrive in treatment highly preoccupied with their appearance. After a trusting therapeutic relationship has been established, the patient will feel comfortable disclosing intimate details, including those that may be related to trauma.

The process of working through the trauma usually begins with the thickest armor, that being the body image symptoms. The body image disturbance exists for a reason and if these symptoms are too quickly removed, the patient becomes directly exposed to the traumatic material that has been buried under years of body related compulsions. If a patient is able to disclose that they have experienced trauma and if they state that they are ready to address it, then the clinician has the green-light to begin the trauma related recovery work. Many times BDD patients who have experienced physical trauma have trepidation about processing the information and either minimize the experience or avoid talking about it altogether. If this is the case, the clinician should delicately address the issue, finding a balance between not overwhelming the patient with the topic and not avoiding the discussion on how its influence may be at the genesis of their body image disturbance.

The psychological and emotional damage resulting from trauma can be passed down from generation to generation (Mohatt et al. 2014). The patient who has entered treatment for a diagnosable mental health condition may have never experienced trauma personally, but there is always the possibility that they are the recipients of emotional shrapnel. A parent, grandparent, or great-grandparent may have endured the initial blatant trauma; if there had never been proper resolution to such an event, there is a high probability that the trauma would have affected how they interacted with the world and with their own children. The child of an untreated trauma victim is likely to indirectly inherit the trauma: The parent who experienced the incident will likely be incapable of providing consistent and sufficient emotional mirroring and attunement. If the child does not receive the basics of parental nurture, this may manifest itself as emotional developmental trauma.

Every human responds to trauma differently. If a parent becomes emotionally disconnected in the wake of the trauma, their child will no longer have a mirror by which to learn how to self-regulate emotions. If the victimized parent becomes very emotionally erratic after the event, this too will significantly impact the child. In the worst-case scenario, the parent re-enacts the trauma by verbally or physically abusing their offspring. Any of these scenarios will inevitably impact the emotional and psychological development of the next generation. Because the family of origin is our blueprint from which we understand interpersonal, intimate, and familial relationships, we superimpose this template onto our children. The child who has been raised by a traumatized parent will likely not have received adequate tools to manage their own internal experiences, so in turn they will parent their children as they were raised. An accumulation effect occurs as the newest generation becomes the repository for emotional pathology that had never been properly addressed.

Case Study: Ian

Ian, a young man in his early twenties, entered psychotherapy with all the classic symptoms of body dysmorphic disorder. He was preoccupied with several aspects of his appearance, but was mainly focused on his right cheek because he believed that it was disproportionally bigger than his left cheek. He also felt as if his facial skin, especially the skin around his cheeks, was abnormally red and made him appear as if he had rosacea. Like most BDD patients who are new to treatment, Ian was hyperfocused on a body part and desperately needed to find a solution for the torment it was causing him.

Ian grew up in a seemingly comfortable middle-class family. Both he and his sister were well provided for by their parents and they never wanted for anything, at least materially. From the outside his family appeared functional, and Ian would frequently receive comments about how he was lucky that he came from such a good family. Ian assumed this was the case because he knew no different. Although his parents would occasionally openly argue with each other, Ian denied ever being physically abused by his parents. His father would almost always attend his basketball games and his mother was usually present when he returned home from school.

Ian also disclosed that he remembers instances as a child where his father could be very scary. He recalled one particular incident that occurred on a Saturday morning when his father had taken him grocery shopping. They had stopped for donuts before going into the grocery store and he remembers his father being in a cheerful and fun mood. After enjoying the donuts, they entered the grocery store and began to shop. They had a tradition that every time they shopped together, his father would push the cart and let him find the grocery items.

As they were turning the corner from one aisle to the next, their shopping cart was accidently bumped by a woman pushing her cart from the other direction. Ian remembers his father flying off the handle: His cheeks turned beet red and he began to shout obscenities at the woman as his eyes bulged out, blood-shot with anger. The woman apologized emphatically, but his father continued to hurl insults at her even after she had continued pushing her cart down the next aisle.

Ian recollected feeling terrified and also very ashamed by his father's impulsive, enraged reaction to a seemingly minor event. He stated that this was not the only time that his father had behaved so erratically while he was growing up. Ian shared that there were occasions when his father would yell at him during his basketball games. If he had a really good game, his father would give him hugs and take him out for pizza afterward. But sometimes if he made a mistake or missed an easy basket, his father would yell at him from the sidelines, something that really embarrassed Ian. After these games, his father would be stone-silent on the car ride home, leaving Ian with the feeling that his father was angry with or disgraced by him.

At the time, Ian interpreted his father's reaction as a result of the mistakes that he had made during the basketball game. Because he was a child, he was not able to comprehend that his father's reaction was about his own demons and not about the performance on the basketball court. Ian internalized these experiences, interpreting them at face value: For his father to get so angry with him after he made even a minor mistake was evidence that there was something wrong with him and that it needed to be corrected to prevent future enraged reactions. Ian loved his father, but also was always on edge when his father was around because he was never able to predict when he would blow his lid.

During the course of psychotherapy for his body dysmorphic disorder, Ian began to better understand the genesis of his father's bursts of rage. Ian's grandfather had been an alcoholic who would become extremely verbally and emotionally abusive when under the influence. Ian's father had never been physically abused, but was raised in an environment where there was the constant threat of a raging parent. Ian's grandfather had been physically abused by his great-grandfather who would hit him with a switch multiple times every week. It is likely that Ian's grandfather turned to alcohol in an attempt to deal with the reoccurring trauma of being regularly hit by his own father.

Although the history of physical abuse had ended with Ian's grandfather, the fall-out from this was far from over. Ian's father would be verbally abused and constantly demeaned by his own father, and this was internalized as somehow he must be a defective and bad person. Ian's father never sought counseling for this because he was unaware that anything he had experienced was inappropriate or abnormal for a parent-child relationship, simply assuming that he deserved to be the recipient of the anger. He dealt with these feelings by over-compensating in school and work and these distractions served to temporarily mollify feelings of inferiority. But emotional wounds that are not actively processed will not properly heal: They continue to fester and rise to the surface when activated by scenarios in the present that mimic the event that initially caused the wound. It was Ian who became the recipient of these festering emotional injuries.

Ian made it very clear that his father never hit him or threatened to do so, but he did admit that as a child he was terrified by his father's bursts of anger. He learned to predict his father's anger outbursts because his cheeks would begin to turn red every time he was about to erupt with rage. As Ian grew up, he became less frightened by his father's anger spells because he had become so used to them over the years. But, he would still cringe every time his father had these reactions in public places. He would feel very embarrassed to be seen with his father during these public outbursts and would study his father's cheeks in an attempt to predict if it was about to happen.

Ian did not recall being preoccupied with his body until he was 17-years-old. It was a sunny and very hot day in the middle of summer and he had gone to the beach with several friends. It was during this beach outing that one of his peers made the comment that he should really put on more sunscreen because his face was getting burned and was turning very red. Ian did not think much of it at the time of the remark, but that evening when he was getting ready for bed he noticed that his face, and especially his cheeks, were quite red from being sunburned. He began to scrutinize his face from different angles and at different distances from the mirror, and began to observe that his right cheek appeared bigger and even redder than his left cheek. That night Ian remained in front of the mirror for hours, trying to figure out why his cheeks did not look symmetrical and why one cheek had more coloration than the other. This was only the beginning of a downward spiral that would eventually lead him into treatment for body dysmorphic disorder.

Like the majority of individuals entering psychotherapy for BDD symptoms, Ian just wanted to fix his uneven cheeks and reddish skin. He admitted that there had been times that he had worn foundation make-up in order to make his skin look less red; he had also researched if he could have an implant placed only in his left cheek so that his cheeks would appear proportional. Objectively there was no noticeable difference between his cheeks, and his complexion looked like that of any other Caucasian man. But to Ian this was certainly not the case as he experienced extreme shame revolving around how he perceived his cheeks and skin complexion.

Ian's journey in recovery from body dysmorphic disorder entailed addressing his symptoms from both behavioral and insight oriented thera-peutic modalities. It was during this process that Ian came to the realiza-tion that throughout the earlier years of his life an association had evolved between his father's angry rants, his father's beet red cheeks, and the fright and shame he would experience during these outbursts. Witnessing his father's cheeks turning red with anger had become Ian's warning signal that an angry reaction was about to occur. The resulting feelings of fright and shame had likely become paired with the physical, facial reddening of his father's face; this in turn solidified the association between particular facial characteristics and very uncomfortable emotions.

Prior to entering treatment Ian had never made this connection, hav-ing previously been so distracted by what he perceived as his obviously ugly cheeks. Ian so badly wanted to just look normal. He felt as if he looked different from everyone else because of what he perceived as his disproportional and discolored cheeks. He also believed that women would never find him attractive if he remained looking this way. Deep down Ian felt as if he was fundamentally defective: This inner experience was something very difficult for him to articulate, thus he would focus on facial features that he could concretely label as blatant defects.

Throughout therapy Ian had the opportunity to process many emo-tions that had never been addressed. Many of these discussions involved the emotions that he would experience when his father was angry. He had never expressed these feelings before because he had assumed that his father's anger was just normal parental behavior, and that any anger that was aimed toward him was justified because he must have been at fault. This completely parallels how his father had felt when he was a boy being demeaned by his own parent. Ian's father had externalized these feelings by over-compensating in performance related behaviors, but Ian had internalized these feelings and blamed his appearance.

Ian's cheeks had become the repository for a multigenerational his-tory of trauma. His great-grandfather physically beat his grandfather. His grandfather verbally and emotionally abused his father. Albeit less overtly abusive, the emotionally erratic behavior of Ian's father became the internalized dialog for Ian. This manifested itself by morphing into the self-deprecating voice of body dysmorphic disorder, constantly reminding him that he was defective. No one on his father's side of the family had ever sought psychotherapy, thus the emotional pathol-ogy caused by trauma had been passed down from one generation to the next. Ian's tormenting BDD symptoms had forced him to seek help outside of his family.

Ian entered treatment convinced that his unattractive cheeks were at the root of him feeling inadequate. As treatment progressed he began to understand that perhaps his cheeks were not actually causing the feelings of defectiveness, but that he had been feeling this way long before he had become preoccupied with his appearance. As an aspect of his treatment protocol, Ian actively participated in exposure and response prevention exercises. These exercises proved to be very valuable in disconnecting the conditioned response between his cheeks and the emotions of shame and fear. He began to focus less on his cheeks and found it much easier to socialize with people without obsessing about his appearance. Although the negative emotions associated with his cheeks began to decrease, he still reported feeling as if he was "somehow just not good enough."

It was during this point in his treatment that he began to gain insight into the possibility that perhaps he experienced an inherent feeling of inadequacy because of experiences unrelated to his appearance. Ian began to understand that when he was a child he would interpret his father's angry explosions not as what was wrong with his father, but as what he was doing wrong to make his father so upset. This internalization of his father's angry reactions had become the template for Ian's fundamental sense of self: That somehow there must be something wrong with him. Ian's new understanding of how this all evolved was not the panacea to his inherent feelings of inadequacy, but it did serve as a significant catalyst in the process of integrating a sense of identity that was no longer influenced by many generations of unhealed emotional wounds.

* * *

When the body becomes a repository for unresolved trauma, it also remains a very vulnerable portal for the reactivation of emotional wounds. Because the body dysmorphic disorder symptoms have in essence become the metaphoric scar tissue covering past trauma, it is not a coincidence that current situations that involve the body may activate emotions similar to those caused by the initial traumatic event. Individuals with BDD are very sensitive to anything involving their appearance, especially in regards to the body area that they believe is defective. Something such as a seemingly innocuous comment about the BDD sufferer's appearance might be the defining moment that activates submerged emotions associated with a particular body part. Sometimes these emotionally activating events are not so innocuous.

For an individual with body dysmorphic disorder and correlating trauma, the invasive nature of cosmetic operations can rapidly become a trigger for the reactivation of traumatic material. To physically alter the area of the body that has held the emotional weight of the trauma will very likely activate negative schemas that had been associated with the reconstructed body part. For individuals who had experienced physical or sexual trauma in their past, the cosmetic operation itself may prove to be re-traumatizing: Not only will this likely lead to a severe exacerbation of body image related symptoms, but there is the possibility that their sense of self will begin to fragment. Although the preoccupation over a supposed defect can be tormenting to the point of opting for cosmetic alterations, it also serves as a filter and distraction from overwhelming, unprocessed emotions. To modify this bodily filter leaves the patient highly vulnerable to the deep emotional wounds that are a result of the physical trauma.

Regardless of the etiology of trauma, it is important that it is acknowledged, examined, and processed with the patient. The behavioral component of treatment for body dysmorphic disorder, specifically exposure and response prevention, also needs to be utilized: This is very important in order to begin disconnecting the association that has been conditioned between the negative emotions and the body areas deemed defective. It is imperative that the clinician works with the BDD patient from multiple angles, not solely focusing on past history while also not over-emphasizing current symptomology. If the clinician only focuses on the patient's history of trauma, this may not be sufficient to reduce the profound feelings of shame, disgust, fear, or anger that have become connected with physical features. Years of engaging in behavioral compulsions in order to ward off these uncomfortable feelings have solidified the association between the emotions and the body.

When exposure and response prevention therapy is done correctly, it can be very effective in disconnecting the negative emotions that have been associated with the body. However, this does not necessarily reduce the patient's experience of feeling inherently defective, different, or bad. Behavioral therapy will contribute to the individual becoming less preoccupied with their body, but unless the history of trauma is thoroughly processed, the patient will remain exposed to either BDD symptoms developing elsewhere on their body or morphing into another diagnosable condition. The trauma is often the source of the fundamental feelings of defectiveness, and to not properly address it leaves the patient very vulnerable to negatively internalizing past, present, and future life events.

13 Personality and Body Dysmorphic Disorder

As a psychotherapy intern I was very interested in behavioral therapy and my initial training and internships reflected this. Behavioral therapy focuses on the symptoms that initially bring a patient into treatment. Therapy is usually intensive and short term and the main goal of treatment is the reduction of overt symptoms. When utilized correctly, behavioral techniques can be highly effective in unlearning maladaptive behaviors and decreasing emotional and psychological distress caused by mental disorders.

When I began to work with body dysmorphic disorder patients, I attempted to apply the behavioral therapy skills that I had eagerly sought out as the foundation of my clinical psychotherapy training. During this time there was minimal literature focusing on the treatment of BDD and the information that was available suggested that cognitive-behavioral therapy was the treatment of choice for the disorder. Naturally I applied what was familiar and what the research was recommending and I began focusing on fixing body dysmorphic disorder symptoms with cognitive and especially behavioral therapy. It was not long before I began to realize that the behavioral techniques that seemed to work so well with obsessive-compulsive disorder and many anxiety disorders were not translating when treating BDD patients.

There were occasions when a body dysmorphic disorder patient would completely cooperate with every therapeutic recommendation and also follow through with all homework assignments. This, though, was the exception and not the norm. The majority of my early body dysmorphic disorder patients either could not follow through with their assignments, could not make it to session, or had such a strong conviction that their appearance was the primary problem that they did not see the point in fully engaging in the therapy process. This did not bode well for employing behavioral therapy. I found myself becoming increasingly frustrated and questioning my capabilities as a clinician and behavioral therapist.

Body dysmorphic disorder patients often enter treatment feeling very, very stuck. This is how I was beginning to feel as a psychotherapist who was supposed to be helping these individuals to become unstuck.

I would observe my BDD patients continuously attempt to fix their problem by way of focusing on their appearance: I would point out to them that they continued to run into the same metaphoric wall time and time again and not get different results. The more they focused on an area of their body, the more frustrated, hopeless, depressed, and stuck they would become. In retrospect it seems so obvious that I was simultaneously hitting my head against a therapy wall trying to fix my patients by emphasizing that their symptoms needed to be fixed. The more they banged their heads against the wall, the more head banging I would do, and this resulted in all of us remaining very stuck.

I also began to notice that the few body dysmorphic disorder patients that were able to follow through with all behavioral recommendations often needed to return to therapy. When they did re-enter treatment it was often for the same symptoms that we had seemingly worked through; it was also not uncommon that they had begun to obsess about another area of their body. For longer than I would like to admit, I continued to use the behavioral therapy formulas that I had so successfully practiced with obsessive-compulsive disorder and related anxiety disorders. I had become stuck in the BDD paradigm: Not as the sufferer trying to fix a supposed bodily defect, but as the clinician attempting to fix the body dysmorphic disorder patient. I finally admitted to myself that the therapeutic modality that was most familiar to me was not overly effective with this patient population. I needed to stop focusing on details and begin to observe the bigger picture.

Behavioral and social learning theory explains the development of personality through the repetition of behaviors that are positively or negatively reinforced, also known as operant conditioning or instrumental learning. Reinforcement may occur in such a way that adaptive responses are interfered with; any behavior that is consistently rewarded during childhood can become difficult to extinguish later in life. Behaviorists also believe that a child's genetically based temperament influences personality development. The psychoanalytical theories about personality development emphasize how childhood experiences can influence personality development (Liebert and Spiegler 1990).

A central concept to psychoanalytical theory is that children unconsciously devise defense mechanisms in order to regulate their emotions. Defense mechanisms are used to guard against the anxiety provoking conscious recognition of unacceptable impulses and desires while satisfying them indirectly. The defenses inhibit or reduce the expression of these impulses by distorting or deflecting them from their original objects. Psychoanalytic practitioners partially explain personality as armor constructed against internal impulses and external assault (McWilliams 1994).

Everyone has their own unique personality that helps distinguish us from others and contributes to our own identity. Personality structure can significantly determine how we interact with others in our surroundings and in turn how others respond to us. When a personality style is very inflexible and impacts many areas of an individual's life it is described as a personality disorder. In the *Diagnostic and Statistical Manual of Mental Disorders*, the American Psychiatric Association defines personality disorders as enduring patterns of inner experience and behavior that deviate markedly from the expectations of an individual's culture, that are pervasive and inflexible, that have an onset in adolescence or early adulthood, are stable over time, and lead to distress or impairment (American Psychiatric Association 2013). I have yet to have a patient walk into my office and proclaim that they have a personality disorder. Patients enter treatment for tangible symptoms such as those we see with body dysmorphic disorder.

Multiple studies have examined the co-existence of personality disorders and BDD. A study by David Veale (Veale et al. 1996) found that 57–100% of body dysmorphic disorder subjects also met the criteria for a personality disorder. Research on 66 people seeking cosmetic procedures who also had body dysmorphic disorder symptoms established that the severity of BDD symptoms correlated to the number of diagnostic criteria for specific personality disorders (Bellino, Zinna, and Paradiso 2003). From my clinical experience, I would have to agree with the outcome of these studies. I have observed that inflexible personality traits and personality disorders are quite prevalent with this population. I have also become very aware that these very rigid personality structures can significantly interfere with the treatment of body dysmorphic disorder.

In the fifth edition of the American Psychiatric Association's *Diagnostic and Statistical Manual of Mental Disorders*, personality disorders are categorized into three clusters. Cluster A includes paranoid, schizoid, and schizotypal personality disorders. Cluster B is defined as the dramatic personality styles including histrionic, borderline, narcissistic, and anti-social personality disorders. Cluster C contains the anxious personality structures of dependent, avoidant, and obsessive-compulsive personality disorders. The personality traits and disorders that I have most frequently observed with body dysmorphic disorder are avoidant, dependent, and borderline personality types. Research studies have varied in the degree to which particular personality disorders co-occur with BDD.

Unlike the tormenting symptoms that patients present with for treatment, personality disorders are often described as ego-syntonic (Reich 1933). This means that even though a disordered personality style may prove to be maladaptive, it is perceived and felt to be appropriate by the individual. When overt body image symptoms are uncomfortable and highly disruptive to a person's life, this becomes an incentive to seek treatment. But if there is an underlying personality disorder, this may soon prove to be a major obstacle in addressing the body image disturbance. I believe that it is very important for clinicians working with body dysmorphic disorder and related body image disturbances to be well versed in the understanding and treatment of personality structure. The frequent concurrence of these disorders necessitates having to address both simultaneously.

My first clue to a personality disorder often arises when I begin to give assignments to my patients. There are instances that I will intentionally give a homework assignment very early in treatment to not only assess the motivation and insight of the patient but to begin probing for characterological themes that may be present. Just because an individual does not follow though with an assignment is not evidence that they are personality disordered; sometimes they are unable to do the assignment because of the severity of their body image symptoms or sometimes they may just forget to do it. But I have found that in more cases than not, an incomplete homework assignment may be a preliminary sign of resistance to therapeutic recommendations. Other signs that personality disorders may be present include arriving late for therapy or missing therapy sessions altogether, help-reject interactions with the therapist, poor medication compliance, and self-damaging, high-risk behaviors such as substance abuse, sexual promiscuity, binge-eating, and compulsive spending or shopping.

It may take many, many sessions with a client, perhaps even months, to discern whether they meet the criteria for a personality disorder. Even though personality disorders do commonly occur with BDD, I am always cautious when jumping to conclusions and usually do not make the diagnosis until I have observed a consistent pattern of behavior that interferes with treatment. For example, a patient may arrive late because they became stuck in the mirror prior to leaving for the therapy session. Or, a patient may not fully comply with medication recommendations because they are concerned (or convinced) that the medication will negatively affect their body area of concern. I always make sure to explore with the patient the source of the behavior so that I can better determine the cause. More often than not if the source of the countertherapeutic behavior stems from the body image disturbance, the patient is able to articulate this and is gradually able to correct the behavior. If an inflexible personality structure is at the origin of the detrimental conduct, rarely will the behavior rapidly dissipate.

New patients frequently ask me how long therapy will take. I always respond that it is definitely a case-by-case basis and is determined by many factors. My answer is always open-ended because I am fully aware that one of these factors may include a very rigid personality structure or possibly a full-blown personality disorder. If this is the case, it is inevitable that the therapy process will take much longer than it would if there was not a personality disorder present. Clinicians should expect disruptions in the therapy process that will probably interfere with the planned course of treatment. These disruptions are often further evidence of a personality disorder and should be utilized as material for the therapy process rather than interpreted as treatment interference. Clinicians must remain mindful of treating the bigger picture of symptom and character pathology and not become hyper-focused on the body image content.

Avoidant Personality and BDD

The American Psychiatric Association's *Diagnostic and Statistical Manual of Mental Disorders* defines avoidant personality disorder as a pervasive pattern of social inhibition, feelings of inadequacy, and extreme sensitivity to negative evaluation and avoidance of social interaction (American Psychiatric Association 2013). It describes people with avoidant personality traits as considering themselves to be socially inept or personally unappealing and likely to avoid social interaction for fear of being ridiculed, humiliated, rejected, or disliked. The prevalence of avoidant personality disorder in the BDD population has been identified as ranging from 38% (Veale et al. 1996) to 82% (Neziroglu et al. 1996). Nirenberg et al. (2002) found 50% of patients with body dysmorphic disorder also have avoidant personality disorder. Regardless of the exact percentage, it is fair to say that avoidant personality disorder or avoidant personality traits cannot be ignored when working with the BDD population because it so frequently co-exists. I conceptualize avoidant personality disorder as being on the extreme end of the social anxiety disorder spectrum where social and interpersonal avoidances go well beyond situational contexts and are pervasive throughout all areas of a person's life. Many characteristics of BDD are similar to that of the avoidant personality structure: Introverted, self-conscious, hyper-vigilant to criticism or judgment, social isolation, and innate sensitivity.

These are the same personality characteristics that inexorably influence the course of treating body dysmorphic disorder. Some BDD sufferers avoid entering therapy, while many who do begin the process are very guarded and highly precautious. The avoidant personality features often become very apparent when the clinician begins to discuss behavioral therapy and related exercises that will entail the patient experiencing emotional discomfort and interacting with others. It is not unusual that during this phase of treatment the patient might be late for therapy or may begin missing sessions. Sometimes the anticipatory anxiety about upcoming behavioral exercises is so profound that the patient abruptly discontinues therapy. This often occurs with opportune justifications such as "not being able to afford to continue therapy" or "I am getting too busy at work." Sometimes the patient just disappears from treatment altogether and does not respond to attempts by the clinician to address the situation.

In my clinical experience, avoidant personality disorder is the personality disorder that most frequently co-occurs with body dysmorphic disorder. This being stated, I think the avoidance behavior that is so prevalent with BDD patients may not always necessarily be avoidant personality disorder or avoidant personality traits, but can also be a symptom of the body dysmorphic disorder itself. There are individuals who enter treatment and meet DSM-5 criteria for avoidant personality disorder, but as their BDD begins to subside, their avoidant tendencies simultaneously decrease. This rapid change would not occur if a diathesis for avoidant personality was present. Thus it can be difficult to discern if an individual's avoidant behaviors are a result of an avoidant personality structure or are symptoms of active body dysmorphic disorder. I have observed that it is often a combination of both that contribute to the individual exhibiting avoidant personality and behavioral characteristics.

It can be difficult to differentiate between avoidance as a result of body dysmorphic disorder and avoidant personality characteristics, but irrespective of the exact diagnosis, it is important for the treating clinician to assume that the patient probably has some tendencies to avoid. I always prefer to pace the treatment process to make sure that I am gaining rapport with the patient rather than racing to fix the symptoms that have brought them into therapy. I find that establishing a connection to the client with avoidant personality traits increases the chances of them remaining in therapy when difficult subject matter arises.

This difficult matter often includes the commencement of exposure and response prevention behavioral exercises. Being exposed to uncomfortable situations is challenging enough for individuals without avoidant personality traits. It is not unusual that patients with avoidant personality characteristics bolt from therapy as certain behavioral exercises are introduced to the therapeutic regimen. Even after discussing this in depth with patients who match this personality profile, this still may not be sufficient to prevent them from abandoning therapy. There are occasions when I have identified patients who have blatant avoidant personality traits that I will not attempt to do exposure and response prevention therapy with, knowing that to do so would likely lead them to discontinuing treatment altogether. This decision needs to be a judgment call made by the clinician and based upon their rapport and overall connectivity with the patient.

Dependent Personality and BDD

Dependent personality disorder is defined as a pervasive and excessive need to be taken care of by others. Individuals with a dependent personality structure have difficulty making everyday decisions and constantly seek reassurance from other people. They may have difficulty initiating daily tasks or life goals, feel helpless when they are not receiving support from other people, and may jump from one relationship to the next in order to avoid the prospect of needing to care for themselves (American Psychiatric Association 2013).

Although comorbidity of dependent personality disorder with body dysmorphic disorder may not appear as prevalent or as overt as other personality traits such as avoidant personality disorder, it does commonly co-occur. This being stated, sometimes it can be difficult to discern whether the individual with BDD has a diathesis for dependent personality traits, or if they have become dependent upon others as body dysmorphic disorder symptoms gradually worsen and interfere with their capacity to function. Sometimes both scenarios exist: The individual with BDD already has a dependent personality structure and the advent of their body image symptoms becomes the rationale for needing to be taken care of by other people.

Individuals with body dysmorphic disorder and dependent personality disorder may remain in relationships that they would admit are not ideal but that are safe and provide excessive reassurance. These relationships do not only include intimate relationships, but often also pertain to parent-child relationships that are highly co-dependent and enmeshed. The reassurance may include both body related concerns as well as support for general life decisions that the individual does not feel capable of solving or completing on their own. Although this may temporarily ease fears of not being self-efficacious, it is definitely not conducive to recovery from body dysmorphic disorder. Recovering from BDD involves participating in life and experiencing the rejections and failures that will inevitably occur. Excessive dependence upon another person will significantly interfere with the process of rehabilitation from body dysmorphic disorder. Because of this, it is important that these personality traits are identified by the treating clinician and openly discussed with the patient.

Narcissistic Personality and BDD

A personality structure that can present with symptomology similar to that of body dysmorphic disorder is narcissistic personality disorder. Individuals with these personality characteristics can present with symptoms that also match the DSM-5 criteria for BDD, having an excessive preoccupation with a perceived or slight defect in their appearance. When these individuals enter treatment, they do not necessarily fit the flashy, attention-seeking, self-centered or aloof stereotype that is commonly associated with the narcissist. Similar to body dysmorphic disorder patients, they enter therapy preoccupied with a body part perceived as defective and are usually very depressed as a result of this. The depressive state masks the more obvious characteristics of narcissistic personality traits as they have been profoundly humbled by the supposed physical defect or perceived change in their appearance.

The narcissist with a body image disturbance feels threatened that the perceived appearance defect will impact how they get their needs met from other people. Their body, how it appears and how it performs in relation to others, has become the apparatus by which their self-esteem is maintained. Image and performance are vital for them to sustain the superficial veneer that conceals fundamental feelings of inadequacy (Young et al. 2003). Although individuals with body dysmorphic disorder also feel essentially flawed, there is much more focus on the body part itself and less emphasis on how it will sustain their overall image to the outside world. The need for external recognition and approbation is much more pronounced with body image disturbances that stem from a narcissistic personality structure. Individuals with BDD usually tend to avoid external interactions because they do not want to draw attention to the body features of concern.

The countertransference that a clinician experiences in the room with body image clients can be useful in discerning the origin of the body image disturbance. The interaction between the patient and the therapist is usually synonymous with how the individual interacts with people outside of the therapy office. Thus the feelings that the clinician has during contact with their client are probably very similar to how other people experience them. When working with body image patients that have a narcissistic personality structure, I often begin to feel as if I am just an object in the room, as if I was a piece of furniture. These individuals have learned that in order to feel worthy they must perform and gain respect and recognition from other people. Even the slightest perceived flaw will be perceived as perilous as it jeopardizes the foundation of self-worth (McWilliams 1994).

Distinguishing between body dysmorphic disorder and a body image disturbance deriving from a narcissistic personality can be very difficult during the initial stages of treatment. Regardless of its origin, the body image disturbance needs to be treated, thus it is important for the therapist to eventually discern the source of the body image concerns in order to determine the direction most conducive for treatment. Psychotherapy with a body focused narcissist will differ from the course of treatment with someone whose symptoms do not derive from a personality disorder. The progression of determining the roots of the body image disturbance occurs as part of the therapy process and sometimes may take weeks or even months to accurately discern. During this process, the therapist-patient interface will most likely reveal truths about how the individual relates to others and how their appearance serves to regulate these interactions.

Narcissists have the capacity to take in admiration and attention but are unable to comprehend true genuine love (Young et al. 2003). The idea of someone authentically caring about who they are rather than how they look or what they do is a concept they cannot relate to. They experience other people as objects that provide a narcissistic supply to maintain their self-worth; to allow other people close enough to establish a sincere intimate relationship comes with the risk of being exposed as inadequate. A body image preoccupation that stems from narcissist personality traits is one of a multitude of manifestations of narcissism.

If it were not expressed through body image, it would appear through other measurable and visible content. Regardless of the subject matter, the narcissistic individual needs to continuously seek external validation in order to support the very fragile façade that camouflages extreme insecurities and intense loneliness. The unending pursuit of exterior flattery inhibits them from ever truly connecting with another person and getting very basic nurture and attachment needs met.

I once evaluated a male patient who came to me self-referred and convinced that he had all the symptoms of body dysmorphic disorder. He described to me that he was concerned that he might be losing his hair and that he wanted me to fix him so that he could stop thinking about it. He stated that women had always found him attractive because of his long, flowing locks and he was worried that if he became bald he would no longer receive this attention. When I asked him what it might mean if he did not receive as much attention from women, he seemed quite baffled, as if I should know the answer to such an obvious question. I explained to him that I did not want to make assumptions because I had just met him and could better understand his concerns if he explained his experience to me. He admitted that even though he was currently in a relationship, he still liked to flirt with other women because this would make him feel good about himself.

This individual reported that he had consulted several dermatologists who had clarified that he was not losing his hair, but that this reassurance did not stop him from compulsively checking his hairline to see if it was receding. He told me that these constant checking behaviors were interfering with his life and that prior to meeting me he had met with two other psychotherapists. When I inquired why he had not stayed with either one of these clinicians and had come to consult with me, he remarked that their feedback had not helped him at all and that he wanted to work with a BDD expert. He then persisted to ask me about where I had attended university, who had supervised my clinical training, and again inquired if I would be able to solve his problem so that he could get back to his normal life as soon as possible. I clarified that psychotherapy would take time and that ultimately it would not be me fixing him, rather, the process would entail us working together to look at a multitude of issues that might explain why he was so distraught about his perceived hair loss. This was obviously not the answer that he wanted to hear: I never heard from him again after this initial session.

This patient was not necessarily incorrect when he stated that he had body dysmorphic disorder because the presentation of his symptoms met the criteria for BDD as defined by the American Psychiatric Association. He was very preoccupied with a body part that he perceived as defective and this was causing significant distress in his life. I would definitely consider this example as a body image disturbance but would hesitate in making the body dysmorphic disorder diagnosis. There is a pattern of externalization in which this individual obtains information about himself and his identity. His hair serves as the interface between himself and his interactions with the outside world, and how he perceives others' reactions to his hair determines if he is fundamentally worthwhile.

Beyond the body themes, the patient is looking to be fixed by someone on the outside who will be able to take away the problem and who has the credentials worthy of such a task. People, in this case women and doctors, are objects which this individual exploits and devalues in order to maintain an equilibrium of sense of self. There is also a lack of capacity to realize that other people have thoughts and experiences different from his, as seen when he became perplexed that I even needed to ask him the question what it would mean if he did not receive attention from women. These overt externalized motifs are the antithesis of the majority of body dysmorphic disorder cases in which individuals regularly internalize thoughts and feelings. There is of course the possibility that this person had both narcissistic personality structure and BDD but, at least based on the initial evaluation, my speculation is that the body image disturbance was a result of pathological narcissism.

Although many body dysmorphic disorder cases involve a preoccupation with an aspect of the face or head, it is not unusual that individuals will also be worried about body parts below the neck. Unlike the head or face, it is much easier to disguise or camouflage other areas of the body, including genitalia. Most male BDD patients that present for treatment do not specify their penis as a main concern, but I have treated a number of men who were primarily distressed about the size and shape of their penis. This preoccupation regarding genitalia not only involved the appearance of their sexual organ but also their performance during intercourse.

Something that stood out to me with these particular cases is that the men were so distracted by a need for reassurance that there was barely any recognition of another person being involved: The sexual partner existed as an object used to acquire admiration rather than for a reciprocal intimate relationship. "Testing out" the genitalia with a partner would take priority over all other relational matters, including the needs and desires of the significant other. This is another example where a BDD diagnosis could be made because the men are preoccupied with a perceived defect in their appearance. With genitalia concerns, I am always cautious about making a body dysmorphic disorder diagnosis if I observe a pattern of externalized issues: I definitely consider the possibility that a narcissistic personality structure might be the genesis of the genitalia fixation.

"I'm Worried That I'm a Narcissist"

I have had many body dysmorphic disorder patients tell me that one of the reasons they did not disclose their body related issues to their previous therapists is that they were worried they would be labeled as vain or narcissistic. When this concern is brought to my attention, I let the patient know that if they truly were a narcissist they most likely would not be having this conversation with me. I explain that individuals who have significant narcissistic traits usually lack insight into this predisposition and usually are the last to notice that they may actually be narcissistic. The narcissist often does not care what the outside world thinks about them. This differs greatly from the average BDD patient who is very concerned about how other people perceive them, most certainly do not want to offend others, and who also have the capacity to empathize.

I once worked with a male BDD client who from his first day in treatment stated that he always thought that he was a narcissist because he could not stop thinking about how unattractive he was and how he felt several of his facial features were so misshapen. He admitted that he was as ashamed of being what he thought was a narcissist as he was about his supposed body defects. He reported that his tormenting body image symptoms had started many years previously and that several years ago he had mentioned this preoccupation to his mother who commented that, "anyone who thinks as much about their appearance as he does must be a narcissist."

This comment by his own mother only validated his belief that he was narcissistic for not being able to stop thinking about how unattractive he felt. He interpreted this comment as meaning that he must be bad if he was so concerned about how he looked; he confided in me that he "so badly just wanted to look normal and that if he could turn off the thoughts about his appearance he would gladly do so." It took almost a half year in psychotherapy for the patient to really believe that not only was he not a narcissist, but that he actually needed more healthy narcissism to counter his constant process of automatically internalizing negative thoughts and emotions.

The majority of patients that come through my practice do not have narcissistic personality disorder. In fact, the majority of them fit the patient profile previously described: They do not want to be judged as narcissistic or entitled and very much care about other peoples' feelings, along with just wanting the constant barrage of self-deprecating thoughts about their appearance to cease. Patients that do have significant narcissistic personality traits are unaware that they might fit this profile and rarely express concern that they might be a narcissist.

One of the methods I use to distinguish between body dysmorphic disorder and narcissistic personality structure is identifying internalization versus externalization: The individual with BDD turns their feelings inward whereas the narcissist externalizes emotional material. The narcissist will blame other people, exterior events, and eventually their clinician for their failures, while the complete opposite is true with the highly self-deprecating body dysmorphic disorder patient. Although narcissism and BDD are on opposite ends of the spectrum, I conceptualize the body dysmorphic disorder experience as narcissism turned inward: Archaic beliefs and inner experiences that activate feelings of shame and inferiority that are diverted inbound. Whereas the narcissist externalizes and attributes their failures to the body, the individual with BDD filters emotions though a body part as this becomes a repository for shameful and other uncomfortable internal experiences.

Because the body dysmorphic disorder patient feels as if they are inherently defective, they very rarely self-aggrandize. They are also very sensitive to rejection and want to make sure that they are liked and are not disapproved of by others. Individuals with BDD interpret self-aggrandizing as "being narcissistic or doing something bad that might result in a person deploring them." This is most certainly not the case with the narcissist who regularly participates in self-aggrandizing conversation or behaviors and can be indifferent to what other people think of them.

Although the narcissist feels fundamentally inadequate at the core, they are unaware of this because they are so well armored by their narcissistic defenses. The individual with body dysmorphic disorder may also be unaware that internal processes may be responsible for such hyperfocus on their bodies, but because they internalize emotional material, they have a greater capacity to look inward during the process of psychotherapy. This is usually not the case with the narcissist and often serves as a clue in determining whether a patient's body image disturbance is actually BDD or a manifestation of a narcissistic personality structure.

Borderline Personality and BDD

In the late 19th century psychiatrists began to describe a group of patients who were not fully psychotic but who also lacked the insight and therapeutic adherence common with neurotic patients. These individuals seemed to exist at the border between psychosis and neurosis (Rosse 1890). By the middle of the twentieth century the terms borderline state, borderline syndrome, or borderline personality were used to refer to these individuals who appeared too sane to be considered psychotic, but simultaneously too disorganized to be classified as neurotic (Grinker, Werble, and Drye 1968). Individuals within the neurotic range of character structure have a much more integrated sense of their identity as is manifested through consistency in behavior and an ability to understand that other people are multifarious and have separate identities (Erikson 1968).

At the opposite end of the continuum from the neurotics are the individuals who are organized at a psychotic level. Unlike the neurotic, they have severe deficits in comprehending their identity and are much more disorganized, frequently including delusions, hallucinations, and referential thinking. A person with borderline personality structure exists on the continuum between neurosis and psychosis. These patients rarely exhibit the hallucinations and delusions present with psychotic individuals, but are much more unstable, unpredictable, chaotic, and more miserable than neurotic patients. They also have identity confusion, but not to the same severe degree as the psychotic does.

I recall a conversation that I had with an associate many years ago regarding the treatment of body dysmorphic disorder. He commented that there seems to be two types of BDD patients: Those that presented more like obsessive-compulsive disorder and the "other" group that did not respond to the classic cognitive-behavioral therapies utilized with the former. I agreed with his opinion because I had also observed that some BDD patients were compliant with behavioral therapeutic interventions and responded to these techniques. Many of the other body image patients had difficulty following through with recommendations or chose not to comply at all even though they had sought out professional expertise. In hindsight, I believe we were in essence defining symptoms of body image disturbance as they existed on the continuum from neurotic to psychotic, as well as in the space defined as borderline.

I use the phrase body image disturbance interchangeably with body dysmorphic disorder. I began using this phrase to define the patients who on the surface appear to have symptoms of body dysmorphic disorder: These particular individuals enter treatment presenting with the same angst and symptomology that I witness with classic BDD cases. They report that their major disturbance and primary reason for seeking treatment is body and appearance related. They also match the criteria for BDD as defined in the fifth edition of the American Psychiatric Association's *Diagnostic and Statistical Manual of Mental Disorders*: A preoccupation with an imagined or very slight defect that clinically causes significant distress or impairment in social, occupational, or other important areas of functioning; and, the individual's symptoms must not be better accounted for by another disorder, for example, an eating disorder.

The subgroup of body image patients that I am alluding to are those who may have borderline personality disorder (BPD). These are individuals who are easily overwhelmed by emotions and affect, lack a stable sense of identity, and usually feel that they are inherently bad. Individuals with borderline personality disorder frequently have unstable relationships that alternate between the extremes of idealizing and devaluing others. They experience chronic feelings of emptiness, fear the possibility of being abandoned, and often are impulsive and self-destructive (Biskin and Paris 2012). Like other personality disorders, these individuals usually enter treatment for symptoms of other disorders, substance abuse, or as a result of impulsive actions such as self-injurious behaviors. Many individuals with borderline personality structure have been in and out of mental health facilities and under the care of multiple clinicians before they are properly diagnosed.

Looking back on my earlier years of treating body dysmorphic disorder, I probably encountered many more borderline personality disorder patients than I was aware of at the time. In retrospect I believe that I had been so focused on the desperate body related presentation of these patients that I erroneously assumed that BDD was the culprit. After all, the majority of patients that sought treatment for body image disturbances would arrive in a tumultuous state. Many of these individuals who I now realize probably had borderline personality structure would frequently be involved with chaotic relationships and usually did not complete the course of therapy. At the time I misinterpreted these symptoms because I was viewing them within the context of body dysmorphic disorder and a cognitive-behavioral therapeutic paradigm.

Over the years I became much more familiar with this group of body image patients who initially appeared to have BDD, but during the course of treatment seemed to more accurately match the criteria for borderline personality disorder. As I became more proficient at making the borderline diagnosis, I also began to notice that there were many similarities between the two diagnoses. Body dysmorphic disorder and borderline personality disorder patients both often lack a developed, integrated sense of self and both often have difficulty in interpersonal and intimate relationships. A theme of borderline personality symptomology is the lack of an integrated sense of self. This includes chronic feelings of emptiness and identity diffusion whereas the self is organized around incongruent internalized representations that do not map onto the individual's actual experience (Bateman and Fonagy 2006). Individuals with BDD have an internalized image of how they should appear that does not match their experience when they see their reflection or see a picture of themselves.

The individual with borderline personality disorder is intolerant of aloneness because the "bad" self is experienced when alone, while the lack of self-cohesion inevitably leads to interpersonal chaos. The borderline experiences others as an extension of themselves rather than as separate and unique entities. These individuals exist in a quandary: When they become close to someone they panic because of fears of engulfment, and when they separate they feel abandoned (Masterson 1976). Individuals with untreated body dysmorphic disorder are also often unable to initiate or sustain intimate relationships. This may be a result of isolation, avoidance, or other related BDD symptoms that blatantly interfere with normalized social interactions that eventually lead to intimacy; or perhaps the body image symptoms are a result of a borderline diathesis in which a body part becomes a safe transitional object. The body not only becomes the lightning rod for the experience of the "bad" self, but it also serves to hinder the individual from connecting with others. This body image dilemma parallels that of the borderline who remains in an endless cycle of fearing both attachment and abandonment.

Suicidal gestures and self-injurious behaviors are very common features of borderline personality disorder. This is often a reaction to real or perceived abandonment and the intolerance of aloneness as the "bad" self is unbearable thus must be punished. There is also a very high rate of suicidal ideation and suicide attempts with body dysmorphic disorder. In a study involving 200 body dysmorphic disorder subjects, it was determined that 27.5% had attempted suicide and 78% had lifetime suicidal ideation (Phillips et al. 2005a). With BDD patients, suicidal ideation is often correlated with a profound hopelessness that they will never achieve their internalized representation of attractiveness; this may also occur after a cosmetic procedure where the physical outcome of the surgery does not match the patient's internal image. Related to this is the belief that unless the body part is corrected they will never be loved and will always remain alone, leaving suicide as a viable option in order to avoid such a bleak existence.

Suicidal ideation and anger at the surgically corrected body part or at the surgeon who performed a cosmetic procedure can be conceptualized as the externalized version of the borderline patient who turns on the "bad" self. It is not uncommon that patients contact me for treatment soon after they receive cosmetic surgeries, some of which have been undertaken impulsively. They present with florid BDD symptoms and are often very angry at themselves for deciding to have the operation as well as being furious at the surgeon for not carrying out the procedure exactly as they described. Often they report "not being able to recognize themselves" and wishing that they had never proceeded in the first place. Individuals who have undergone procedures that entail implants, such as breast, chin, or cheek implants, sometimes report the experience of having a "bad foreign object" within them that they want expelled.

Undergoing plastic surgery and other cosmetic procedures is so prevalent in many areas of the United States that it has become a socially acceptable behavior within the culture. It is not currently viewed as deviant conduct and is much more accessible to the mainstream because of an abundance of cosmetic surgery practitioners along with technological advances in medicine. Within the context of our culture these procedures are considered to be acts of beautification, altering the aesthetic to more closely resemble what is currently viewed as attractive.

It needs to be considered that perhaps certain individuals who undergo cosmetic operations and who are also predisposed to a body image disturbance might well be partaking in an act of mutilation under the guise of socially acceptable behavior. Patients with borderline personality symptoms that engage in self-mutilating acts such as cutting themselves with a razor blade are promptly categorized as participating in self-harming behaviors. This behavior is not considered socially acceptable thus rarely goes under the radar. On the other hand, cosmetic procedures that are impulsively sought out may also be a form of self-mutilation and an act of punishing the "bad" self, while soothing unpleasant emotions connected with aloneness and abandonment fears. This might help to explain why so many individuals with body image disorders only experience ephemeral relief after receiving a cosmetic procedure. If a behavior is not culturally interpreted as mutilation, it can much more easily be construed as an act of self-improvement rather than as a self-destructive behavior.

The borderline personality adheres to what is described as a teleological stance in which physical evidence rather than a person's intentions provides the foundation of interpersonal judgment (Bateman and Fonagy 2006). This means that the borderline patient understands interpersonal motives in terms of the physical, tangible actions rather than mental outcomes. Individuals with body dysmorphic disorder have great difficulty with the internal representation of how they look thus frequently turn to visible physical feedback—such as their reflection, reassurance from others, and cosmetic procedures—to confirm that they are acceptable. BDD sufferers frequently lack the capacity to accurately interpret others' expressions and reactions, and thus return to the familiarity of a body part, albeit a source of distress, shame, and disgust.

Sometimes patients who have seriously considered cosmetic surgeries, but have yet to follow through, want reassurance from me that this will remain an option if therapy does not prevail. Although I do not condone the cosmetic route, I also do not tell the individual that it will never be an option. The patient is more inclined to remain focused on their BDD treatment when they have the knowledge that the surgical alternative still exists. This is analogous to individuals with borderline personality structure who cling onto the fantasy of suicide knowing that within the depths of their misery there will always be an escape if all else fails.

Natural physical changes that occur with ageing, such as real or perceived male pattern balding, wrinkles, and the loss of skin elasticity, are often very disconcerting for those with body image disturbances. Many patients have admitted to me that physical changes from ageing activate their body image issues and in turn lead to depression, suicidal ideation, and even suicide attempts. If an area of the body is considered to be fundamentally flawed and has become the transitional focus for the "bad" self, it must not have been an integrated and solid source of identity to begin with. The body becomes the most tangible form of self for those with identity diffusion, thus any unwanted aesthetic changes to the body will inevitably destabilize the teleological stance. A disruption in the teleological mode threatens cohesion and may lead to self-harming behaviors or impulsive surgical procedures as the individual desperately attempts to re-establish coherence.

Bodily changes that are not related to ageing can also be highly disturbing for these individuals. It is much easier to observe daily changes with the skin and hair than with other areas of the body such as the nose that only gradually alters shape over a lifetime. Hair can look and feel different when wet or styled with various products, when blowing in the wind, and at different lengths. The skin is also never constant as most people experience blemishes and other natural variations with the epidermis.

This is highly disconcerting for individuals who rely on object constancy to discern a sense of self. Skin picking in an attempt to correct an undesirable change that might also be conceptualized as a self-mutilating behavior. As the individual picks at their skin, they become more distraught as they witness further damage created by their own doing. This only deepens their sense of self-loathing and misery as the bodily object, the skin, appears further from their internalized representation of it.

Whether change in appearance is a result of the ageing process or whether it is self-induced, it often elicits a sense of fear and panic. For those individuals with a body image disturbance and an underlying borderline diathesis, the solidity of the body has become the transitional object defining identity and connecting them with the outside world. As previously described, the borderline fears abandonment while simultaneously dreading the possibility of becoming engulfed as they alternate between the experience of idealizing and devaluing others (Masterson 1976). The consistency of the body, although perceived as defective and bad, provides a tangible source of connectivity with the outside world because their internalized experience is so empty. Fluctuations in this bodily consistency can elicit the same panic and terror that a borderline patient experiences from changes in an interpersonal relationship.

Borderline Character Structure Versus Body Dysmorphic Disorder

The following examples describe the differences between body dysmorphic disorder and borderline personality disorder, and then compare the similarities between the two diagnoses. These can serve as possible clues that the presenting individual may have borderline personality traits or may even have borderline personality disorder as their primary diagnosis. It is important to distinguish the etiology of a body image disturbance in order to determine the therapeutic route most beneficial for the patient. Body image disturbance cases are usually complex thus by no means should these criteria alone be utilized to make a final diagnosis of a personality disorder.

Differences Between Body Dysmorphic Disorder and Borderline Personality Disorder

Emotional Dysregulation Versus Habituation

Patients with borderline personality disorder lack the capacity to tolerate the emotions that arise during behavioral therapy, specifically exposure and response prevention (ERP). This is usually a clue that the individual presenting with a body image disturbance might have borderline personality disorder. In my experience in practicing exposure and response prevention therapy with body dysmorphic disorder patients, even individuals with very severe BDD symptoms have the capacity to tolerate the emotions activated during these behavioral exercises. This is not the case with individuals with borderline personality disorder: These individuals frequently become emotionally dysregulated when participating in ERP exercises and rarely ever habituate to the stimuli presented. The individual without the borderline predisposition can tolerate the spike in emotional discomfort long enough to experience a decrease in discomfort. This does not happen with the borderline patient who often becomes confused, frustrated, and discouraged that they are not feeling any better.

Anger: Externalization Versus Internalization

Patients with borderline personality disorder generally externalize emotions, for instance, "this is happening to me because of you" or "you the therapist must fix me." Intense anger is frequently the emotion that is externalized. The majority of individuals with body dysmorphic disorder internalize their emotions: They automatically turn inward in an attempt to find an explanation for many situations, especially interpersonal scenarios that they believe are a result of some personal, internal deficit. Many individuals with BDD avoid expressing anger because they do not want other people to disapprove of them. The avoidance and suppression of anger will inevitably be directed inward and will eventually manifest as indignation toward aesthetic features of the body.

Feedback: Help-Reject Versus Receptive

A pattern of help-reject interactions with the clinician can frequently be observed with patients who have borderline personality disorder. This is not usually the case with BDD patients without a borderline personality diathesis. With the exception of the rigidly held beliefs associated with their supposed physical defects, BDD patients are often quite receptive to feedback from the clinician.

Abandonment and Rejection

The individual with a borderline personality diathesis usually experiences terror surrounding the possibility of rejection or abandonment. Even perceived abandonment can activate the feeling of spiraling out of control as if they are falling into oblivion. Individuals with body dysmorphic disorder are also very rejection sensitive but their reaction to actual or perceived rejection is one of a profoundly internalized feeling of despair; this experience is usually interpreted as a result of the perceived physical flaw.

Inflexible Thinking

Patients with borderline personality disorder often present with an extremely rigid, all-or-nothing, absolute thought process that extends beyond body image related themes and almost always interferes with interpersonal relationships. Individuals with BDD may also have all-or-nothing thinking, but the inflexibility usually involves the body area of concern or matters associated with it. They are usually much more amenable to considering alternative possibilities regarding content that is not body related.

Cosmetic Procedures: Impulsive Versus Discrete

It is not unusual for patients with a borderline personality related body image disturbance to impulsively undergo multiple, simultaneous cosmetic procedures. This differs from the body dysmorphic disorder patient without a borderline diathesis who carefully weighs the pros versus the cons of having a cosmetic procedure performed. Also, individuals with BDD who do receive cosmetic procedures are often significantly more discrete about it; they are already very ashamed of the supposed defect and the last thing they want to do is draw further attention to it. This differs from patients with borderline personality disorder who after receiving a cosmetic procedure may share this information indiscriminately.

Self-Destructive Behaviors

Patients with borderline personality disorder often have a history of self-destructive behaviors, many that are done impulsively, and may include polysubstance abuse; poor judgment in sexual encounters; binging behaviors regarding any content from shopping to eating; skin picking (see below); socially acceptable self-injurious behaviors such as impulsive cosmetic procedures, body piercings, and tattoos (see below). Individuals with body dysmorphic disorder and without a borderline diagnosis usually do not have a history of self-destructive behaviors. If there is a history of substance abuse, it is usually directly correlated with the BDD sufferer's attempt to ameliorate the body related intrusive thoughts.

SKIN PICKING

The preoccupation with skin is one of the most common body dysmorphic disorder concerns, and the act of picking is usually an attempt to make the skin appear less defective. Skin pickers with a borderline diathesis also want to improve the appearance of their skin, but often report needing to pick in order to "remove the bad stuff from inside their pores" and report that they will not feel better until they accomplish this. These individuals have extreme difficulty tolerating the experience that something "foreign" is within their body and usually report that they will only feel soothed once they can remove the "yucky stuff" from their skin. Individuals with body dysmorphic disorder who pick at their skin and who do not have a borderline personality diathesis usually do so in an attempt to make their skin look better, or at least less defective: The behavior is not driven by an impulsive need to expel an internal experience of disgust, badness, or evil.

TATTOOS AND BODY PIERCINGS

Within the timeframe that this book was published, excessive body piercings and tattoos have become a socially acceptable form of body modification and self-expression and are by no means an indicator that an individual has borderline personality disorder. But something that I am observing much more frequently, and patients with border-line personality are reporting to me, is that the pain associated with body piercing and the tattooing process provides the same release and relief that less socially acceptable behaviors, such as cutting, may have previously served. Sometimes patients with borderline personality disorder get tattoos to cover scars from where they had previously cut themselves.

I have worked with individuals with body dysmorphic disorder who meticulously organize and plan where they want a tattoo placed on their body, sometimes to distract from an area of their appearance that they dislike. They are usually very cautious about making any changes to their body out of the concern that they might be dissatisfied after the fact. This differs from the random, unorganized display of tattoos impulsively inked onto the body, something I have observed with individuals who do have borderline personality traits. I would never make a diagnosis of a personality disorder based on tattoo patterns, but it is sometimes a clue that I might be working with an individual with borderline personality characteristics.

Relationships: Chaotic Versus Avoidant

Many patients with borderline personality disorder have a history of cha-otic interpersonal relationships that fluctuate between the extremes of idealization to devaluation. Individuals with body dysmorphic disorder do not fit this profile. Patients with BDD often have difficulty with inter-personal relationships, but this is usually because the BDD symptoms interfere with them attaching to someone to begin with. Once they do connect with someone, there are rarely the chaotic, whirlwind interper-sonal interactions that occur with individuals with borderline personality traits. Often there is a deficit of quality relationships because of avoid-ant behaviors, but the relationships that they do have rarely vacillate between idealization and devaluation.

Identity: Vacuous Versus Preoccupied

Individuals with borderline personality disorder may experience a very vacuous sense of emptiness and missing identity that seemingly cannot be filled unless their "defective" body part is corrected. They experience their sense of self and others as fragmented, distorted, and superficial and this leads to difficulty reading other people. Body dysmorphic disorder patients are preoccupied and tormented by aspects of their appearance, but they do not usually present with the same level of misery and intensive vacuity experienced by those with borderline personality disorder. In body dysmorphic disorder, a body part that the individual believes is defective takes on an extensive identity of it's own. Although so much of how the BDD patient feels about himself is filtered through the body part, it is not unusual that they have a semblance of a sense of identity beyond their appearance.

Multiple Diagnoses

Many borderline personality disorder patients have a long history of multiple physical and psychiatric diagnoses that often morph from one to the next but never get fully resolved. Body dysmorphic disorder patients may have a history of multiple misdiagnoses, for instance obsessive-compulsive disorder, social anxiety disorder, or even attention deficit disorder: The abstruse nature of BDD frequently leads to inaccurate diagnoses. This differs from the borderline patient who may report an extensive history of ambiguous physical and mental health diagnoses, including body image disturbances and often a long list of failed medication trials.

Clinging Versus Filtering

Borderline personality disorder patients may "cling onto a diagnosis." A diagnosis is something that is tangible and has a definition and substance. For the individual with borderline personality disorder who experiences a very diffuse sense of self, a diagnosis is a concrete object that can help organize an empty internal experience. Both a body part and a diagnosis can provide a solid object onto which the borderline patient can make sense of their existence. To let go of the diagnosis might leave the individual feeling absolutely bereft of any identity whatsoever. A body dysmorphic disorder diagnosis can quickly become an identity and the object to which the individual with borderline personality disorder attaches.

Many patients with body dysmorphic disorder do not believe that they have BDD because they are certain there is something factually defective with their appearance. With the patients who do acknowledge and accept that they may have a psychological condition called BDD, the diagnosis does not become their identity. Rarely do individuals with BDD want or need to have the diagnosis of body dysmorphic disorder: If they are in acceptance that they match BDD criteria, they most certainly do not want to openly share this diagnosis because the last thing that they want to do is draw attention to the body areas that they consider to be defective. Whereas the patient with borderline personality disorder "clings onto" both the supposed aesthetic defect and the diagnosis of BDD, the body dysmorphic disorder patient without a borderline diathesis experiences their supposed defect as a conduit by which they filter uncomfortable emotions.

Devaluing Versus Misunderstood

Individuals with borderline personality disorder have often worked with many different psychotherapists and psychiatrists and usually only for a brief period of time, after which they frequently devalue the services of these mental health practitioners. There is often a history of lack of compliance with treatment. This is always a red flag that the individual may have borderline personality traits. Body dysmorphic disorder patients may change mental health practitioners if they feel that they are not understood or if they are too ashamed to discuss the body image related material with the practitioner; this differs from the borderline pattern of behavior of looking to be rescued and fixed by a clinician who ultimately can never meet the expectations of the patient.

Victim Versus Self-Blame

The borderline personality disorder patient often exists in the perpetual role of victim and blames external factors such as people and events as the cause of their suffering. The individual with body dysmorphic disorder exists on the complete opposite end of the continuum: They attribute fundamental internal defects, or their appearance, as the source of their issues.

Deficits in Mentalization

Individuals with borderline personality disorder are not able to mentalize. Mentalization is a person's ability to understand that other people have experiences, thoughts, and feelings different from their own (Bateman and Fonagy 2004). The individual with body dysmorphic disorder may have poor insight with regards to the body related symptoms, but in other areas of their life they are able to distinguish that how they experience the world is different from the next person. The individual with borderline personality disorder is unable to mentalize and discern whether their issues derive from disruptive interpersonal relationships or from their body image symptoms. The observation that the patient lacks the ability to mentalize can often be a clue that the individual may have a borderline or related Cluster B personality diathesis. Note: Individuals with body dysmorphic disorder can also have difficulty mentalizing if they have active symptoms with referential thinking. For instance, automatically assuming that another person must be thinking about their "physical flaw" and losing the capacity to consider that maybe this thought never crossed the other person's mind.

Transparent Versus Concealed Bodily Shame

Patients with body dysmorphic disorder that do not have a borderline personality character structure are usually very discrete about their body area of concern because of the profound shame associated with it; they are also very hesitant to disclose that they have a body dysmorphic disorder diagnosis. This is often not the case with individuals who have a body image disturbance related to borderline personality disorder: They may be very open about their perceived aesthetic defects, the cosmetic procedures that they have received, and about their diagnosis, which they are usually convinced is body dysmorphic disorder. This is not to say that they are void of shame, but in my opinion the experience of shame associated with a supposed physical defect is significantly more pronounced in patients with body dysmorphic disorder. BDD is frequently misdiagnosed and under-diagnosed because patients may not disclose information necessary for an accurate diagnosis due to the significant shame associated with their appearance.

Similarities Between BDD and Borderline Personality Disorder

Interpersonal Hypersensitivity

Both populations are highly sensitive to interpersonal rejection. Individuals with body dysmorphic disorder often interpret rejection as evidence that their supposed aesthetic defect must truly be the problem. The fear of interpersonal rejection usually revolves around the belief that they are getting rejected because of how they look. With borderline personality disorder the hypersensitivity to rejection is more frequently associated with fear of abandonment.

Misinterpretation of Facial Affects

Hand-in-hand with a hypersensitivity to interpersonal rejection, individuals with BDD and borderline personality disorder often misinterpret facial affect and nonverbal forms of communication. Untreated body dysmorphic disorder patients often interpret facial cues inaccurately. For instance, seeing someone smile could be interpreted that they are being laughed at because of their supposed defect. The BDD patient may interpret lack of eye contact from another person as concrete evidence that they are too ungainly to look at.

Extremely Rigid or Absolute Thoughts and Beliefs

Individuals with borderline personality disorder are often extremely absolute with many of their thoughts and beliefs. This is also frequently the case with body dysmorphic disorder, but usually the inflexible thoughts revolve around the preoccupation with the body part deemed defective.

Teleological Stance

The borderline personality interprets physical evidence rather than a person's intentions as the foundation of interpersonal judgment (Fonagy 2000). Individuals with body dysmorphic disorder regularly utilize what they interpret as physical evidence, their aesthetic features, to confirm that they look acceptable.

Existing on a Continuum From Neurotic to Psychotic

Not all body dysmorphic disorder sufferers are delusional, but many experience symptoms described as overvalued ideation. Individuals with overvalued ideas about the perceived defect fluctuate between acknowledging the possibility that symptoms may be a result of a psychiatric condition, to beliefs that are held with unwavering conviction. Those with borderline personality disorder also experience a vacillation between neurotic and psychotic level thoughts and beliefs, thus existing on the border between these two states.

* * *

If a clinician who is treating a BDD patient determines that borderline personality disorder is present, the biggest challenge during treatment may be associated with the borderline personality characteristics, thus it needs to be identified. Body dysmorphic disorder is considered a separate diagnosis from borderline personality disorder, but like all psychiatric disorders, comorbidity does occur. Sometimes what may at first appear to be body dysmorphic disorder might actually be a body image disturbance deriving from a borderline character structure. It might be valuable to conceptualize both of these body image disturbances on a continuum rather than viewing them as two distinct disorders: To view them on completely opposite ends of the spectrum without any middle ground might mimic the extremely inflexible thinking that occurs in both body dysmorphic disorder and borderline personality disorder.

Individuals who present with body related disturbances that match the DSM-5 criteria for body dysmorphic disorder will be given a BDD diagnosis because the symptoms are concrete, overt, and can easily be quantified. This differs from the ambiguity of personality disorders that tend to take much longer to diagnose because the criteria for making an accurate diagnosis can only usually be observed by working with a patient over a long period of time. Thus when an individual enters treatment and immediately expresses dissatisfaction about their appearance, most clinicians will hear that the patient is experiencing distress because of a perceived aesthetic defect and will usually conclude that this must be body dysmorphic disorder. Could it be possible that the symptoms for body dysmorphic disorder that have been defined in the fifth edition of the *Diagnostic and Statistical Manual of Mental Disorders* might be very similar to body image disturbance symptoms that derive from an etiology of borderline personality disorder?

According to the DSM-5, individuals with borderline personality disorder may experience an identity disturbance characterized by markedly and persistently unstable self-image or sense of self. It is explained that these identity disturbances can include sudden shifts in self-image, values, sexual identity, or at times a self-image with feelings that they do not exist at all. In the DSM-5, the criteria required to make the diagnosis of body dysmorphic disorder are: A preoccupation with one or more perceived defects or flaws in appearance that are not observable or appear slight to others; at some point during the course of the disorder, the individual has performed repetitive behaviors in response to the appearance concerns; the preoccupation causes significant clinical distress or impairment in social, occupational, or other important areas of functioning; the appearance preoccupation is not better explained by concerns with body fat or weight in an individual whose symptoms meet diagnostic criteria for an eating disorder (American Psychiatric Association 2013).

If a patient with borderline personality disorder has an identity disturbance that can include drastic shifts in sense of self, sexual identity, or even their existence, might it not be possible that this could include a very diffuse sense of their appearance and a fluctuation in how they perceive their physical self? If this was the case, then the individual could easily become preoccupied with a perceived defect in appearance, perform repetitive behaviors related to this body image concern, and be preoccupied with it to an extent that it affects important areas of their functioning. The DSM-5 also states that some individuals with borderline personality disorder may develop psychotic-like symptoms such as body image distortions and ideas of reference during times of stress (American Psychiatric Association 2013). A clinician who is versed in obsessive-compulsive and related disorders could easily interpret this particular individual's preoccupation with appearance as having obsessions because of the constant, continuous nature of their experience. But perhaps what might initially look like obsessions about appearance could be a pervasive sense of lack of identity that manifests itself by way of appearance: The individual's physical self might be the only object that they can desperately hold onto in order to maintain some semblance of sense of self.

Body dysmorphic disorder is currently classified in the DSM-5 under Obsessive-Compulsive and Related Disorders: What if the etiology of the body image disturbance stems from a very ambiguous sense of self such as in borderline personality disorder rather than from intrusive thoughts that have been defined as obsessions as in obsessive-compulsive disorder? If the etiologies of the body image disturbance are different, can the diagnosis be the same? Something that I have questioned for a long time is if the current diagnosis for body dysmorphic disorder is possibly valid for two separate body image disturbances but, because of the similarities in symptom presentation, they have been lumped together under the BDD diagnosis. Perhaps these body image disturbances exist on a continuum but currently are all classified as body dysmorphic disorder: On one end of the continuum exists a body image disturbance deriving from borderline personality disorder; on the complete opposite end of the spectrum is a body image disturbance associated with negative, intrusive thoughts about appearance, what we currently call BDD; and in the middle exists those individuals who experience both BDD and a borderline personality diathesis.

How a clinician defines the body image disturbance may have a lot to do with their training and the psychological modality from which they operate: Psychiatrists, academic psychological researchers, and cognitive-behavioral therapists tend to value evidence based information and identifying and fixing overt symptoms. Psychiatrists and academic researchers are usually the individuals who are chosen to contribute to the discussions on what criteria define a particular psychiatric disorder. Many psychotherapists and psychologists who do not utilize a cognitive-behavioral model usually focus less on the conspicuous symptoms and more on the therapeutic process; they frequently utilize intuition over science and emphasize the connection with the patient rather than pursuing diagnoses.

Regarding the possibility of two body image disturbances that have both been classified as body dysmorphic disorder, I would expect fervent resistance from clinicians or researchers who operate within precise, evidence based symptoms. It is difficult to publish research in a peer reviewed academic journal that is not evidence based; it would also be very difficult to quantitatively measure something as abstract and diffuse as a body image disturbance caused by a rapidly fluctuating sense of identity or even a nonexistent identity as in the case of borderline personality disorder. I would also expect psychotherapists who interpret symptoms as a process of the patient's life history to be much more amenable to the idea that perhaps the current body dysmorphic disorder diagnostic criteria occurs on a continuum: Two body image disturbances with similar presentations but different etiologies existing on opposite poles of a body image disturbance continuum.

Why is it important to have the conversation regarding the origins of a body image disturbance? Currently there is only one established definition for body dysmorphic disorder, but this definition does not take into account the possibly that the genesis of these body image disturbances might be dissimilar. If there is a distinction in the etiology of body image symptoms, the course of treatment might need to be different. Also, a more precise definition of the origins of the body image disturbance can assist communication between clinicians.

For instance, if a psychiatrist meets with a patient once or twice and the patient describes a preoccupation with his appearance and denies having an eating disorder, the psychiatrist will probably diagnose BDD because the symptoms reported match the DSM-5 diagnosis for body dysmorphic disorder. If this psychiatrist then refers the patient to a psychotherapist for treatment of BDD, the clinician (if not experienced in treating body image disturbances) will likely also follow the BDD symptom route. This would be less problematic if the origin of the patient's symptoms derived from an obsessive-compulsive or related disorder. But, if the etiology of the patient's supposed BDD symptoms stem from a very diffuse sense of identity, such as in borderline personality disorder, the treating clinician will quickly become disoriented regarding how to manage the patient's symptoms. If the origins of the body image disturbance were better defined, this would assist in communication between clinicians.

More precise criteria for body dysmorphic disorder, including defining the etiology of the body image disturbance, would also greatly assist in patient care. The psychotherapeutic modality utilized as well as the medication regimen employed could be more rapidly individualized for each patient if the origins of the body image symptoms were more clearly defined. If a patient appears to have BDD symptoms because they report intrusive negative thoughts about their body, a psychiatrist who is using the current DSM-5 definition of body dysmorphic disorder and the published evidence based research will likely prescribe a SSRI and recommend cognitive-behavioral therapy. If this patient's body image symptoms exist on the end of the continuum similar to obsessive-compulsive and related disorders, then chances are they will receive sufficient treatment. But if the body image symptoms that appear to mimic BDD are a result of a borderline personality diathesis, the patient's treatment will be off the mark from the onset.

Mental health clinicians need to be highly attuned to their patients when establishing rapport and while identifying symptoms. The current DSM-5 definition of body dysmorphic disorder may not be conducive to truly tuning into the etiology of every patient's body image disturbance. To categorize all body image patients who match the very broad definition of BDD may actually contribute to the patient and clinician being out of sync from the very beginning of treatment. Many patients, especially those with a borderline personality diathesis, are highly sensitive to people and are acutely aware when their mental health clinician is even slightly off the mark: They already feel as if no one truly understands their experience, and for their clinician to not be attuned to them only confirms the deeply held internal experience that they are inherently different from everyone else. This lack of attunement can never be good for the development of the patient-therapeutic relationship that is imperative when working with complex body image disturbance cases.

I have observed throughout the years that although the majority of patients that enter treatment for body dysmorphic disorder present with remarkably similar symptoms, the response and prognosis to treatment correlates to the greater etiology of the symptoms. Patients who present with what might appear to be classic body dysmorphic disorder symptoms but who are significantly personality disordered do not respond to treatment nearly as well as those without rigid personality traits. To the seasoned clinician, or anyone who has worked with personality disordered patients for that matter, this might read as a very obvious statement. In my experience, it is very difficult to treat the body image disturbance unless the personality disorder material is also addressed simultaneously.

If a patient presents with symptoms that appear to be body dysmorphic disorder but does not respond to treatment, could it be possible that the symptoms are actually that of another disorder other than BDD and this is why they are not responding to the usual BDD treatment protocol? Are they not responding to treatment because they are personality disordered? Are their symptoms that of body dysmorphic disorder, or is there a combination BDD and a personality disorder? I feel that these are questions that need to be asked in order to better understand clients with body image disturbances. From a clinical psychotherapy perspective, I feel that if we automatically label every patient who matches the DSM-5 criteria with body dysmorphic disorder, we may become oblivious to clues that would allow the clinician to conceptualize treatment more comprehensively. A more flexible conceptualization of body dysmorphic disorder can only contribute to improved patient care.

14 The Family System

I am frequently contacted by individuals who are concerned about a member of their family who they believe may have body dysmorphic disorder. The shame, secrecy, and poor insight characteristic of BDD is such that the sufferer often avoids seeking treatment or believes that the cosmetic route is the solution to their distress. Thus it is not unusual that first contact might be from a family member or significant other reaching out for help rather than the individual with the body image symptoms.

I have not observed one specific type of family system that is unique to body dysmorphic disorder patients, but in my years of working with this patient population I rarely encounter individuals from a family without notable psychopathology and emotional dysfunction. Although it is not uncommon that individuals with BDD come from families that place premium importance on image and appearance, this is by no means always the case. I have worked with patients whose parents have blatantly under-emphasized appearance, as well as patients from family systems in which external appearances were not a significant theme one way or another.

As I have discussed in previous chapters, a clinician treating body dysmorphic disorder can very easily become hyper-focused on the symptoms that their patient presents with. The patient is so distraught and panicked by their perception of their appearance that it can be challenging for a therapist not to be easily distracted from the bigger picture. In my experience this picture often includes the patient's family system.

The majority of body dysmorphic disorder patients that I have worked with have a family history of psychiatric disorders. Bienvenu et al. observed that 8% of individuals with body dysmorphic disorder also have a first-degree family member with a lifetime diagnosis of BDD which is three to eight times as prevalent compared to the general population (2000). In a study conducted by Phillips et al. (2005b), body dysmorphic disorder occurred in 5.8% of first-degree relatives. There is also a higher lifetime prevalence of BDD in families of those with OCD compared to control probands (Beinvenu et al. 2000). Sometimes a person may not be aware of their family's psychiatric history because generational or cultural factors mean it may have been taboo to discuss such topics. The family history of mental illness can be very valuable information for the treating psychiatrist whose position is to address the psychiatric and medical components of the disorder. It is also salient material for the psychotherapist who needs to begin reconstructing when and how the patient's symptoms developed.

At the beginning of treatment it may be very difficult to redirect the individual from exclusively focusing on their perceived physical flaw. This does not mean that I do not acknowledge their tormenting thoughts and feelings: I make sure they know that I believe they are having the experience they describe. During this early stage of therapy I need to learn about their family of origin so that I can better comprehend how members of this system related to one another. Our parents are our first two relationships, one being our first male and the other our first female relationship. The extent to which an infant attaches to his parents can become a template for how they relate to males and females as they get older. This information is very important because it sets the stage for the germinating therapeutic relationship between the clinician and patient.

A pattern that frequently emanates in the exploration of the body dysmorphic disorder patient's family history is that of deficits in parental emotional attunement. Albeit this is often the case with many individuals who seek out psychotherapy, I have noticed a significant incidence of this with patients seeking treatment for body dysmorphic disorder. The capacity to be emotionally attuned is learned and passed from parent to child. If a parent never received adequate attunement from their own parents, it would be impossible for them to be aware that this is a critical aspect of parent-child attachment. A parent cannot teach what they do not know, thus these deficits in parenting are passed down from one generation to the next.

Even if a parent did receive sufficient attunement when they were a child, this is not a guarantee that they will be emotionally attuned with their own children. A parent who is contending with an untreated psychological or psychiatric ailment, an addiction, or any other distraction cannot be fully present for their child. Even with their best intentions, a distracted parent cannot completely provide the mirroring and nurture that is essential for healthy attachment. This does not mean that an infant will not thrive because each person is born with a different temperament: Some infants need much less attention and coddling than others. For individuals with a highly sensitive temperament, deficits in connectivity with caregivers may contribute to an insecure attachment (Kerns and Brumariu 2014). Insecure attachments during infancy and childhood could very well contribute to certain individuals hyper-focusing on their bodies in an attempt to self-regulate emotions. This may not necessarily be the defining factor in the development of body dysmorphic disorder, but for those predisposed to BDD, fragile early attachments may affect the individual's capacity to self-soothe later in life.

A particularly insidious source of inadequate child attunement occurs within the context of parental narcissism. In a healthy relational dyad between parent and child, the adult will ideally serve as an emotional mirror: The seeds of a sense of self are cultivated as the child realizes he exists by seeing a reflection of himself by way of his parent. In the relationship between an adult narcissist and their child, the human mirror is reversed as the child becomes the reflection for the parent. The narcissist experiences their child as an extension of themselves rather than a unique and separate individual. A parent cannot be fully emotionally attuned if the child is serving to compensate for their own emotional needs. The deficits in ample mirroring and attunement will inevitably interfere with the development and integration of the child's identity.

Children of narcissists are usually unaware that a narcissistic parent raised them and often describe their childhood as "the perfect childhood" (Young et al. 2003). Our family of origin is the template from which we understand the world. If this template involves parental-child attachments based upon conditional love and one-way emotional mirroring, then the majority of a child's identity formation will be founded upon external rather than internal processes. The narcissistic parent will almost always report that they provided everything for their child, but they are also unaware that they were not able to provide unconditional love because it is unlikely that they ever received it themselves. Performance, external approbation, and maintaining an image to satisfy the needs of the narcissistic parent become the foundation of the child's identity. All the material trappings of a comfortable childhood might have been in place, but this can never replace and will never be more valuable than a genuine parental-child attachment.

It is not unusual for the narcissistic parent to become over-involved with the treatment of their child's symptoms. Every parent wants the best for their child and has difficulty seeing them distraught. However, the narcissistic parent has much more difficulty tolerating the emotional distress of their offspring; because the child is an extension of their identity, they experience their child's emotions as if these were their own. The narcissistic parent rarely has the capacity to self-reflect or identify that their reaction to their child's emotional state is because they are unable to tolerate these feelings. Because the feelings become too overwhelming for the parent, they often become very enmeshed with the child's treatment. Sadly, this often impacts the healing process because the child will still not be given the opportunity to develop their own identity even in the context of their recovery.

Deficiencies in parental-child attunement may interfere with healthy identity development, as is the case in family systems where a parent is over-involved with a child. If a parent is overly anxious and is constantly hovering over their infant, the child will never learn that they are a separate being (Cooper-Vince, Pincus, and Comer 2014). Becoming enmeshed with a child is not adequate attunement because the parent is attempting to compensate for their own anxieties rather than becoming attuned to and reflecting the needs of the child. Children of over-involved parents frequently have difficulty with emotional self-regulation and identity formation; this may leave a child with no other option other than to turn outward toward their physical appearance in an attempt to understand internal feelings of emptiness.

A theme that I have observed in many of the family systems of body dysmorphic disorder patients is that of a parent who is emotionally unavailable, while the other parent is either very emotionally erratic or emotionally fused with their child. These extremes in emotional connectivity can be very confusing for a child because on one end of the spectrum there is absolutely no emotional mirroring, and on the complete opposite end exists the experience of being emotionally engulfed. Neither scenario provides healthy attunement for the child who learns that emotions are either nonexistent or are overwhelming and are best to be avoided altogether. Because there is not a safe place to learn how to process feelings, the child will either internalize or externalize their emotional states. Children that externalize their feelings act out, whereas children who internalize feelings may become avoidant and isolative: Those that turn inward often attempt to solve emotional experiences by way of intellect.

These intellectual interpretations of emotional states may serve as an adaptive method of self-soothing during childhood, but will eventually evolve into maladaptive patterns of thinking later in life. All-or-nothing thinking is an example of an absolute and erroneous thought that can develop when a child is raised in an environment with parents who are on either side of the emotional spectrum. The child's interpretation of these drastic extremes of emotions may transform into beliefs that the world is either all good or all bad and that there is no middle ground. Individuals with body dysmorphic disorder usually internalize their emotions and also hold extremely rigid all-or-nothing beliefs about their bodies. Not every BDD patient grows up in a family with parents on opposite poles of the emotional continuum, but many do. Perhaps it is not a coincidence that this pattern of parental emotional extremes often transpires in the family systems of patients with body dysmorphic disorder.

Case Study: Kyle

Kyle, a 22-year-old man was brought into treatment by his mother who had contacted me stating that her son had very severe symptoms of body dysmorphic disorder and needed help immediately. When I first met with Kyle he presented with a shy and pleasant demeanor, and although not guarded, he was slow to disclose personal information. His particular bodily preoccupation involved the belief that his nose was too wide. He stated that previously he would obsess about his hair—that it did not "look right"—but that this thought had subsided and now he was very concerned about the width of his nose. He was also very depressed and reported to me that his mood was determined by what he saw in the mirror; he mentioned what I hear from many BDD patients which is that his mood would usually plummet after he viewed the body areas that he believed looked defective.

When Kyle began therapy with me, he was already under the care of a competent psychiatrist whose medication recommendations had appeared to assist in mollifying some of his depressive symptoms. Although he had previously met with several different psychologists, he had never stayed in therapy for any significant period of time. He appeared to suffer from what I considered to be moderate body dysmorphic disorder symptoms: He had insight that the symptoms that had brought him into therapy might be the result of a psychiatric and psychological disorder rather than solely a problem with his nose.

Throughout several meetings Kyle shared with me how his preoccupation with his nose had caused him to become very isolated and depressed. Because he had moderate insight into his symptoms he was capable of discussing other material besides his body image concerns. He shared with me that his parents divorced when he was very young and that he was currently very close with his mother but had not had contact with his father for a long time. This missing relationship in his life caught my attention and I asked him to elaborate about why he was not communicating with his father.

He explained that after his parents had divorced he lived with his mother during the week and would visit his father on weekends. He described his father as very self-involved, inconsistent, and highly emotional: He stated that communication entailed his father "being aggressive and a very one-way conversationalist." He conveyed to me that he learned early on not to speak much around his father and to certainly not express how he was feeling in order to not upset him. He expressed how lonely, neglected, and isolated he would feel on the weekends when he was visiting his father: Turning inward as to insulate himself against his father's erratic behavior became his way of avoiding conflict. As we explored his relationship with his father, Kyle also discerned that it was around this time in his life that he began to internalize information, interpreting the way that his father had treated him as evidence that he must be bad.

Kyle disclosed that ever since he was a child his father would attend to the needs of girlfriends before his needs and that he "always felt secondary and inferior like a step-child." He noted that he would always yearn that maybe his father might change and connect with him, but he was disappointed time and time again when this did not occur. His relationship with his mother was the complete antithesis of that of his father: She was always present, overly protective, and very nurturing.

After a month into the therapy process Kyle had become more relaxed and much more expressive. During one session he stated to me that how he viewed his nose was very similar to how he would perceive himself as a child in the presence of his father. He explained how scrutinizing the size and shape of his nose was analogous to how he would search for deficiencies within himself when interacting with his father. He also articulated that the internalized disparaging voice of his father that would lead to self-denigrating thoughts and feelings as a child was identical to his hypercritical perception about his appearance. As a child he quickly learned to isolate himself, physically, mentally, and emotionally, in order to avoid conflict and chaos; as a young adult the preoccupation with his nose led him to become isolated from people and disconnected from his emotions.

Body dysmorphic disorder symptoms often deprive sufferers of quality relationships and sometimes all relationships. Kyle was no exception: He admitted to having disconnected with most of his friends from high school and even though he still did have one good friend, he rarely communicated with him. Kyle described a profound loneliness, sadness, and lack of friendships that he attributed directly to the width and size of his nose. As he became more immersed in therapy and began to connect and trust me as his therapist, his beliefs about his nose began to change. He also appeared to seem very relieved that someone believed his experiences and was willing to listen to him.

Kyle gained insight that it was not his nose that was causing his life to flounder, but rather the preoccupation with his supposed nose imperfections that were directly interfering with how he interacted with others. The more he concentrated on his nose the more isolated he would become and this would only reinforce the deeply held belief that he was a failure and fundamentally defective. As he connected the therapeutic dots he discerned that the self-degrading thoughts that he held toward himself and his nose were completely analogous to how his father had interacted with him. It was during this series of therapeutic revelations that Kyle began to notice a decrease in his intrusive thoughts about his appearance. Simultaneously his depression also began to lift.

Although I was thrilled to learn that Kyle was beginning to experience a reduction in body dysmorphic disorder symptoms, I was mildly apprehensive because in my experience with even moderate BDD cases, symptoms rarely dissipated this rapidly. We began to discuss the prospect of him getting back on his feet and participating in life, including getting a part-time job so that he could at least be around people. He stated that he really wanted to begin getting his life back and that he felt he needed to become more autonomous from his mother. As his nose obsessions and his depression decreased, we were able to begin exploring what it would look like for him to become an independent adult. Kyle declared that he was ready to begin living his own life.

It was barely over two months since I had began working with Kyle and since he was doing so well I suggested that perhaps it was appropriate to decrease the frequency of therapy sessions from twice a week to one visit per week. The next morning I received a voicemail message from Kyle's psychiatrist: He stated that Kyle's mother had contacted him and reported that Kyle had taken a dozen Klonopin the previous evening and that she had taken him to the emergency room. He was deemed okay by the emergency room staff and released back into his mother's care later that night. This message confounded me because when I had seen him the previous day he was on an upward trajectory toward recovery. His mood had been good and he had been quite optimistic about his future.

The next evening I met with Kyle for our scheduled appointment. He entered my office with a sheepish look on his face; his psychiatrist had already informed him that I had been made aware of the incident. When I inquired about what had occurred he said that he had been feeling overwhelmed, anxious, and disappointed with life choices that he had made. He reported that he was not attempting suicide but had been feeling out of control and had lost track of how many Klonopin he was taking. I expressed to him my concern about what had occurred and that I was very happy to hear that he had not damaged himself. I also expressed that I was confused where this came from because he had been reporting for weeks that things were only getting better and that he had a bright future. The treating psychiatrist had also noted that when he had met with Kyle most recently that he was doing well.

Kyle confided in me that he was feeling very smothered by his mother who he admitted he knew loved and cared about him but that she made him irritable. He explained that he really wanted his independence from her but he felt as if she was stifling this and this frustrated and annoyed him. He stated that she believed he was much more mentally challenged than he truly believed he was and that he needed more space to "do his own thing." When he would get frustrated with his mother, she would interpret this as him not doing well and then react by worrying about him, which would only exacerbate his experience of not having enough freedom. I began to believe that perhaps this was a case of a mother who was having her own anxieties about her child leaving the nest; that is until I met with Kyle and his mother together. I requested that at the next session the three of us meet to discuss what had transpired the previous evening.

When I met with Kyle and his mother during our next session it did not come as a complete surprise that she viewed the Klonopin binging incident very differently: She stated that Kyle had begun talking with her regarding his recovery from BDD and depression and during the conversation he would go back and forth, in and out of his bedroom. She said that she had observed his speech begin to slur and had become suspicious, and soon observed that he was taking multiple doses of Klonopin. I asked Kyle what this was about since he had stated that it was not a suicide attempt. He voiced that he was feeling out of control, and that the more he spoke with his mother the more overwhelmed and hopeless he had become and that he had completely lost track of the number of Klonopin he was consuming.

His mother stated that she had observed improvements in Kyle compared to when he had entered therapy, but that she still considered him mentally ill. Her report differed greatly from what I had observed for many weeks, which was that Kyle was on a relatively fast track to recovery. In my mind I was running through possible different scenarios: Had Kyle been lying to me about how well he was doing? Had I become over-zealous about his improvement and been lulled into missing the bigger picture? Was there something else going on besides the symptoms of body dysmorphic disorder and the comorbid depression?

Kyle's mother stated that she wanted him to move out of her home, have his own life, and become independent. She admitted that she was waiting for him to show her some evidence that he was improving before she would allow him more autonomy, but now she was more fearful than ever before because of the impulsive behavior that had occurred right in front of her. I stated to the duo that I was wondering if perhaps something else was going on besides the body dysmorphic disorder that had initially brought Kyle into treatment. I was very curious why Kyle presented himself as much improved in front of me but at home he continued to be depressed and act out. This discrepancy made me very suspicious that something was going on in their family system or at least in the relationship between mother and child. It also made me reflect upon Kyle's rapid recovery from his body image issues.

A picture began to emerge of an individual who craved independence from his mother but simultaneously doubted his ability to achieve autonomy. On the surface Kyle reported feeling smothered by his mother's over-protectiveness and believed that this was interfering with moving forward with his life. His behaviors at home were counter to what he had been reporting to me—the Klonopin overdose being the most overt example—and these were activating his mother's fears which translated into her becoming even more worried and preoccupied with her son's mental health. This would only perpetuate the pattern of Kyle acting out in front of her, which she would interpret as evidence that he was not ready to leave the nest.

I explained to Kyle that I believed him that he really wanted to become independent and move out on his own, but I also believed that perhaps subtly he was very scared to do so. I have observed that this ambivalence with independence and relationships is a quite prevalent theme with many individuals with body image disturbances. They intellectually seek autonomy and intimacy but emotionally they have become suspended in an earlier psychosocial stage of development. Kyle was not an exception: As we began to process the material associated with his ambivalence about growing up, he began to become aware that he was very fearful of moving forward in life. He acknowledged that when he was a child his father was very detached from him while his mother was enmeshed; because of his mother's over-involvement he had never learned how to do many things on his own thus doubted his ability to take care of himself. He had not been fully self-aware that many of his behaviors were contradictory to his intellectual goals of moving out of his mother's home.

A push-pull dynamic between mother and son had maintained an equilibrium in the family system, in which Kyle would remain as the identified patient. The more he struggled against his mother to gain his independence, the more this solidified the cycle of him feeling frustrated and remaining stuck. The blatant symptoms of body dysmorphic disorder and depression had existed, but also served as a smoke screen for the underlying themes permeating the family system. With the symptoms no longer available to divert attention, other symptoms had to arise to replace them and to maintain the familial pattern of codependency. I believed Kyle when he stated that he was not attempting suicide; I also believe that he was not intentionally trying to provoke his mother. I do believe that much more subtle and salient fears of maturation and autonomy were active in maintaining a family system that would guarantee the identified patient, Kyle, would remain stuck.

This case is unusual in that the patient's body dysmorphic disorder disappeared rather quickly, but it is not uncommon that the family system is somehow intertwined with the identified patient who presents with the symptoms. There was no behavioral therapy applied to this case, including exposure and response prevention, and minimal cognitive therapeutic techniques were utilized. Although we did explore the patient's background and family history, there was minimal interpretation involved. The patient really began to participate in the therapeutic process when he felt heard, understood, and was experiencing adequate mirroring and attunement. Something that may be very normal to most people was an unprecedented experience for him: The therapeutic environment provided unconditional positive regard and a forum where he could discharge years of negative internalized thoughts and feelings.

It is possible that if I had concentrated on the body dysmorphic disorder, I may have encountered a similar scenario witnessed in the patient's family system: The same push-pull dynamic Kyle had with his mother may have been re-enacted in the therapy milieu with me had I attempted to over-emphasize the body dysmorphic disorder symptoms. If we had focused mostly on the symptoms, there is the possibility that they would not have dissipated as easily. Kyle had unknowingly participated in behaviors that maintained the status quo of his family system; this cycle may have been perpetuated within the therapeutic realm if the sole focus of treatment had been about fixing the body dysmorphic disorder symptoms.

Dysfunctional family systems can be extremely difficult to alter. Years, decades, and even generational patterns of behaviors have become intricately ingrained in how family members interrelate. Attempts to modify a family system can be met with overt resistance or can also be unconsciously undermined. If the identified patient in the family begins to recover from his ailment, this will consequently create a shift in the system. This alteration will deem an imbalance in the family and this is frequently countered by behaviors to equilibrate familial conformity. The excessive focus by the family to fix the identified patient may actually be what maintains the familiar family patterns and simultaneously keeps the patient ill (Minuchin 1974).

In the case of Kyle, he clearly stated the need for independence from his mother. As he struggled for autonomy his mother would worry more about his mental health disorders. Most concerned and caring family members would react similarly; in this particular family system the over-reaction to Kyle's behaviors only fueled further behaviors that would demonstrate that he was unstable and needed to be cared for. If his mother had not reacted to his behavioral symptoms, the role of identified patient would inevitably have subsided because it would no longer have been positively reinforced. This, though, might have had implications for other dynamics in the family system: If Kyle fully recovered from his symptoms and moved on with his life, his mother's role of caretaker would end. In less pathological family systems the caretakers are able to surrender their roles and the family system evolves. But in family systems that are saturated with multiple layers of psychopathology, change is usually a long and arduous process.

Case Study: Kyle—Part II

I explained to Kyle and his mother what I believed was occurring in their family system. Although Kyle did not fully agree with my assessment, his mother recognized that perhaps this pattern was taking place. She questioned if maybe she had become too involved with rescuing her son and began to blame herself for his predicament. I pointed out that my observation of their family system was not coming from a place of condemnation, and blaming herself for her son's ailments may actually contribute to the family pathology. I explained that the guilt she was experiencing from self-blame might actually manifest in attempts to further rescue Kyle, and this would only perpetuate the cycle that the duo had been stuck in for years.

I told Kyle's mother that the best thing she could do for her son would be to do something very counterintuitive and that would be to not continue to try and fix him. Her need to always save him not only maintained his role as identified patient, but it interfered with him learning how to care for himself and also prevented her from addressing her own fears and guilt surrounding her role as a mother. I explained that resisting the urge to always rescue Kyle, albeit counterintuitive, was actually how he would recover and be able to move forward with his life. I emphasized that I expected there to be further symptoms and crises, whether these be body dysmorphic disorder related or otherwise, as she withdrew from the her traditional role of caretaker.

I suggested that she speak with her own psychotherapist in order to help her regulate feelings regarding giving up her parental function. If Kyle began to act out or manifest body image symptoms, I recommended that she send him to either myself or his psychiatrist and not play the role of his therapist and caretaker. This would allow Kyle to turn elsewhere besides his mother when he was in crisis and by doing this would not activate his mother's anxieties. By utilizing his clinicians as external sources of support, he would not be rescued by his mother when in distress; this would give him the opportunity to make decisions on his own while simultaneously learning how to self-soothe. To become self-efficacious is invaluable in the process of individuation.

This case is a prime example of how viewing the bigger picture, including understanding a patient's family system, is imperative when treating body dysmorphic disorder. If my attention had been diverted by Kyle's BDD symptoms then I would have completely missed what was going on in his family of origin. Likewise, if I had become distracted by attempting to fix Kyle's symptoms, then I would have been mimicking as well as colluding with his BDD symptoms that were already distracting him from viewing the bigger picture of the family system. Just as Kyle had become preoccupied with fixing his perceived nose defect, his mother had become preoccupied with fixing him. Every family member's attempt to correct something that was presumed faulty actually served to hinder their ability to alter the dysfunctional family patterns. Without bringing this to the attention of the family and without altering behaviors in the family system, Kyle likely would have continued to fixate on his nose and remained convinced that the width of his nose was responsible for why he could not move forward with his life.

Family Psychosocial Education

A child that does not receive satisfactory mirroring from a parent will eventually seek other external sources to provide a reflection. In the case of body dysmorphic disorder, literal reflective surfaces as well as comparisons to other people often become the primary replacement for these deficits. Both of these provide the child with concrete evidence that they exist; without an internal sense of self having been instilled, the physical body can easily develop into the primary means by which the individual comprehends their identity. If a person's physical appearance becomes so significant to how they understand their existence, this would likely become very self-reinforcing because the individual would constantly turn toward the mirror or to other people when attempting to understand internal experiences. Not only does this fortify the association between the body and identity but it simultaneously further hinders the individual from learning how to regulate emotions from within.

It is always important for clinicians to have knowledge of the patient's family system and attachment history in order to discern if elements of their BDD profile derive from this source. For body dysmorphic disorder patients that live with their immediate families or are enmeshed with them, I recommend BDD psychosocial education for the family— of course with the patient's consent. These educational sessions should include the patient and incorporate the following topics:

- Family members should not participate in BDD reassurance seeking compulsions. If the individual with body dysmorphic disorder asks if their supposed defect looks acceptable, the family members are to respond that this is a question that needs to be taken to the psychotherapist. It needs to be explained to the family that by participating in the reassurance seeking compulsion, the family is actually colluding with and strengthening the BDD. Also, when constantly giving reassurance, neither the patient nor the family will learn to tolerate the emotions that prompt them to give reassurance in the first place.

- Family members should be mindful not to have conversations about the appearance of the patient, of each other, or of other people. The body dysmorphic disorder patient is acutely attuned to any comments about aesthetic appearance and often misinterprets these comments in such a way that only reinforces their overvalued beliefs.

- Family members should not fund cosmetic procedures, especially without consulting the patient's therapist. Besides being one of the more extreme body dysmorphic disorder compulsions, cosmetic procedures do not improve the BDD prognosis and usually exacerbate the symptoms. If the patient is an adult and chooses to work to pay for their own cosmetic procedures, this is their choice. The clinician should allow the patient to openly discuss this decision without judgment; if the patient proceeds with the operation, they will most likely need the emotional support of the therapist post-procedure. It is acceptable for the therapist to educate the patient and family regarding why cosmetic procedures are contraindicated for individuals with active body dysmorphic disorder symptoms.

- The clinician should consider making an outside therapy referral for family members who are having difficulty in tolerating the emotional distress of the BDD patient or who are over-involved with their treatment. Referring family members to their own therapy can assist in the bigger picture of the patient's recovery. If a family is over-involved in the patient's rehabilitation, this may mimic certain patterns in the family system that initially contributed to the patient's body image disturbance. Sometimes an over-involved parent is unaware that they are regulating their own feelings by trying to fix their child. Whereas the child is overly preoccupied with their appearance, the parent becomes too fixated on rescuing their child from BDD. If the treating clinician identifies this pattern, it definitely needs to be addressed with the patient and the parent. Recovery from BDD includes becoming an autonomous adult, and this cannot happen if a parent is constantly hovering over their child while desperately attempting to shield them from the body image symptoms.

- The clinician should encourage disengaged family members to make their best effort to better educate themselves about body dysmorphic disorder. Individuals with BDD already feel alone and disconnected from others, so at least making an effort to better understand their experience can greatly contribute to them feeling less misunderstood.

- If the parents of a child with body dysmorphic disorder are experiencing dysfunction within their own relationship, it is very important that this be addressed. Way too often a child can become the identified patient in a family system that is experiencing dissension between parents: Yes, the child may have body dysmorphic disorder and of course this should not be ignored, but sometimes symptoms can serve the purpose of rallying family members together. The parents and other family members communicate in order to fix the child with BDD; although this may be necessary, it also fortifies the BDD sufferer into the role of the identified patient and also serves as the adhesive that delays the parent's relationship from completely deteriorating. I have worked with multiple cases of body dysmorphic disorder where the patient's symptoms gradually began to abate once they were no longer in the role of the identified patient. Although addressing the condition of the parental relationship while a child is in crisis might seem counterintuitive, remaining cognizant of the less obvious crises in a family system might ultimately be the missing piece to a complicated body dysmorphic disorder case.

15 Group Therapy for Body Dysmorphic Disorder

The body dysmorphic disorder experience can be a very lonely and isolated existence. Individuals with untreated body dysmorphic symptoms frequently report feeling as if no one truly understands their experience, and this in turn makes them feel even more dissimilar and detached from other people. It is exactly this reality that makes BDD group therapy such a highly therapeutic adjunct to individual treatment. Like any support group, the affinity stemming from sharing similar and intimate experiences can be invaluably cathartic.

Many body dysmorphic disorder patients have never received adequate mirroring and attunement, thus the BDD psychotherapy group not only provides a supportive environment but also serves as a corrective emotional family experience. If a person has not experienced sufficient emotional mirroring, an intellectual explanation of what it is will not suffice because mirroring is something that is learned through interpersonal interactions. I conceptualize the psychotherapy group as a recreation of the early family experience but with a heavy emphasis on the process of attuning to, mirroring, and ultimately genuinely attaching to other people.

In April 2003 I began a weekly body dysmorphic disorder therapy support group. I was already working with numerous BDD patients so I had a broad selection of individuals to choose from. Fortunately, I had four patients who had been steadily progressing in individual therapy, were motivated, had reasonably good insight into their symptoms, and who were also interested in participating in a group experience. This group was one of the first ever body dysmorphic disorder therapeutic support groups that would meet on a weekly basis. I remember wondering why there were not more BDD support groups, something that has not changed up to the publication of this book. It was only a matter of time until I began to realize why there was such a paucity of groups available for this patient population.

When I began informing my body dysmorphic disorder patients that I was now running a group specifically for those with BDD, they would often express curiosity about meeting other people who were having a comparable experience; there was also trepidation that everyone else in the group would look normal and that they would be the only person with a real aesthetic defect. Every time this was expressed to me, I would explain to the patient that almost every other BDD sufferer who I had informed about the group had stated the exact same concern. This involved the fear that they would receive the ultimate confirmation that they really did not have a psychiatric condition and that they were just unattractive. Just the thought of the possible corroboration from others that one has a physical defect is sometimes enough to deter a patient from even considering joining a body image group. I also observed the opposite extreme: Body image patients who were desperate to connect with a group because they felt so fundamentally different from other people and believed by meeting others like them they would not feel as insulated. Although getting them into the group was easy, I was soon to realize that their extreme eagerness to participate was frequently a red flag for things to come.

The body dysmorphic disorder group experience serves as a bridge between the relationship the patient establishes with the therapist and the goal of improved connectivity with people outside of the therapeutic milieu. It is a natural adjunct to individual therapy and also allows the clinician to observe the patient outside of the safety of the patient-therapist relationship. The group initially bonds through the medium of the body dysmorphic disorder symptoms: It is the process of the group members' interactions and inevitable attachments that define the ethos of this experience.

Group discussions will of course include conversations regarding body dysmorphic disorder symptoms, but this should not be the exclusive theme during meetings. The reason for this is because the greater purpose of the group process is to alter the relationship that the patients have with their appearance by replacing the body focus with genuine, authentic, and healthy relationships with other human beings. If the majority of the group content revolved around body image issues, this would effectively undermine the entire point of the group that exists to assist individuals in learning how to trust, connect, and receive nurture from other members. If the preoccupation with their appearance had already served to fill these needs, the individual would not be in treatment; they would not be having the experience that somehow they look or feel fundamentally different from everyone else.

The group experience is a microcosm of how individual members interact with people in the outside world. When an individual begins the group experience, they are usually very internally focused except when they are fixated on their perceived flaws or on the physical features of other people. This significantly hinders them from mentalizing or comprehending that other people have thoughts and experiences different from their own. The deficits in the capacity to mentalize will inevitably interfere with the formation of relationships (Bateman and Fonagy 2006). The individual with BDD automatically assumes that other people think about them as they think about themselves and this equates to "how can I be liked or loved if I look so heinous?" The process of the group focuses on the interactions between group members rather than on their appearances, thus the main content of the group is about relationships.

My early body dysmorphic disorder groups were open to all BDD sufferers in the community as long as they were in their own individual therapy. At the time this seemed ideal because the group could meet the needs of more people looking for a venue where they could share their BDD experiences. Although this open policy provided a continual stream of group members, it soon became apparent that many of these individuals were not ready for the group experience. Some had yet to receive sufficient individual therapy and badly needed medication management, presenting with overvalued ideation and even delusional beliefs about their appearance. Other individuals had significant personality disorders that had not been detected by their individual therapists but became very evident when interacting with other group members. And others had considerable social anxiety and avoidant personality traits that resulted in evading numerous group sessions. The numerous issues associated with and secondary to the body image disturbances created an atmosphere of inconsistency that was not conducive to forming a safe and secure environment. This was the opposite of what the group members needed, many who already had considerable issues with trust, attachment, and intimacy.

In the initial years of the group there became a culture of the group members going out for dinner after the weekly meeting. Quite a few of the attendees lived very isolated lives so I encouraged this in order to increase social interactions and to provide practice for interpersonal skills. What began as a seemingly innocuous and even therapeutic social outing soon proved to be just the opposite: Because group members were becoming comfortable with one another, many began using each other as a source of reassurance about their appearance, a common BDD compulsion.

My intention of having group members communicate outside of the group was to give them the opportunity to sharpen rusty interpersonal skills and perhaps even begin to connect with one another. It soon became apparent that although these post-group outings provided some socialization practice and an opportunity to further bond with other BDD sufferers, it also became a venue for body preoccupation and reassurance seeking rather than the intended goal of improved interpersonal communication. Another problem with the communication of members outside of the formal group setting was that issues between participants were often not being processed during the group, instead becoming fodder for gossip. Inevitably this would result in the recipient of the gossip feeling on the periphery of the group experience and yet again feeling different from other people. This was the antithesis of the message I was attempting to disseminate when urging group members to interact outside of the weekly meeting.

Group Recommendations

When I created the initial weekly body dysmorphic disorder group there were very few examples to use as a template, thus the group today is the result of years of learning from trial and error. The following recommendations are for clinicians who are considering starting a BDD group:

- Begin with no less than five members. There will be individuals who are not able to tolerate the group experience and will leave the group, thus starting with more participants will provide room for the waxing and waning in membership.
- Require that all group members are actively attending individual therapy. The activation of group participants' material should be expected and needs to be processed during the meeting. The issues that arise as group members interact also provides valuable information and insight into how the individuals interact with others outside of the office. The group experience cannot be a replacement for one-on-one psychotherapy, although it can be a valuable adjunct to individual treatment. There still needs to be the therapeutic forum to which the individual returns in order to identify and work through their own issues that are activated when having interpersonal interactions.
- Group members should not communicate with each other outside of the group setting. This might appear contradictory to the pervasive theme of the group that emphasizes attachment and relationships, but it also assures that all interpersonal experiences within the group can be processed between all group members. One of the main points of the BDD group experience is to foster healthy relationships, thus an open dialog and the expression of each person's feelings is paramount. Having no contact outside of the group also means that participants will not be utilizing one another as a source of reassurance about their appearance. Communication includes, but is not limited to, meeting in person, using the telephone, e-mail, Internet message boards, video chatting, instant messaging, and texting.
- No contact outside of the group includes no dating or flirting between members. Individuals with body dysmorphic disorder already have enough difficulties with attachment and connectivity with plutonic relations, thus the group setting needs to create a forum in which participants do not feel intimidated or anxious about the possibility of romance between one another. Another reason for not permitting romantic relationships between group participants is that if two

members were to become involved, this would leave others feeling excluded which only propagates the BDD theme of feeling different and on the periphery of the group. Group discussions should frequently include the topic of intimacy, and if a member begins an intimate relationship outside of the group, they should be encouraged to openly speak about this during sessions.

- A four-month minimum attendance, or approximately 16 meetings, is recommended for individuals interested in entering the body dysmorphic disorder group. If there are not any guidelines regarding how long a member has to remain in group, there is the probability that group members may leave as soon as they begin feeling uncomfortable expressing themselves and getting emotionally close to other people. Also, frequent transition of group participants makes it difficult for members to establish a consistent and trusting bond with one another, especially if they know at any given time a member might disappear from the group. The reasons behind the four-month attendance requirement should be explained to the patient prior to them starting the group.

- The group experience is metaphoric for relationships in the outside world. An individual's excessive tardiness or lapses in attendance needs to be processed with the other group participants: Inconsistency with group attendance creates discontinuity between meetings as well as possible resentment from members who consistently attend. The lack of consistency ultimately interferes with relationships within the group, and of course the same erratic behavior affects relationships in the individual's personal life.

- Group attendees need to be encouraged to express their experiences and feelings with each other during the meetings. This includes when they are annoyed, frustrated, or angry at another group participant as well as articulating positive interactions that they may have. A major point of the group is for participants to learn how to communicate interpersonally in order to get their emotional needs met and to understand that other members have thoughts and experiences very different from their own. The only way that this can be learned is through direct communication. Many BDD patients have become very removed from other people thus the process of learning how to effectively express oneself with others usually takes time.

- A 90-minute group meeting, once a week is satisfactory. Most patients who are also attending individual therapy will not have the time to attend a group that meets more than once a week. It is not recommended that the body dysmorphic disorder group meet less than once a week because too much of a gap between meetings interferes with attachment between the members.

- The group rules should be explained to new members prior to them joining: Any hesitation by the individual regarding their ability to comply with the rules might indicate that they are not yet prepared to participate in and benefit from a group scenario.

I would recommend caution with patients who are too eager to join the body dysmorphic disorder group. This may simply be the reaction of an individual who has felt so isolated and alone for such a long period of time that they just want to connect with people who have had similar experiences. But, it is sometimes the individuals that rush into the group who then abruptly state that they still feel very different from everyone else. They often have expectations that everyone else will know exactly how they feel and can completely relate to them. Even though other group members might have a preoccupation with the exact same body area, their life experiences and BDD history cannot be an exact replica of the next person. This realization may leave the individual feeling even more dissimilar to others; sometimes they interpret this information as further proof that no one can relate to or understand them and that they must be fundamentally different from the rest of humanity. They conclude that if they are in a group of people who share BDD symptoms but who also cannot fully relate to them, then this must be evidence that they will always be alone and misunderstood.

It is well advised to have worked with a patient prior to permitting them to join the body image group. Not all individuals are appropriate for a group setting, especially those with pronounced personality disorders such as borderline or narcissistic personality structures. Patients with these personality profiles have significant difficulties in interpersonal relationships and this will undoubtedly surface in a closed group of people. One group member with a borderline or narcissistic personality can abruptly dismantle a cohesive and functioning therapeutic support group. Although these individuals may have presented with what appears to be body dysmorphic disorder, the chaos that ensues when they begin getting close to other people is far too distracting and even intimidating for many BDD patients who tend to be introverted and avoidant. Having worked with a patient, or communicating with a clinician who has, can assist in identifying personality types that are not suitable for the group experience.

Because psychotherapy is an inexact science, it is impossible to perfectly ascertain how any given patient will react in a group setting. Sometimes there are patients who in individual therapy present with all the outward signs of body dysmorphic disorder and do not demonstrate any obvious signs of considerable personality disturbance; that is, until they become involved in group therapy. Within the confines of the patient-therapist relationship, these individuals may be more able to tolerate the interpersonal interactions and the clinician may miss tell-tale signs of borderline personality disorder.

Borderline personality characteristics may rapidly emerge once the patient enters a group setting and their capacity to tolerate multiple interpersonal relationships deteriorates. This of course creates a paradoxical situation: If the group moderator allows the personality disordered patient to remain in group, the other members will likely be overshadowed by the chaos and the rhythm of the group will be significantly affected. If the moderator expresses to the individual that they are not appropriate for the group experience, the patient will internalize this as another rejection and as evidence they do not belong and are different. If the individual's presence becomes too unsettling, it may be necessary for the moderator to remove the individual from the group in order to maintain a non-chaotic milieu that permits the majority of the group to thrive.

Although the body dysmorphic disorder group may not be ideal for all patients, for many it can provide a very valuable therapeutic experience, especially for those with social anxiety, trust issues, deficits in interpersonal skills, and for patients who have never received adequate attunement and mirroring. The group may not be imperative for a patient's recovery, but it certainly can be a very beneficial addition to individual psychotherapy. Many BDD symptoms evolve within the context of negative interpersonal interactions, thus the group provides a secure environment in which healthy human connections are cultivated and in turn replace the pathological relationships that body dysmorphic disorder patients have with their bodies.

References

American Psychiatric Association. 1994. *Diagnostic and Statistical Manual of Mental Disorders* (4th ed.). Washington, DC: Author.

American Psychiatric Association. 2013. *Diagnostic and Statistical Manual of Mental Disorders* (5th ed.). Washington, DC: Author.

Bateman, Anthony W. and Peter Fonagy. 2004. *Psychotherapy for Borderline Personality Disorder: Mentalization Based Treatment.* Oxford: Oxford University Press.

Bateman, Anthony W. and Peter Fonagy. 2006. *Mentalization-Based Treatment for Borderline Personality Disorder.* New York: Oxford University Press.

Beck, Aaron T. 1976. *Cognitive Therapy and Emotional Disorders.* New York: International Universities Press.

Bellino, Silvio, Monica Zizza, Erika Paradiso, Luca Patria, Alberto Rivarossa, Mario Fulcheri and Filippo Bogetto. 2003. "Body Dysmorphic Disorder and Personality Disorders: A Clinical Investigation in Patients Seeking Cosmetic Surgery." *Italian Journal of Psychopathology* 9:149–156.

Bienvenu, O. Joseph, Jack F. Samuels, Mark A. Riddle, Rudolf Hoehn-Saric, Kung-Yee Liang, Bernadette A.M. Cullen, Marco A. Grados and Gerald Nestadt. 2000. "The Relationship of Obsessive-Compulsive Disorder to Possible Spectrum Disorders: Results from a Family Study." *Biological Psychiatry* 48(4):287–293.

Biskin, Robert S. and Joel Paris. 2012. "Diagnosing Borderline Personality Disorder." *Canadian Medical Association Journal* 184(16):1789–1794.

Bizamcer, Aurelia N., William R. Dubin and Bernadette Hayburn. 2008. "Olfactory Reference Syndrome." *Psychosomatics* 49(1):77–80.

Bowlby, John. 1969. *Attachment and Loss.* London: Hogarth Press.

Bowlby, John. 1988. *A Secure Base: Parent-Child Attachment and Healthy Human Development.* London: Routledge Press.

Buhlmann, Ulrike, Nancy Etcoff and Sabine Wilhelm. 2006. "Emotional Recognition Bias for Contempt and Anger in Body Dysmorphic Disorder." *Journal of Psychiatric Research* 40(2):105–111.

Cooper-Vince, Christine E., Donna B. Pincus and Jonathan S. Comer. 2014. "Maternal Intrusiveness, Family Financial Means, and Anxiety Across Childhood in a Large Multiphase Sample of Community Youth." *Journal of Abnormal Child Psychology* 42(3):429–438.

Cororve, Michelle B. and David H. Gleaves. 2001. "Body Dysmorphic Disorder: A Review of Conceptualizations, Assessment, and Treatment Strategies." *Clinical Psychology Review* 21(6):949–970.

Diehl, Manfred, Helena Chui, Elizabeth L. Hay, Mark A. Lumley, Daniel Gruhn and Gisela Labouvie-Vief. 2014. "Change in Coping and Defense Mechanisms Across Adulthood: Longitudinal Findings in a European-American Sample." *Developmental Psychology* 50(2):634–648.

Erikson, E.H. 1968. *Identity: Youth and Crisis.* New York: Norton.

Feusner, Jamie, Arie Winograd and Sanjaya Saxena. 2005. "Mirror, Mirror, on the Wall . . . Treating Body Dysmorphic Disorder: A Multimodal Approach Appears Most Effective for this Distressing Somatoform Disorder." *Current Psychiatry* 4(10):69–82.

Foa, Edna B. 2010. "Cognitive Behavioral Therapy of Obsessive-Compulsive Disorder." *Dialogues in Clinical Neuroscience* 12(2):199–207.

Fonagy, Peter. 2000. "Attachment and Borderline Personality Disorder." *Journal of the American Psychoanalytic Association* 48(4):1129–1146.

Gardner, Fiona. 2004. "To Enliven Her Was My Living: Thoughts on Compliance and Sacrifice as Consequences of Malignant Identification with a Narcissistic Parent." *British Journal of Psychotherapy* 21(1):49–62.

Grant, Jon E., William Menard, Maria E. Pagano, Christina Fay, and Katharine A. Phillips. 2005. "Substance Use Disorders in Individuals with Body Dysmorphic Disorder." *Journal of Clinical Psychiatry* 66(3):309–316.

Grinker, Roy R., Beatrice Werble and Robert C. Drye. 1968. *The Borderline Syndrome: A Behavioral Study of Ego Functions.* New York: Basic Books.

Gunstad, John, and Katharine A. Phillips. 2003. "Axis I Comorbidity in Body Dymorphic Disorder." *Comprehensive Psychiatry* 44(4):270–276.

Herman, Judith. 1992. *Trauma and Recovery: The Aftermath of Violence—From Domestic Abuse to Political Terror.* New York: Basic Books.

Hoffman, Lois, Scott Paris, Elizabeth Hall and Robert Schell. 1988. *Developmental Psychology Today* (5th ed.). New York: McGraw-Hill Publishing Company.

Jaeger, Jeff, Katie M. Lindblom, Kelly Parker-Guilbert and Lori A. Zoellner. 2014. "Trauma Narratives: It's What You Say, Not How You Say It." *Psychological Trauma: Theory, Research, Practice and Policy* 6(5):473–481.

Kerns, Kathryn A. and Laura E. Brumariu. 2014. "Is Insecure Parent-Child Attachment a Risk Factor for the Development of Anxiety in Childhood or Adolescence?" *Child Development Perspectives* 8(1):12–17.

Krypotos, Angelos-Miltiadis, Marieke Effting, Merel Kindt and Tom Beckers. (2015). "Avoidance Learning: A Review of Theoretical Models and Recent Developments." *Frontiers in Behavioral Neuroscience* 9(189):1–16.

Levine, Peter A. 1997. *Walking the Tiger: Healing Trauma.* Berkeley: North Atlantic Books.

Liebert, Robert M. and Michael D. Spiegler. 1990. *Personality Strategies and Issues* (6th ed.). Pacific Grove, CA: Brooks/Cole Publishing Company.

Masterson, James F. 1976. *Psychotherapy of the Borderline Adult: A Developmental Approach.* New York: Brunner/Mazel.

McGrath, Patrick B. 2007. *The OCD Answer Book.* Naperville, IL: Sourcebooks, Inc.

McWilliams, Nancy. 1994. *Psychoanalytic Diagnosis.* New York: The Guilford Press.

Minuchin, Salvador. 1974. *Families & Family Therapy.* Cambridge, MA: Harvard University Press.

Mohatt, Nathaniel Vincent, Azure B. Thompson, Nghi D. Thai and Jacob Kraemer Tebes. 2014. "Historical Trauma as Public Narrative: A Conceptual Review of How History Impacts Present-Day Health." *Social Science & Medicine* 106:128–136.

Neziroglu, Fugen, Dean McKay, John Todaro and Jose A. Yaryura-Tobias. 1996. "Effects of Cognitive Behavior Therapy on Persons with Body Dysmorphic Disorder and Comorbid Axis II Diagnoses." *Behavior Therapy* 27:66–77.

Nirenberg, Andrew A., Katharine A. Phillips, Timothy J. Petersen, Karen E. Kelly, Jonathan E. Alpert, John J. Worthington, Joyce R. Tedlow, Jerrold F. Rosenbaum and Maurizio Fava. 2002. "Body Dysmorphic Disorder in Outpatients with Major Depression." *Journal of Affective Disorders* 69:141–148.

Pavlov, Ivan. 1927. *Conditioned Reflexes* (G.V. Anrep, Trans.). New York: Liveright.

Phillips, Katharine A. 2007. "Suicidality in Body Dysmorphic Disorder." *Primary Psychiatry* 14(12):58–66.

Phillips, Katharine A., Meredith E. Coles, William Menard, Shirley Yen, Christina Fay and Risa Weisberg. 2005a. "Suicidal Ideation and Suicide Attempts in Body Dysmorphic Disorder." *Journal of Clinical Psychiatry* 66(6):717–725.

Phillips, Katharine A. and Susan F. Diaz. 1997. "Gender Differences in Body Dysmorphic Disorder." *Journal of Nervous & Mental Disease* 185(9):570–577.

Phillips, Katharine A. and Raymond G. Dufresne. 2002. "Body Dysmorphic Disorder: A Guide for Primary Care Physicians." *Primary Care* 29(1):99–vii.

Phillips, Katharine A. and Eric Hollander. 2008. "Treating Body Dysmorphic Disorder with Medication: Evidence, Misconceptions, and a Suggested Approach." *Body Image* 5(1):13–27.

Phillips, Katharine A., William Menard, Christina Fay and Risa Weisberg. 2005b. "Demographic Characteristics, Phenomenology, Comorbidity, and Family History in 200 Individuals with Body Dysmorphic Disorder." *Psychosomatics* 46(4):317–325.

Pope, Harrison G., Katharine A. Phillips and Roberto Olivardia. 2002. *The Adonis Complex: How to Identify, Treat, and Prevent Body Obsession in Men and Boys.* New York: Simon & Schuster.

Reich, Wilhelm. 1933. *Character Analysis.* New York: Farrar, Straus, and Giroux.

Rosse, Irving C. 1890. "Clinical Evidences of Borderland Insanity." *Journal of Nervous and Mental Disease* 15(10):669–683.

Sarwer, David B., Canice E. Crerand and Elizabeth R. Didie. 2003. "Body Dysmorphic Disorder in Cosmetic Surgery Patients." *Facial Plastic Surgery* 19(1):7–17.

Saxena, Sanjaya, Arie Winograd, Jennifer J. Dunkin, Karron Maidment, Richard Rosen, Tanya Vapnick, Gerald Tarlow and Alexander Bystritsky. 2001. "A Retrospective Review of Clinical Characteristics and Treatment Response in Body Dysmorphic Disorder Versus Obsessive-Compulsive Disorder." *The Journal of Clinical Psychiatry* 62(1):67–72.

Strathearn, Lane. 2011. "Maternal Neglect: Oxytocin, Dopamine and the Neurobiology of Attachment." *Journal of Neuroendocrinology* 23(11):1054–1065.

Thompson, J. Kevin and Leslie J. Heinberg. 1999. "The Media's Influence on Body Image Disturbance and Eating Disorders: We've Reviled Them, Now Can We Rehabilitate Them?" *Journal of Social Issues* 55(2):339–353.

Veale, David, Anne Boocock, Kevin Gournay, Windy Dryden, Fozia Shah, Robert Wilson and Jessica Walburn. 1996. "Body Dysmorphic Disorder: A Survey of Fifty Cases." *British Journal of Psychiatry* 169(2):196–201.

Veale, David and Fugen Neziroglu. 2010. *Body Dysmorphic Disorder: A Treatment Manual* (1st ed.). Chichester, UK: John Wiley & Sons Ltd.

Wolpe, Joseph. 1990. *The Practice of Behavior Therapy* (4th ed.). Elmsford, NY: Pergamon Press.

Young, Jeffrey E., Janet S. Klosko and Majorie E. Weishaar. 2003. *Schema Therapy: A Practitioner's Guide.* New York: The Guilford Press.

Index

For Product Safety Concerns and Information please contact our EU
representative GPSR@taylorandfrancis.com
Taylor & Francis Verlag GmbH, Kaufingerstraße 24, 80331 München, Germany